MW01193412

STEVE CUSHION is a retired university lecturer with a Ph.D. in Caribbean Labor History who lives in the East End of London. For twenty years, he worked as a bus driver in London, and has been an active socialist and trade unionist all his adult life. He is currently adviser to the Museum of Labor History on the digitization of their archives.

# A Hidden History
—— *of the* ——
# Cuban Revolution

*How the Working Class Shaped the Guerrilla Victory*

*by* STEVE CUSHION

MONTHLY REVIEW PRESS
*New York*

Copyright © 2016 by Steve Cushion
All Rights Reserved

Library of Congress Cataloging-in-Publication Data available from
the publisher
—

Monthly Review Press
146 West 29th Street, Suite 6W
New York, New York 10001

www.monthlyreview.org

5 4 3 2 1

# CONTENTS

*For Mary Turner (1931–2013),*
*historian, teacher, comrade, and loyal friend*

## FOREWORD

The war constitutes an encouraging example of what can be achieved by the tenacity and revolutionary will of the people. The revolutionary armed combatants, in the final phase of the struggle, scarcely numbered three thousand men. . . . Our workers and peasants, integrated into the Rebel Army, with the support of the middle class, pulverized the tyrannous regime, destroyed the armed apparatus of oppression, and achieved the full independence of the country. The working class, with its revolutionary general strike in the final battle, contributed decisively to the triumph [of the Revolution]. This brilliant feat of our Revolution in the military terrain is little known outside the country. It has been published in anecdotal and sporadic form, but a documented and systematic history of it remains to be written.[1]

—FIDEL CASTRO

Fidel Castro's retrospective analysis of the insurrectionary phase of the Cuban Revolution, delivered at the first Congress of the Cuban Communist Party in 1975, recognizes the contribution of the working class to the revolutionary struggle, but confines this contribution to two areas: active service in the rebel army and the general strike of January 1, 1959. Whereas the latter receives minimal attention in historical accounts of the Revolution, the deeds of the small band of revolutionary guerrillas continue to exert a powerful hold on popular and scholarly depictions of its eventual triumph. Despite the rhetorical invocations of the *pueblo* (the people) by the revolutionary leadership, and despite the official embrace of Marxist-Leninist ideology from 1961, there remains surprisingly little documented and systematic analysis of the contribution of Cuban workers to the eventual overthrow of the detested Batista regime. Yet, as this engaging and meticulously researched book amply demonstrates, a militant and well-organized labor movement, often operating independently of union leaders, played a pivotal role in the victory of the Cuban insurrection, not only through the final *coup de grâce* of the 1959 general strike, but in myriad actions that served to defend workers' interests, resist state repression, and materially support the armed struggle. Thus there was a third arm to the revolutionary forces, a labor movement, which has been consistently ignored by both general and labor historians of Cuba alike.

Scholarly neglect of the role of organized labor in the Cuban Revolution can be partly explained by the nature of the official trade union organization, the Confederacíon de Trabajadores de Cuba (CTC), under the leadership of Eusebio Mujal. As this book vividly describes, the CTC leadership, working hand in glove with the Batista regime, was responsible for gross abuses including interference in union elections, removal from office of elected officials, expulsions of troublesome officials from the unions, and discrediting individual leaders by false or exaggerated accusations of Communism.[2] By 1957, in the wake of further anti-communist purges carried out with the full backing of state security forces, the CTC was openly operating as Mujal's personal fiefdom. However, in conflating organized labor with the corrupt bureaucracy of the CTC, scholars have overlooked or underestimated the activities of ordinary workers and the critical role they played in resisting not only the corrupt trade union leadership but also the iniquities of the Batista regime. Steve Cushion's work calls for a broader definition of organized labor, looking beyond the formal structures of the trade union federation to include the multiplicity of unofficial, informal structures through which ordinary workers defend their interests. This includes the activities of shop stewards, independently minded union officials, strike committees, regional committees, mass meetings, and unofficial, as well as clandestine, networks of militants, all of which make up the wider labor movement and interact together to produce the dynamic of industrial action.

What emerges in this book is a lively and variegated picture of working-class activism that sheds new light on the struggles of workers, ranging from those employed in the more traditionally proletarian sectors of sugar, transport, textiles, and utilities to those in shops, department stores, and white-collar professions in offices and banks. Drawing on a wealth of untapped sources including material from local and provincial archives, interviews with veterans of the labor and revolutionary movements, clandestine publications, leaflets, pamphlets, and other political ephemera encompassing previously unused collections from activists' personal archives, the book offers a rich and detailed account of labor activism in 1950s Cuba. This activism, often undertaken at considerable risk to its protagonists, took multiple forms, from slowdowns, walkouts, and solidarity strikes to mass meetings and street demonstrations, to sabotage and the formation of clandestine cells that would form the basis of the workers' section (*sección obrera*) of the guerrilla movement. Thus, for example, we see railway workers in Guantánamo developing the tactics of *movimiento obrero beligerante* (trade unionism on a war footing), which combined mass action with acts of sabotage, an approach that led telephone workers to cut phone lines, sugar workers to burn fields, and railway workers to derail strikebreaking trains during strikes. Further west, in Matanzas, we see a textile workers' strike leading to the complete shutdown of the city, with female workers in the Woolworth's store playing a central role in enforcing the *ciudad-muerta* (city-wide general strike) in defiance of state security forces who attempted to force them to reopen the store.[3] And in Oriente Province, we see mass demonstrations and a general strike initiated in response to the murder of Frank País, one of the leaders of the Movimiento Revolucionario 26 de Julio (MR-26-7, Revolutionary Movement of July 26), which constituted probably the biggest public demonstration of opposition during the entire Batista dictatorship. As Cushion argues, this strike, so often characterized as spontaneous, suggests the existence of a high level of clandestine organization that was able to react quickly and seize an opportunity without requiring orders to do so.[4]

This attention to local contexts constitutes one of the many contributions of this book. Looking beyond Havana to consider actions right across the island, Cushion highlights the existence of an energetic and independent milieu of local labor activism, acting autonomously from, and indeed in defiance of, the central labor leadership. For example, sugar workers at the Delicias y Chaparra mills in Las Tunas undertook strike action on their own terms after the *mujalista* union officials melted away at the first sign of trouble. These workers organized themselves in the absence of their official leaders by holding daily mass meetings, despite the presence of Rural Guardsmen on horseback with drawn sabers.[5] In Santiago, members of the local PSP, the communist Partido Socialista Popular (Popular Socialist Party), acted in defiance of direct instructions from the leadership in Havana, calling strikes to support the November 1956 *Granma* landing by MR-26-7 rebels, an action considered adventurist by the party's national leadership.[6] This attention to local traditions of activism, local networks, and solidarities, and local responses to national events, contributes to a more variegated picture of working-class activism that highlights the differences and tensions between and within the trade union and political leadership and the rank and file, as well as between the capital and the provinces. It also helps to explain the different outcomes across different sectors and regions, for example, contributing to our understanding of why strikes in some sectors succeeded in achieving their goals while others were defeated. Hence Cushion's regionally differentiated analysis of the August 1957 strike suggests that it was more effective in areas where the M-26-7 and the PSP had a history of established collaboration.[7]

Taken together, the workers' struggles provide a compelling account of how organized labor contributed directly and indirectly to help shape the course of revolutionary struggle in 1950s Cuba. As Cushion depicts so vividly here, workers provided valuable material support for the rebel guerrillas in a number of ways, including organizing significant strike action in support of the *Granma* landing and armed uprising in Santiago. Workers in shops, warehouses, and distribution depots proved valuable by large-scale pilfering of essentials, railway workers were able to move those supplies under the noses of the police, and bus drivers formed propaganda distribution networks, while telephone operators eavesdropped on police conversations, providing vital intelligence for those more directly engaged in the armed struggle.[8] Others organized clandestine networks involved in acts of sabotage such as derailing an armored train carrying soldiers sent to protect the vital railway system, and helping disaffected soldiers to desert. Such actions depended on a high degree of organization that reached its apotheosis in the revolutionary general strike of January 1, 1959. Overlooked in much of the literature, this strike is reassessed here for its decisive contribution to the triumph of the revolution, securing the capital, heading off a potential army coup, and ensuring the victory of the revolutionary forces. This analysis aligns with Castro's own estimation of the strike's significance. Thus, for Cushion, the final victory of the revolutionary forces should be viewed as the result of a combination of armed guerrilla action and mass support.

Cushion's analysis also casts a fresh eye on working-class politics in the period, assessing the relationship between organized labor and the two main organizations seeking to mobilize the working class: the PSP and the M-26-7. In so doing, he brings a new perspective to both, highlighting for example how local traditions of labor militancy directly contributed to the development of the M-26-7's network of clandestine workplace cells (the *secciónes obreras*), and showing how mistakes made at the leadership level derived partly from their lack of experience of labor organizing, contributing to the failure of the general strike called for April 9, 1958. And though the PSP has often been considered a latecomer to the revolutionary struggle, Cushion underscores the immense contribution made by rank-and-file communists in sustaining levels of working-class discontent in areas where they had influence, often at considerable risk to their lives. Meticulously tracing the evolution of the relationship between the M-26-7 and the PSP, this book provides a much more nuanced picture of the internal debates within and between these two organizations, the points of commonality and difference in their respective approaches to confronting the Batista regime, and the local specificities informing the mixture of competition and collaboration that characterized relations between the two. Cushion's detailed analysis of joint endeavors such as the Comités de Unidad Obrera and the Frente Obrero Nacional Unido (FONU) suggests that the coming together of the M-26-7 and the PSP started at the working-class base of both organizations. Local grassroots collaboration between PSP and M-26-7 members in the workplace provided a solid base for unity on which to construct the attempted national organization of a workers' united front.[9]

In foregrounding the courageous struggles of Cuban workers and their families in the face of increasing state brutality, this rich and engaging book makes a welcome addition to the literature on the Cuban Revolution.

—KATE QUINN, *Institute of the Americas,*
*University College, University of London, June 2015*

# INTRODUCTION

The fiftieth anniversary of the Cuban Revolution, in 2009, was marked by the appearance of two films: *Che* and *Ciudad en Rojo*.[1] The first, described as "a grand Hollywood war movie," depicts the revolution as the work of a band of heroic guerrillas with little or no reference to the ordinary people of the island.[2] The second, a Cuban production, shows a day in the life of Santiago de Cuba during the final days of the Batista dictatorship. It portrays the brutal state terror, the organization of the underground resistance and its relationship with the rebel army, as well as the political disagreements and class tensions within the revolutionary movement. These two films represent divergent views of the Cuban insurrection: that of the heroic guerrilla struggle, which is the one most widely held, and that of the middle-class urban underground resistance, which has more recently come to the fore. However, archival research has revealed an additional dimension to the struggle that has been almost universally ignored, the participation of militant organized labor.

Over the years, the Instituto de Historia de Cuba (IHC) in Havana has painstakingly amassed a collection of leaflets, pamphlets, clandestine newspapers, and similar agitational material from the 1950s, most of which were produced by typing directly on thin paper stencils for duplication by a mimeograph machine such as a Gestetner or Roneo. These evoke images of small groups of militant workers, perhaps aided by revolutionary students, meeting in the home of one of their number, secretly producing a few hundred copies of a leaflet to be passed from hand to hand at work, scattered from the windows of passing cars, or left on the seats of public transport. The written content shows a lively working-class political milieu, where the way forward was hotly debated between different tendencies, where strikes and demonstrations were commonplace, and where ordinary workers played an active part in shaping their own destiny. The number of leaflets to have survived is in itself astonishing, given that such material could be a death sentence if discovered during a police raid or at an army checkpoint. As yet no one had made a systematic examination of this remarkable collection.

The center of such action was in all likelihood not Havana, but rather Oriente Province, which was distant from the seat of power and the heartland of the guerrilla struggle. I chose, therefore, to explore in particular detail the provincial archives in Manzanillo, Guantánamo, and Santiago de Cuba. These largely untapped reservoirs of locally produced material testify to a revolutionary process far from the capital in which party political lines often counted for less than workplace and neighborhood solidarity. The written documents from these and other holdings form the bedrock of this study, yet they required contextualizing, and this came from interviewing surviving veterans in different parts of the country. It was an honor to speak to these remarkable men and women; I hope I have done justice to their story.

This book will examine the activities of the organized working class in the period leading to the victory of the Cuban revolutionary forces in 1959. An analysis of these activities in the Cuban case can add to the wider debate about the relationship between working-class mass action and the armed struggle in the context of opposition to an authoritarian regime. The political economy of Cuba in the 1950s will be examined to determine the extent to which economic considerations affected the course of the revolution. The book will analyze why some groups of workers supported the rebels from an early stage, while others stayed loyal to their official leaders or to the Communist Party. The role of the Communist Party has been shrouded in an ideological mist arising from the Cold War. An examination of the party's public statements and details from primary sources about the manner in which party members applied these policies paint a more nuanced picture than is usually given.

It is not my intention here to deny the importance of the guerrillas or the middle-class underground in the fight to overthrow Batista, but rather to argue that neither view presents a complete picture, that there was a third arm to the rebel forces, a revolutionary labor movement. The findings of my research clearly suggest there has been a silencing of this third dimension, intentional or otherwise. One obvious reason for this is that the story of a few heroic guerrillas overcoming seemingly impossible odds makes for a romantic story, whereas the recounting of dogged labor activity does not have the same appeal. In the early days of revolutionary Cuba, this romance was a weapon in the hands of the more radical elements in the leadership in their battles with those, often associated with the urban underground, who wished to slow the pace of change. From the other end of the political spectrum, the idea that the Cuban Revolution was the work of a few individuals without mass support also suited its enemies in the United States, and this helps explain their apparent belief that the death of Fidel Castro was all that was required to reverse the changes.

This book therefore challenges the notion that the revolution emerged from a rural guerrilla struggle in which the organized working class played no role and that the workers who did participate did so as individual citizens rather than as part of an organized labor movement. It will document substantial labor organizing, which played a pivotal role in key places and times in the 1950s, especially outside Havana and markedly in eastern Cuba. It is my intention to give organized labor its due credit for the role it played in the overthrow of the Batista dictatorship.

By focusing on the period from 1952 to 1959, my emphasis is on the insurrection rather than the outcome of the Cuban Revolution and thus the eventual effect on the structure of the state, the economy, and society. Nevertheless, understanding the social forces involved in the insurrection phase of a revolution is essential to an understanding of the subsequent changes in the structure of society. It is a question of examining the level of participation of workers in the events of the time, acting collectively rather than as individual citizens, and analyzing how workers' class interests fitted into the wider class structure, national politics and the economy.

A picture emerges of a vibrant clandestine milieu in which working-class militants debated, collaborated, and competed for influence, but always in the context of organizing active opposition to the dictatorship. In order to recount the events considered vital to the analysis of the role of the Cuban working class in the insurrection, this narrative is organized on a chronological basis. Such an approach requires a periodization in order to be intelligible and, in terms of working-class politics and activity, we can divide the Batista years into distinct periods, divided by qualitative changes in the level of state repression. Tony Kapcia, writing about fifty years of the Cuban Revolution, punctuates this account by the various crises affecting Cuban society.[3] This approach also proved useful as a method of dividing the period leading up to the rebel victory. Of course, it may be argued that the period was one of continual crisis, but within this, there were peaks and troughs that provoked changes and turns in the tactics of both the government and the rebels.

From Batista's coup in March 1952 until the fraudulent elections of November 1954, little changed from the days of Batista's predecessor, President Carlos Prío Socarrás. The fall in the price of sugar caused a crisis in the economy, and from the end of 1954 until the end of 1956, there was a concerted effort by the government and the employers to increase productivity by reducing workers' wages and decreasing staffing levels. This was achieved by a combination of collaboration with the trade union bureaucracy and relatively low levels of state repression, with police habitually beating workers with clubs and dousing them with fire hoses but with very few deaths. The arrival of the *Granma* and the start of the rebel insurgency was a crisis for the regime, whose approach changed in early 1957 as the forces of the state began to confront the armed guerrillas in the mountains. From this point in time, the regime used death squads, routine torture, and "disappearances" in an attempt to make organized resistance cower to its rule. April 1958 proved to be a crisis point for the rebels as their attempt at a general strike failed disastrously. This crisis caused both the Movimiento Revolucionario 26 de Julio (MR-26-7, Revolutionary Movement 26 of July) and the communist Partido Socialista Popular (PSP, Popular Socialist Party) to rethink their tactics and their relationship with each other. It also gave increased confidence to the government and, during the summer and autumn of 1958, Batista launched a full-scale military attack on the rebels in their mountain strongholds. The failure to destroy the rebel army was the regime's final crisis and created a situation in which a successful general strike would force the dictator from office. The chapter structure follows this periodization, with chapters 1 and 2 forming an introductory background, chapters 3 and 4 examining the period 1954 to 1956, chapters 5 and 6 dealing with 1957 to mid-1958, chapter 7 the second half of 1958, and chapter 8 taking the history into the first year of the revolutionary government.

Chapter 1 examines the nature and history of the Cuban working class, its political and industrial organization, informed by a discussion of the historical role of the trade union bureaucracy.

Chapter 2 considers the state of the Cuban economy in this period. Given the overwhelming importance of sugar in the national economy, the falling price on the world market led to an economic crisis. This in turn led Cuban employers to seek to maintain their profit margins by means of a productivity drive, which, given the strength of the trade unions, could only be achieved under an authoritarian regime. This is offered as an explanation for the support from business interests for the 1952 coup and subsequent dictatorship.

Chapter 3 recounts the history of the class struggles of the year 1955 and stresses the importance of these strikes for the relationship between militant workers and the July 26 Movement. In particular the battles of that year are analyzed in terms of the success or failure of the employers' productivity drive.

Chapter 4 argues that the defeat in most of the 1955 disputes led some militant workers to draw the conclusion that they needed armed support if they were to be able to resist the government and their employers in order to defend their wages and conditions. In particular, a group of experienced trade union militants from Guantánamo in eastern Cuba started to build a clandestine cell structure in support of their aims. This network had its first real test at the end of 1956 when it was able to organize significant action in support of the *Granma* landing, when Fidel Castro returned from Mexico.

Chapter 5 examines working-class responses to the government's increased use of arbitrary arrest, torture, disappearances and death squads. This campaign of state terror affected both the July 26th Movement and the communists. The political and organizational response of both organizations is outlined and analyzed, with particular emphasis on the way in which local activists interpreted their own group's line, and how this new situation affected their relationship.

Chapter 6 subsequently examines two general strikes, August 1957 and April 1958, the first a success, the second a failure. It analyzes the reasons for the different outcomes and shows how these outcomes affected the politics of the PSP and MR-26-7. These two strikes are reassessed in the light of the process of convergence between the two groups.

Chapter 7 continues this theme of convergence and traces its organizational form. In particular it gives details of workers' congresses in territory under the control of the rebel forces. These two congresses show the true level of working-class organization in support of the revolution and refute the arguments of those who say that such support was merely passive. In the process, it becomes clear that the trade union bureaucracy was marginalized by the activity of the rebel army and by grassroots trade union activists.

A revolution does not succeed with the seizure of power, but with its consolidation. In the first year of the new Cuba, organized labor played an important role in that process of consolidation and in the final triumph of the more radical wing of the revolutionary forces. Chapter 8 therefore returns to the theme of trade union bureaucracy, as the disputes within the rebel leadership on the future course of the revolution are fought inside the trade union federation.

A concluding section draws together the main themes of the book and answers the question of what exactly the role was of the organized working class in the Cuban insurrection of the 1950s.

I WOULD LIKE TO THANK Kate Quinn and Jean Stubbs for their help, support, encouragement, and constructive engagement. I am also extremely grateful to Angelina Rojas and Jorge Ibarra Guitart of the Instituto de Historia de Cuba, my mentors in Cuba and the source of much encouragement and advice. I also acknowledge the generous help of Alcibíades Poveda Díaz, Alejandra Lopez, Alejandra Serpente, Alex Ostmann, Alfredo Menéndez, Barry Carr, Beatriz Rajland, Belkis Quesada, Bill Booth, Brian Pollitt, Camillia Cowling, Carrie Gibson, Clem Seecharan, Colin Lewis, Daniel Kersffeld, Delio Orozco and the staff of the Manzanillo Archives, Fernando Carcases and the staff of the Library of the University of Oriente, Dylan Vernon, Emily Morris, Erin Clermont, Felipe Pérez, Francis Velázquez Fuentes, Francisco Monserrat

Iser, Gary Tennant, Gloria García, Hal Klepak, Ian Birchall, Inés Enoa Castillo, James Dunkerley, Jana Lipman, Jerry Hagelberg, Jon Curry-Machado, Jorge Giovanetti, Jorge Ibarra Cuesta, José Puello Socarrás, José Sanchez Guerra and the staff of the Guantánamo provincial archive, Juan Carlos Gomez, Juan Venegas, Julio Garcia, Liz Dore, Ken Fuller, Kevin Middlebrook, Kristine Hatzky, Leonie Jordan, Luis Figures, Luis Suarez, Maily Acosta and the staff of the Archivo Historico Provincial de Las Villas, Maku Veloz, Mandy Banton, Margarita Canseco, María Celia Cotarelo, María Victoria Antúnez Salto, Maritza Mendez and the staff of the IHC archives, Martin Paddio, Mary Turner, Maxine Molyneux, Michael Yates, Mildred de la Torre Molina, Murray Glickman, Natividad Alfaro, Nicolás Iñigo Carrera, Olivia Saunders, Oscar Zanetti, Paulo Drinot, Pedro Machado, Philip Mansfield, Rafael Duharte and the staff of the Oficina del Historiador de Santiago de Cuba, Reinaldo Suárez, Robert Whitney, Robin Blackburn, Servando Valdés Sánchez, Silvia Blanca-Nogales, Shirley Pemberton, Sue Thomas, Tony Kapcia, Vicente Perez, and Victor Bulmer-Thomas.

Without their help, this study would not have materialized. The responsibility for amassing and interpreting the material, however, lies with me.

# 1. ORGANIZED LABOR IN THE 1950S

In the early 1950s, the Cuban trade union federation, the Confederación de Trabajadores de Cuba (CTC, Cuban Workers' Confederation), headed by General Secretary Eusebio Mujal, was widely seen as corrupt and undemocratic. It had not always been like this, but the Cold War attack on organized labor, which affected the whole of the Americas, north and south, was particularly successful in Cuba. Following the 1947 CTC Congress, the communists had been removed from their previous position of leadership and replaced by a new bureaucracy that seemed more interested in enhancing their own comfortable existence than in defending workers' wages and conditions. However, the actions of the trade union leadership cannot be explained solely by corrupt practices but must be understood in relation to analysis of their politics, which prevented them from seeing beyond the parameters set by the capitalist system. In the difficult economic circumstances facing postwar Cuba, the CTC leadership was prepared to restrict the demands they put forward on behalf of their members to the employers' "ability to pay." But though the leadership accepted that trade union demands had to be "affordable" and "realistic," growing numbers of Cuban workers did not see it that way. This resulted in tensions within the unions between the rank and file and the bureaucracy, which led militant Cuban workers to build unofficial structures in order to defend their interests.[1]

Nevertheless, trade unions are never monolithic, relying on voluntary officials such as shop stewards and branch secretaries to maintain local organization. There is therefore nearly always a space in which militants can organize to counteract the domination of the bureaucracy. During the crisis in which Cuba found itself during the 1950s, there was still a lively independent milieu within the labor movement at the local level, where the authority of the CTC bureaucracy was contested and became a battleground between the various currents competing for influence within the working class.

*Historical Background*

The organized labor movement in Cuba dates back to the guilds and craft unions of the nineteenth century, but the first nationwide trade union federation, the Confederación Nacional Obrera de Cuba (CNOC, Cuban National Labor Confederation), was not founded until 1925. In the same year, Gerardo Machado was democratically elected president, but his regime became increasingly repressive as the effects of the economic crisis of the late 1920s raised the temperature of the class struggle. Cuba's sugar-based economy was already suffering from reductions in U.S. purchases as a result of political pressure from mainland producers, with the result that the Wall Street Crash of 1929 had a particularly devastating effect on the island.[2]

The situation came to a head in 1933 when a strike by Havana bus drivers developed into a general strike that, in conjunction with a rebellion by students and an army mutiny led by Sergeant Fulgencio Batista, brought down the government. It is worth noting that the Cuban Communist Party (PCC), which had progressively gained control of the CNOC toward the end of the 1920s, tried unsuccessfully to call off the strike in return for minor concessions from the Machado government, and this may be seen as confirmation of the politically moderating effect of having control of a trade union apparatus. The government of Ramón Grau San Martín, which took office after the uprising, proved to be neither capable of satisfying the aspirations of the workers nor being able to bring them under control. The state of dual power that resulted from this contradiction was brought to a close by Batista, who, working closely with the U.S. ambassador, used his control of the army to defeat a general strike in 1935. Initially ruling through puppet presidents, Batista imposed a regime that has been described as both co-optive and repressive, a model that operated by combining a mixture of nationalist demagogy and minor social reforms with repression of any attempt by workers to exceed the boundaries established by the government.[3]

The CNOC did not recover from the defeat of the 1935 general strike, while the PCC, itself considerably weakened by police repression, reached an understanding with Batista whereby, in return for legalization, they worked to broaden its narrow social base. One of the outcomes of this arrangement was the replacement of the CNOC by a new organization, the Confederación de Trabajadores de Cuba, which was, from the outset, a state-sponsored trade union. A low level of subscription payment led to dependency on the state, a dependency that was increased by the CTC's approach to defending its members' interests, which mainly depended on the leadership's relationship with the Ministry of Labor, rather than industrial action or collective bargaining.[4] This relationship left the CTC leadership vulnerable to a change of government.

Batista finally tired of indirect rule and, in 1940, with the support of the communists, won the first honest general election in Cuban history. The PCC, now renamed the Partido Socialista Popular (PSP), under the influence of Moscow, declared a class truce during the Second World War, which resulted in a wage freeze and no-strike deal. This reduced its credibility among the general CTC membership, the majority of whom were more interested in their material conditions than in the war in Europe. Thus, when Batista's chosen successor stood for election with PSP support in 1944, he was defeated by Grau San Martín and his Auténtico Party.[5] The communists' wartime "non-political" approach made them superfluous, while their trade union practice, a combination of undemocratic bureaucratic control and a reliance on government patronage, left them in a weak position. The logic of dependence on a relationship with the state is that with the arrival of a new government other factions could offer a closer relationship and thereby gain popular support. The Comisión Obrera Nacional Auténtica (CONA, National Labor Commission of the Auténtico Party) led by Eusebio Mujal and linked to the ruling Auténtico Party, did just this. Throughout the spring of 1947, the Auténticos made gains in the sugar and port workers' unions, while some PSP officials defected to CONA.

There were some armed skirmishes between members of the PSP and the CONA in 1944–45, but matters came to a head at the 5th CTC

Congress in 1947 when, following a violent dispute over credentials, the Minister of Labor, Carlos Prío, suspended the congress and then used the powers of his ministry to give control of the federation to the CONA, although initially the general secretary was an independent, an official of the electrical workers' union named Angel Cofiño. The PSP did not have sufficient active support to prevent the takeover of the CTC and an attempted general strike called by the displaced communist leadership failed, with only the Havana dockworkers and tram drivers coming out in support. In areas where government intervention proved insufficient to impose a new leadership, gangsters linked to the Auténticos used violence to enforce the change of officials. This included the murder of three of the most respected communist workers' leaders, the dockworker Aracelio Iglesias, the cigar-roller Miguel Fernández Roig, and the sugar worker, Jésus Menéndez.[6] An attempt to form a communist-controlled breakaway federation failed when a new law required a union to be affiliated to the official federation before it could sign a collective agreement and this led many previously PSP-led unions to reenter the official CTC controlled by the Auténticos in order to preserve their legal status.[7]

Thereafter, Mujal, who quickly succeeded Cofiño as general secretary, used his links to Carlos Prío, who was elected president in 1948, to secure enough economic gains for his members to maintain his position and to prove that his grouping, referred to as *mujalistas*, were at least as effective as the communists they had replaced.[8] Thus, in 1950, a Havana tram strike, led by communists, was defeated by police repression, while bank workers were granted their demands on condition that they affiliate with the CTC(A). Reports from the British ambassador in 1952 are full of criticism of the "endless irresponsible demands of the labor movement," which he blamed on Mujal, who "imposed his will on President Prío and secured satisfaction for his every whim, however irresponsible and prejudicial to the long term interests of the country it might be." The U.S. embassy made similar complaints; they used more moderate language, but their frustration with the strength of organized labor comes through just as clearly.[9]

Cuba in the 1950s had the highest percentage of unionized workers in Latin America (see Table 1.1).[10] The Cuban labor movement was organized in a single confederation, the CTC, which had a membership of over one million workers out of a total national population of six million. This membership was divided into industrial federations with the sugar workers' federation, the FNTA, accounting for half the membership. These federations were in turn divided into local unions covering either a geographical area or a single employer depending on the structure of the industry. There were also provincial and city-wide confederations of all of the CTC unions in the area covered. The Cuban trade union movement was highly centralized, with the CTC leadership claiming and exerting authority over the individual federations. By the mid-1950s, this centralized control was exerted with the support of the Ministry of Labor, backed up by the police where necessary. The removal of the communists from office may have suited the Cold War foreign policy objectives of the U.S. government, but did little in itself to improve the productivity of Cuban workers. This would require a more structural weakening of their industrial organization.

Much of the Cold War was fought on the battleground of organized labor and the *mujalista* takeover of the CTC,

## TABLE 1.1: CTC Membership

| Industrial Federation | Membership |
| --- | --- |
| Sugar | 550,000 |
| Tobacco | 98,000 |
| Transport | 80,000 |
| Construction | 75,000 |
| Commerce | 65,000 |
| Textiles | 50,000 |
| Maritime | 35,000 |
| Food Processing | 32,000 |
| Petroleum | 27,000 |
| Railways | 25,000 |
| Cattle Farming | 22,000 |
| Flour Processing | 20,000 |
| Shoes | 19,000 |
| Medicine | 19,000 |
| Gastronomy | 16,800 |
| Metallurgy | 16,000 |
| Barbers | 15,000 |
| Beverages | 12,000 |
| Printing | 10,000 |
| Furniture | 8,500 |
| Electric, Gas, Water | 7,300 |
| Cinema | 5,200 |
| Insurance | 5,200 |
| Banking | 4,000 |
| Shows | 4,000 |
| Musicians | 4,000 |
| Salesmen | 4,000 |
| Telephone | 3,500 |
| Aviation | 2,000 |
| Medical Sales | 2,000 |
| Telegraph | 600 |
| TOTAL | 1,237,100 |

Source: U.S. Embassy, Havana, Dispatch 1309 (June 29, 1955).

and the subsequent purges can be seen as part of the Cold War anti-communist offensive. The 1950s were a period of great tension in the Cold War and the extent of communist influence in Cuba was a matter of great concern, often verging on paranoia, as can be seen by the British embassy's pleasure that the singer Josephine Baker, "this hot gospeller of racism, Peronism and communism," fell afoul of the military intelligence authorities and was deported from the island.[11] The Western powers had a firm public ally in the International Congress of Free Trade Unions (ICFTU), which had its origins in an anti-communist split from the World Federation of Trade Unions (WFTU) in 1949. The CTC affiliated to the ICTFU at its 6th Congress and would go on to organize the anti-communist work of the ICTFU's Latin American section, the Organización Regional Interamericana de Trabajadores (ORIT, InterAmerican Regional Organization of Workers), using money provided by Batista, who acted as a "laundry service" for the U.S. State Department.[12] A major figure in this process was Serafino Romualdi, who was employed openly by the AFL and covertly by the CIA.[13] In retrospect, Romualdi's 1947 article "Labor and Democracy in Latin America" can be seen as a declaration of Cold War within the international labor movement.[14] This resulted in the pro-U.S. ORIT splitting from the Latin American section of the WFTU, the Confederación de Trabajadores de America Latina (CTAL, Latin American Confederation of Workers). Romualdi worked closely with Mujal and Bernardo Ibañez of the Chilean union federation in the setting up of ORIT. He explains in his autobiography that the role of ORIT was not just political anti-communism, but also to create "a new type of Latin American trade union leader who, abandoning the customary concept of the class struggle, would substitute constructive relations between the workers and the employers."[15]

This may explain why the ICFTU was completely satisfied with the situation in Cuba under Batista, with the British Foreign Office noting the "refreshing spectacle of an American dictator enjoying the support of ICTFU."[16]

Mujal's anti-communism should not be seen as coming from any principled political position; indeed, he had once been a Communist Party member, but he always managed to be affiliated with the group that most favored his career prospects. His rapprochement with Batista should not therefore have been a great surprise. The logic of a trade union whose practice is based on maintaining a good relationship with the state requires a change of allegiance with each new government. This happened very quickly following Batista's coup. Apart from a few isolated strikes in particularly well-organized workplaces such as the Matanzas textile industry and some Havana bus routes, there was little response from organized labor to the March 10, 1952, coup. Such working-class resistance that did occur was quickly isolated and crushed.[17] The official trade unions made a token show of resistance, with Mujal first calling a general strike and then rapidly calling it off before most workers even heard.[18]

The majority of the trade union bureaucracy quickly came to an accommodation with the new regime,[19] and Mujal went on to become one of Batista's most loyal collaborators. In return for this collaboration, the government turned a blind eye to corruption and obliged employers to deduct trade union dues from workers' wages by means of a compulsory check-off, which isolated the CTC leadership from rank-and-file pressure.[20] This measure was to prove deeply unpopular, and, throughout Batista's period in office, the demand for the abolition of the *cuota sindical* appeared on every list of workers' demands. The Havana dockworkers, despite police intervention, made such an issue of the matter that the employers eventually paid the money over to the CTC without deducting it from their wages.[21] Its abolition was one of the first acts of the revolutionary government on seizing power in 1959.

This, therefore, is the context in which *mujalismo*, nationalism, and communism, the three major tendencies within Cuban organized labor, came to contest the leadership of the movement.

## *Mujalismo*

The *mujalistas*, as the leadership of the CTC around Eusebio Mujal have come to be known, were widely seen as being extremely corrupt. Their corruption was indeed a contributing factor in their support for the Batista regime, but another equally important factor can be found in the nature of trade union bureaucracy in a capitalist society.

Trade unions, as their name implies, are organized around sectional divisions that reflect the economic structure of capitalism, which in turn institutionalizes the divisions between different groups of workers. This allows the government to confront workers sector by sector and thereby avoid a generalized response, which could otherwise overwhelm the forces of the state deployed in support of the employers. As long as the role of a union is seen as defending workers' interests within the capitalist mode of production, with its differential wage structure, these divisions will remain. It would appear impractical in this context to discuss the wages of bank clerks and sugar workers in the same negotiations. Trade union bureaucracy is based on the sectional nature of the unions and arises from a division of labor between the ordinary workers and those who negotiate on their behalf. This bureaucracy has developed interests of its own, different from the mass of workers it represents, which depend on the ability to mediate between capital and labor. This leads to a more conservative social view, even among those who started their trade union career as class-conscious militants, with a resulting propensity to vacillate. The actions of full-time trade union officials will largely depend on the balance of conflicting forces; employer or state pressure from above and rank-and-file pressure from below.

One of the common traits of trade unions everywhere is a tendency to avoid mass working-class involvement in politics, as any such involvement must raise the question of state power and on whose behalf it is being used. This in turn would bring the economic structure of society into question and threaten the comfortable position of full-time officials, who depend upon having two antagonistic classes to mediate between. This, of course, does not prevent individual trade union leaders from pursuing personal political careers, but this is normally kept separate from their industrial functions, maintaining the fiction of a distinction between the "political" and the "economic" that lies at the heart of reformist labor politics. None of this is to say that individual trade union officials cannot rise above these pressures and act in a militant class-conscious fashion, but for them to do so requires a firm political position, which is normally only possible when they have considerable support and/or pressure from below.

It might be thought that the formation of a national confederation of unions, such as the Cuban CTC, would give the officials a more universalist approach and highlight the common interests of the working class. Indeed, this has always been the justification for forming such national federations. However, the leaders of a national federation form another bureaucracy that sits on top of the bureaucratic layer that already exists in the federating unions. Rank-and-file pressure on the national federation leaders is mediated by that intermediate layer. As a result, national federations tend to be more conservative than their component parts. The fact that they are balancing between two social classes allows a certain room for maneuvering, and this partial independence presents the bureaucracy with the possibility of working for their own interests.

In the case of the Cuban Republic, this self-interest expressed itself in the form of a level of corruption on a par with the corrupt nature of society as a whole, and the CTC general secretary, Eusebio Mujal, was no exception. Not content with his salary of $280,000 a year, he was susceptible to manipulation by a government prepared to use public finances to corruptly advance its policies. Mujal and his associates therefore became an important prop of the dictatorship. The role they played arose from a combination of factors, with the position of the trade union bureaucracy in capitalist society and the corrupt nature of the individuals concerned becoming pressures that were pushing in the same direction. Most writers on the period speak of the evident corruption of the leadership of the CTC, but the idea that this merely reinforced the tendency toward caution and compromise inherent in trade union bureaucracy is normally neglected.[22]

Mujal's arguments had a logic and were not incompatible with the economic nationalist politics that dominated working-class political discussion, on condition that the necessity of operating within the prevailing economic and political system was accepted. Thus he was able to report to a May Day meeting in 1952 that he had called off the March 10th strike against the coup in return for Batista's guarantee of workers' rights and the confirmation of existing trade union officials.[23] He argued for the trade unions to stay out of politics and claimed that his friendly relationship with Batista was merely pragmatic and was the best way to advance workers' interests, thereby avoiding any discussion of the nature of the regime.[24] He constantly spoke of increasing productivity to help create new jobs and argued that it was true solidarity for those workers in employment to make sacrifices to help create jobs for the unemployed: "Anyone who does not cooperate in promoting the prosperity of the nation is a traitor to Cuba. The workers' movement is inclined to reach agreements and compromises which lead to more work and greater production."[25]

A typical example of the *mujalista* method was Mujal's relationship with the trade union organization in the U.S. base in Guantánamo Bay. In 1950, the trade union for the base workers was set up jointly by the American Federation of Labor (AFL) and the CTC as a moderate, bureaucratic, anti-communist organization with a no-strike policy, membership of which was confined to permanent staff, thereby excluding the daily-paid contract workers and potentially establishing the permanent employees as a sort of labor aristocracy. U.S. Navy authorities were reluctant to recognize the union at first, but following the establishment of the Batista dictatorship in 1952 and under pressure from the State Department via Romualdi, saw that a moderate organization that could channel workers' resentments along harmless paths would be to their advantage. Mujal initially threatened to mobilize the whole Cuban labor movement in support of the base workers' union if it were not recognized, but, as soon as he obtained this recognition, he ensured that the union was run by moderate men, confining themselves to occasional nationalistic rhetorical outbursts, while practically achieving little to improve the material conditions of the membership. When even this rhetoric proved too much for the base commander in 1954, Mujal "intervened" and called fraudulent union elections to ensure that his own people organized matters without troubling the employer.[26]

The CTC in the 1950s did manage to prevent some of the employers' worst excesses, but if a trade union accepts the principles of capitalism, then during an economic crisis, if the employer really cannot afford to pay, the reformist trade union leader has no choice but to accept a cut in his members' wages. This is of course easier for the trade union bureaucrat to accept as he does not himself have to lose money. In the world economic situation of the 1950s, particularly given the falling world price of sugar, Cuban capitalism could neither afford to pay the existing level of wages nor maintain manning levels as they were. So, opposition to productivity increases required a revolutionary perspective at odds with the normally cautious attitude of most full-time trade union officials. Such a revolutionary perspective had its deepest roots in Oriente Province, particularly in the town of Guantánamo, which, ironically, was also Eusebio Mujal's hometown. It was in Oriente that Cuban anti-imperialism found its strongest base.

## Nationalism

Some sections of the Cuban manufacturing bourgeoisie were attracted to ideas of economic nationalism such as protective tariffs and import substitution, but they were hampered in their campaign for such measures by two main factors. Firstly, there was considerable intermingling of commercial and manufacturing capital, which caused a conflict of interest because commercial capital was strongly attached to the link with the United States.[27] Secondly, both national and foreign manufacturing capital suffered from the same problems of low productivity, and this would push many Cuban employers into an alliance of self-interest with American capitalism.

At a Conference for the Advancement of the National Economy in 1947, Cuban industrialists called for higher productivity and for easier dismissal of unwanted employees, linking this with measures to attract foreign capital. There was also a trend toward the merger of foreign and national capital in joint ventures, thereby increasing the convergence of interests between the Cuban industrial bourgeoisie and U.S. capitalism as foreign investment increased in the hope of larger profit margins.[28] This structural integration led to a lessening of nationalist sentiment among Cuban industrialists that was not reflected in working-class attitudes.

Although the integration of U.S. and Cuban capital resulted in a more positive view of the United States among the elite, the attitudes of working-class people, who often bore the brunt of U.S. economic domination, became more hostile. Charles Page comments: "For years, the Cuban workers' bloodiest strikes were against the intransigence of certain American enterprises."[29]

This close relationship between U.S. and Cuban capital could inflame nationalist passions when that relationship seemed to the detriment of other classes. An example of this is the *Canal Vía Cuba*. This was an American project to build a canal that would cut across the whole island, from the Bay of Cárdenas in the north to the Bay of Pigs in the south. This elicited considerable opposition from many different sections of the community, but was most unpopular among the workers and students.[30] Thus the newly elected president of the university students union, the Federación Estudiantil Universitaria (FEU, Federation of University Students), José Antonio Echeverría, described it as a direct attack on the

**TABLE 1.2: Direct U.S. Investment in Cuba (millions of dollars)**

| Investments | 1929 | 1936 | 1946 | 1950 | 1953 | 1954 | 1957 |
|---|---|---|---|---|---|---|---|
| | | | | | | (1) | (4) |
| Agriculture | 575 | 265 | 227 | 263 | 263 | 272 | 275 |
| Petroleum (2) | 9 | 6 | 15 | 20 | 24 | 27 | 81 |
| Manufacturing | 45 | 27 | 40 | 54 | 58 | 55 | 76 |
| Public Services | 215 | 315 | 251 | 271 | 297 | 303 | 353 |
| Commerce | 15 | 15 | 12 | 21 | 24 | 35 | 49 |
| Other industries (3) | 60 | 38 | 8 | 13 | 18 | 21 | 118 |
| **TOTALS** | **919** | **666** | **553** | **642** | **686** | **713** | **952** |

NOTES:  (1) Preliminary figures.
(2) Includes investments in refineries and market facilities
(3) Does not include direct U.S. government investments in mineral plants.
(4) Includes previous figures plus later investments largely made through Cuban banks and finance agencies such as BANFAIC, BANDES, Financiera Nacional de Cuba, and others, to June 1957.

Source: Through 1954, U.S. Department of Commerce.

island's sovereignty, and the railway workers of Guantánamo organized an opposition meeting jointly with the city's student federation that attracted many of the city's leading citizens.[31] *Carta Semanal*, the Communist Party's clandestine newspaper, called it a military project, which was designed to enable the United States to deploy its fleet and which would make Cuba a nuclear target in time of war. The paper went on to condemn the proposed canal as an 80-km-long port with lower wages and bulk loading of sugar where Cuban employment law would not apply.[32] This last aspect drew the virulent opposition of the dockworkers' union, the Federación de Obreros Marítimos Nacional (FOMN, National Federation of Maritime Workers), whose conference unanimously opposed the project, comparing it to the Panama Canal.[33] Juan Taquechel, leader of the Santiago dockers, sent a letter to all his fellow workers condemning the project in terms that combined anti-imperialism, nationalism, and anti-militarism with a promise to resist the canal's threat to jobs and conditions.[34] The outcry was such that the project was quickly abandoned, an indication of widespread Cuban anti-imperialist sentiment just below the surface.

**FIGURE 1.2: Direct U.S. Investment in Cuba**

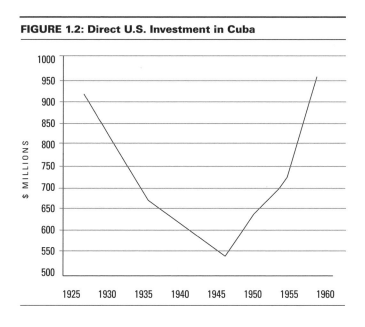

Any nationalist movement requires a mass base to advance its policies and, given the island's gross economic inequality, a Cuban nationalist program had to address the region's social problems if it were to attract support from the impoverished peasants and workers. This gave Cuban nationalism its characteristic nature as a mass popular movement. Such arguments attracted considerable working-class support, with the close relationship between the Cuban bourgeoisie and U.S. imperialism leading many workers to see the national question in class terms. However, this did not often lead to the posing of socialism as an alternative, but merely to seeing the ruling class as "traitors." Indeed there was no organization in Cuba in the 1950s advocating an openly socialist perspective. While nationalist sentiments dominated Cuban working-class politics in the 1950s, there were various forms they could take, ranging from the revolutionary to the reformist. The labor movement was to be one of the battlegrounds within which the competing approaches would seek support.

In addition to a well-structured bureaucratic trade union organization, there also existed a long tradition of independent action organized unofficially at the rank-and-file level. The informal organization behind this was still actively operating in the early 1950s, despite the *mujalista* takeover of the official structure. This was particularly true in eastern Cuba where, far from the union head offices in Havana, militants found the need for a greater level of self-help. Insofar as the workers who organized this independent activity were politically affiliated, they tended to be associated either with the PSP, or else with the Auténticos and the Ortodoxos.[35] However, the behavior of Eusebio Mujal and his associates largely discredited the Auténticos, with whom he had previously been affiliated, and the death of Eddie Chibas deprived the Ortodoxos of much of their attraction, which was largely based around his charismatic leadership.[36] In any case, the Ortodoxos had little to offer workers faced with an employing class and a government concerned to increase profitability. Therefore, the tendencies previously associated with the reformist parties, or at least those who rejected the collaborationist policies of Mujal, were increasingly searching for a militant alternative. The newly formed Movimiento Revolucionario 26 de Julio (MR-26-7) would gain many of its first working-class members from the disillusioned ex-supporters of these reformist organizations, whose anti-communist political trajectory prevented them from seeing the PSP as a potential alternative. In order to understand the political development of these local activists, who were used to operating independently of the union bureaucracy, it may be useful to look at the earlier history of one particular group's involvement in the Cuban class struggle.

In 1924, the Havana leadership of the Hermandad Ferroviaria (Railway Brotherhood), the main railway trade union, refused to support the railway workers employed by the Ferrocarril del Norte de Cuba (North Cuba Railway) in Morón, members of an independent union who had walked out in solidarity with striking Camaqüey sugar workers. Nevertheless, despite the official attitude, the *delegaciones*[37] in Santiago and Guantánamo soon also walked out in support of their colleagues in Morón and put pressure on the national leadership to change its position. This incident is an example of the level of independence existing in the eastern end of the island where local loyalties were often stronger than formal affiliations to national organizations. Thus in 1943, by which time the CTC was under communist control and had signed a no-strike truce with the first Batista government for the duration of the war, the Guantánamo *delegaciónes* launched a strike in an attempt to enforce the payment of a 15 percent wage increase that had been decreed by the government, but from which they were excluded.[38] A strike during the Second World War was considered unpatriotic by the PSP, given their priority of maximum support for the Allied war effort following the German attack on the Soviet Union. They denounced the strikers' leaders as "Trotskyites," and for once this often misused accusation was true.[39]

In the 1930s, Cuban Trotskyism had its principal base in Guantánamo, where the Partido Obrero Revolucionario (POR, Revolutionary Workers' Party)[40] was led by a railwayman, Antonio "Ñico" Torres Chedebaux.[41] Torres was an experienced working-class militant who started his working life in the sugar industry in the Guantánamo region, but was victimized in 1931 for his involvement in a strike against the Machado dictatorship. In 1934 he joined the POR, along with Gustavo Fraga Jacomino, in time to participate in the party's intervention in the peasant struggles at Realengo 18, in the mountains near Guantánamo.[42] Unemployed and blacklisted for the remainder of the 1930s, Torres finally secured employment on the railway, and in 1942 was elected Secretario de Correspondencia by the members of Delegación 11, from which position he became one of the acknowledged leaders of the Guantánamo labor movement.[43] By the mid-1950s, he was part of a loose network of militants that operated very effectively in the Guantánamo region. This network would go on to play a significant role in the developing revolutionary resistance to Batista and would later provide the organizational framework and develop the tactics of the July 26 Movement, led by Fidel Castro.

Statements made at the founding conference of the Cuban Communist Party indicate that when Fidel Castro and 135 others attacked the Moncada army barracks in Santiago de Cuba on July 26, 1953, it was with the intention of provoking an armed popular insurrection aimed at overthrowing the dictatorship.[44] A letter written by Castro to Luis Conte Agüero in December 1953 nuances this by suggesting the intention was to provoke a mutiny of army officers who were members of the Ortodoxo Party and that this would, it was hoped, provide a backbone to the popular uprising.[45] Whatever the attackers' motivations, the action itself failed disastrously. However, the torture and murder of many of the attackers revolted a large number of ordinary Cubans and won a measure of sympathy for the young rebels. Castro himself was sentenced to fifteen years in prison, but he was released in May 1955 following an amnesty campaign.[46] However, finding it impossible to operate in Cuba with his life under threat from agents of the regime, he left for Mexico on June 24.[47] He was still technically a member of the Ortodoxos and started organizing the MR-26-7 as a faction inside that party, issuing the first manifesto from Mexico on August 8, 1955.[48] This proposed a solution to the country's problems based on agrarian reform, reestablishing workers' rights, profit sharing in industry, rent reduction, social housing, the nationalization of foreign-owned utilities, the establishment of a social security system and measures for the state to aid industrialization. This was a radical program, but not one that crossed the bounds of economic nationalism, nor was it explicitly anti-imperialist.

At the founding meeting of the MR-26-7 on June 12, 1955, it was agreed to set up a workers' section, or *sección obrera*, to coordinate the movement's activities among organized labor, national responsibility for which was given to a sugar worker from Camagüey, Luis Bonito.[49] Thereafter, every local group of the MR-26-7 that was formed appointed one or more of the leadership team to be responsible for setting up a local *sección obrera*. The process was uneven at first, with greater initial success in the east. The group of Guantánamo railway workers around Ñico Torres affiliated in September 1955, and the Santiago *sección obrera* was set up by a worker in the soft drinks industry, Ramón Alvarez Martínez, who, by the middle of November, persuaded the entire workers' section of the local Ortodoxo Party to join the MR-26-7.[50] There were also early organizational moves in Matanzas Province around the textile workers' leader, Julián Alemán.[51] Small and uneven as the MR-26-7 *sección obrera* was, it had an initial membership with sufficient experience and contacts to be able to recruit from the series of strikes that would break out in 1955. This expansion would force the MR-26-7 to consider its relationship with the PSP, with which it would find itself in competition for influence among the militant working class.

## Communism

The Cuban Communist Party was founded in 1925. In common with the other official Communist parties in Latin America, it supported a stage-by-stage approach to politics that required the establishment of a "Bourgeois-Democratic" regime before a start could be made on the road to socialism.[52] During the early 1930s, the Cuban Communists attempted a sectarian implementation of this policy and refused to work with other organizations that opposed the Machado dictatorship.[53] Nevertheless, the party increased its influence and membership by its support for workers in the sugar industry from 1930 to 1933 and thereafter played an important role in the Cuban trade union movement.[54] But the party leadership was taken by surprise when, in 1933, a stoppage by Havana bus drivers turned into a revolutionary general strike. The party tried to settle the dispute in return for concessions from the government, but when the strike continued despite these attempts at compromise and successfully brought down the Machado government, the party sacrificed much of its credibility.

After the Nazi victory in Germany, the Communist International (Comintern) became increasingly concerned by the growth of fascism and changed course, adopting the policy of calling for *popular fronts*, or alliances between the working class and progressive elements in the bourgeoisie. Communist parties began to speak in terms of national unity against fascism and imperialism, and minimizing the significance of the class struggle.[55] This tendency was exacerbated in Cuba as a result of the influence of the leader of the U.S. Communist Party (CPUSA), Earl Browder, who, in December 1943, argued that all social problems could be solved through peaceful compromise. This approach, which became known as Browderism, argued that capitalism and communism could march hand-in-hand to a future of peaceful collaboration.[56] This provided theoretical justification for the particular interpretation of the popular front policy that was adopted in Cuba, which resulted in an alliance with General Batista during his first government in the 1940s. Memory of this alliance would further reduce the party's credibility among Batista's opponents during his second regime in the 1950s, despite the party having repudiated Browderism in 1945 along with the rest of the world communist movement. It has become common to apportion blame for this political approach entirely to Earl Browder, but it should be recalled that Vicente Lombardo Toledano, leader of the CTAL, though not a communist, also spoke of the progressive nature of the Roosevelt administration and advocated alliances with right-wing governments as long as they were anti-Fascist. Fortunately for his historical reputation, Lombardo rejected the logic of the Cold War and denounced U.S. imperialism after the Second World War, and Browder was purged and sank into obscurity.[57]

This relationship with Batista did, in fact, allow the Communist Party to claim credit for some reforms, such as the labor protection clauses in the 1940 constitution, which provided a space within which the CTC could function. It should be said that the PSP was probably the only consistently honest force in Cuban politics during the 1940s.[58] Nevertheless, their approach left the PSP dependent on its relationship with the state and, when Batista lost the election in 1944, the communists were dangerously exposed, particularly given the U.S. pressure to repress communism in the new atmosphere of the developing Cold War. They were eventually purged from the CTC leadership during 1947–48.

Therefore, the PSP could not be under any illusions that their previous good relations with Batista could be reestablished following his 1952 coup, which they immediately condemned placing the blame on U.S. imperialism.[59] They called for the setting up of a *frente democrático nacional* (national democratic front) with the aim of uniting the whole opposition in a popular front to resist Batista by legal means. Unfortunately for them, the Havana leadership of most of the rest of the opposition was more anticommunist than it was anti-Batista and the call fell on deaf ears.[60] This was not always the case in the provinces with, for example, the local newspaper in Santiago de Cuba publishing a joint declaration by all the political parties, including the PSP, condemning the coup.[61] Generally speaking, such was the disillusion with politics felt by most Cubans that the only organized social group to actively oppose the coup were the students, with whom the PSP had little influence. Thus the party failed to see any significance in Fidel Castro's attack on the Moncada Barracks.

Having been falsely accused of complicity in the Moncada attack, the PSP was included in the generally increased repression that followed the incident. Their newspaper *Hoy* was closed down; the party was formally banned; and the purge of the remaining communists in the CTC was intensified.[62] In the widely circulated pamphlet entitled *Carta Abierta a los Putchistas y Terroristas* (Open Letter to the Putschists and Terrorists), they argued that individual action, such as the Moncada attack, disorientated the masses and gave the government an excuse for brutal repression.[63] There were, however, some signs of disagreement within the party, although mainly confined within the leadership. The following year, a well-known member of the National Committee of the PSP, César Vilar, who had once been general secretary of the first national trade union federation, the CNOC, and had been both a National Assembly representative and a senator, was expelled for persistently criticizing the manner in which the party handled the situation.[64]

It is easy with hindsight, given the eventual victory of the MR-26-7, to think that the PSP made an avoidable political mistake in criticizing the Moncada attack. However, such an attitude does not take into account the real situation at the time. Fidel Castro was not the prominent figure he would become, and he did not have a track record of success. Indeed, there was considerable confusion as to who the actual attackers were. Juan Arauco, writing immediately after the events on behalf of the PSP in the New York *Daily Worker*, seemed to think that ex-president Prío was behind the attack and went on to criticize him for the loss of life and for giving the regime an excuse for repression.[65] This last point is expanded in an open letter from the PSP national committee that lists the measures taken in the aftermath of the attack. Despite the regime being well aware that the PSP was not involved, the attack provided an excuse to arrest and harass communists, to close the party's newspaper, to impose censorship on all the opposition press, and to implement wage cuts and redundancies.[66] The footnotes of history are littered with forgotten glorious failures, and there was no way of knowing that Castro would be able to turn this apparent disaster to his immense political advantage. At the time, as far as militants in the workplaces were concerned, the attack must have seemed irrelevant to their struggle, if not positively dangerous.

By the end of 1953, the Communist Party had reorganized and adapted to underground operation in the increased repression following the Moncada attack. Its main tactic in 1954 was to appeal to the leaders of the "bourgeois opposition," mainly through open letters published in the party's clandestine press, for unity against the government.[67] This initiative reached its most unlikely position when they proposed, at the end of May, a Frente Democrático Nacional, which was to include progressive sectors of the bourgeoisie and would oppose the provisions of the 1951 report from the World Bank, known as the Truslow Plan. It strains credulity to think that even progressive sectors of the bourgeoisie would oppose a report that called for increased productivity. However, by July 1954 the regime's proposed elections in the coming November gave the PSP a more concrete slogan: "*Voto negativo*" (negative vote), a vote against Batista.[68] The pages of *Carta Semanal* became increasingly dominated by this idea, while militants were urged to set up *comités de voto negativo* (committees for a negative vote) in their neighborhoods as the basis for a future *union popular*.[69] Those other oppositionists who called for abstention were roundly attacked as playing Batista's game, while the federation of university students, the Federación Estudiantil Universitaria (FEU), was accused of "petit-bourgeois desperation."[70] There were, however, inherent problems with this approach, not least in the naïveté displayed in believing that there was the slightest possibility that Batista would allow himself to lose the election; after all, the original coup was staged because he had no chance of winning an election honestly. This time the only opponent was Ramon Grau San Martín, who undercut the PSP's strategy still further by withdrawing from the contest at the last minute, leaving Batista as the sole candidate, despite which his supporters still fraudulently increased his vote to a scandalous degree. Faced with this farce, the PSP national committee reassessed its position and, recognizing that there was little future in electoral politics for the foreseeable future, turned its attention to the working class.[71]

Under the slogan ¡*Unión y Lucha, Obreros!* (Workers, Unity and Struggle!), *Carta Semanal* would report in great detail the increased level of industrial disputes that followed the 1954 elections.[72] The PSP's new alignment to the working class, therefore, came at a propitious time and the November 1954 decision to set up locally based Comités de Defensa de las Demandas Obreras (CDDO, Committees for the Defense of Workers' Demands) created a useful vehicle to intervene during 1955.[73] The demands in the manifesto published on the thirtieth anniversary of the founding of the party, under the title of "A Democratic Solution to the Crisis," provide a useful resumé of PSP policies at this time:

- Defend workers' and peasants' incomes
- Eliminate the Truslow Plan

- 80 pesos/month for the unemployed
- Agrarian reform that gradually distributes the land to the peasants
- Nationalization of foreign-owned public services
- Control of bank credit in the interests of the country
- Protection of national industry
- Unrestricted sugar harvest
- Relations with the United States on the basis of mutual respect and equality
- Diplomatic relations with the socialist countries
- Eliminate racial discrimination
- Democratic rights, independence, and peace
- Establish a National Democratic Front[74]

The new approach would enable the party to develop a sufficient base in February 1956 to be able to organize a national conference to set up the Comité Nacional de Defensa de las Demandas Obreras y por la Democratización de la CTC (CNDDO, National Committee for the Defense of Workers' Demands and for the Democratization of the CTC).[75] With their wholehearted adoption of the rhetoric of national unity and a "bread and butter" approach to their work in the trade unions, the Cuban Communist Party did not offer a socialist alternative to challenge the hegemonic nationalist politics. As a result, they remained content with tailing other, more militant nationalist currents such as the MR-26-7.[76]

Thus, though there were considerable differences in the tactics that the PSP and the MR-26-7 proposed to implement their programs, there was no great difference in the basic politics behind the programs, with a shared concern for economic justice, national independence, and an end to corruption. Both groupings also sought to unite the Cuban "people," a nebulous term that included workers, peasant farmers, the unemployed, small businessmen and professionals along with patriotic industrialists. However, while the MR-26-7's tactics for the revolutionary overthrow of Batista centered on a general strike, they differed markedly from the PSP in stressing the need to combine that strike with an armed insurrection.[77] The importance of these tactical differences would become clear as the struggle developed.

## Trade Union Bureaucracy

There is a contradiction in the nature of trade unions under capitalism. They are both hierarchical and bureaucratic, with a top-down structure, as well as being democratic, voluntary organizations whose authority comes from the base. However, there is a danger of oversimplification if we solely equate the bureaucratic side of unions with the full-time officials and the democratic side with the rank-and-file membership and their local leadership. On the one hand, the full-time apparatus of a trade union depends on the support, or at least acquiescence, of local officials such as secretaries of local unions and workplace representatives and their wider support among the general membership. On the other hand, full-time officials sometimes respond to pressure from below and lead militant action in defiance of instructions from their hierarchical superiors. Nevertheless, the tendency for the trade union bureaucracy to be cautious and conciliatory in their dealings with management and government is an important factor in all industrial disputes and one that is often neglected by many writers.

The Cuban government appeared to be in a strong position in the 1950s and was recognized as being very pro-business. The legal political opposition was weak, corrupt, incompetent, and divided, with little interest in defending workers' wages and conditions, being composed of the traditional representatives of business interests. In any case, the de facto powers adopted by the government since the coup left little public political space in which the legal opposition could operate. The trade union movement seemed to be firmly under the control of a corrupt bureaucracy which, given that incomes were guaranteed by the compulsory deduction of subscriptions from workers' wages, were more dependent upon their good relations with the Ministry of Labor than on the support of the ordinary union members.

The employers and their allies neglected the tradition of independent militancy. The workplace activists who would be responsible for reviving this tradition provided an alternative pole of attraction within working-class politics opposed to the *mujalista* bureaucracy. This milieu was not politically homogeneous with the PSP and the MR-26-7 competing for influence. However, both groups were pushing in the same direction as the competition for influence and membership would be won by the group showing that its strategy was best able to advance the workers' cause.

When a regime becomes involved in industrial relations, the class struggle becomes overtly political, and so the government's close relationship with the United States, which still dominated the economy, would give credence to nationalist politics among militant workers. The domination of the Cuban trade unions by a corrupt clique exacerbated the normal trend of a trade union bureaucracy to reach an accommodation with the existing regime, yet despite this radical popular nationalism provided a political base for internal opposition within the labor movement. Thus the labor movement was divided. On one side was the pro-government *mujalista* bureaucracy and, on the other, the anti-government forces within organized labor, principally represented by the communists and the 26th July Movement, which were in competition for political influence.

Was the Cuban working class of the 1950s capable of acting as a "class for itself" and intervening in events to assert its own interests? The Cold War offensive appeared to have been successful in Cuba. It not only removed the communists and their allies from their controlling position in the CTC, but also replaced them with new leaders who were far more focused on their own interests than those of their members. This new bureaucracy seemed firmly entrenched, having subverted the internal democratic structures of the unions and marginalized the internal opposition. Thus at first sight it would appear that those who doubt the political importance of the working class at this juncture might seem justified.

Nevertheless, by the middle of the decade, there were signs of life among militant workers who were unhappy with this state of affairs. The PSP still had a base and, having recovered some confidence following the defeats of the late 1940s, was embarking on a new approach, based on the CDDOs, which were aimed at reconnecting with organized labor. There were also other, less formal networks of militants who were working to overcome the stranglehold of the bureaucracy, and the MR-26-7 was starting to seem an attractive home for these activists.

The tension between bureaucracy and democracy becomes more obvious at times of heightened class struggle, and by the middle of 1954 the scene was set for industrial confrontation. The fall in the price of sugar and the consequent crisis of profitability made the question of raising the level of productivity crucial for the Cuban employing class. In order to achieve this, they had to reduce staffing levels and wage rates. This did not seem to present too great a problem for the employers.

However, though workers may tolerate an undemocratic and corrupt leadership of their unions when their livelihoods are not in jeopardy, they can be much less tolerant when they see their wages and working conditions in jeopardy. The increasing difficulties faced by the Cuban economy, along with the employers' determination to maintain their profit margins at their employees' expense seemed to call for a more robust response than the CTC leadership was prepared to organize. Thus the question of working-class action can be reformulated to ask whether rank-and-file militants were able to overcome the dead hand of the bureaucracy and organize their fellow workers to fight for their interests.

## 2. A CRISIS OF PRODUCTIVITY

The assumption that economic conditions were not a significant factor in developing mass opposition to the Batista regime has resulted in a neglect of the class struggle in the period leading up to the regime's overthrow, and the argument that Cuba was prosperous compared to other Latin American countries leads to the revolution being seen as an anomaly. This approach fails to look at the Cuban economy with particular reference to the way in which workers were affected by changes in economic conditions. This is important in assessing the role of organized labor in the Cuban Revolution, for if changes in the political economy of the island resulted in a deterioration of the working and living conditions of workers, then this will have a bearing on the form and degree of their involvement in the revolutionary process.

The whole Cuban economy was dependent on sugar, which in the 1950s provided 80 percent of the island's exports. There was some other industry, but the tobacco industry was the only other major exporter, with the result that it was commonly said that "*sin azúcar, no hay país*" (without sugar, there is no nation).[1] There was a large civil service, but this required a buoyant sugar market to finance it. This situation left the country highly dependent on the international price of sugar. As a result of sugar's overwhelming importance, any deterioration in the price or the amount that could be sold in export had serious consequences for the rest of the economy. It is therefore logical to set any investigation of the Cuban economy in the context of Cuba's position in the international sugar market and to ask whether the price fluctuations of the 1950s were serious enough to merit reference to an economic crisis. Yet, if there were indeed severe problems, why do many authors refer to Cuba being "prosperous" during this period?[2]

The real question is how one defines "prosperity." It can be seen either as an environment in that business can make large profits, or alternatively as a system that provides a high standard of living for the whole society, not just for the middle and upper classes. In Cuba in the 1950s, the productivity measures that business interests wished to implement in an attempt to maintain their profit margins were achieved by layoffs and by increasing workloads for the same or lower wages. An approach that considers only GDP and similar broad indicators gives a distorted view. As Jorge Ibarra Cuesta demonstrates, an increase in per capita income, when combined with higher unemployment and wage cuts for many of those in work, results in an increase in inequality.[3] The struggle over the surplus produced by labor frequently takes ideological form in a discussion of the need for productivity increases, which can be portrayed by the employers as contributing to the common good. This argument was rejected by militant sections of organized labor, who had a tradition of fighting to defend what they saw as their rights, irrespective of the economic problems faced by their employers. This led many employers in Cuba at this time to feel that they needed an authoritarian regime to defeat working-class resistance to measures that would increase productivity. There is, therefore, a link between the fall in the price of sugar, the resulting crisis of profitability, and the employers' need to increase productivity that provides an explanation for the 1952 military coup and the support given to the resulting dictatorship by business interests.

### Economic Dependence and the Power of Sugar

Following U.S. intervention in the Cuban War of Independence, known to the North Americans as the Spanish-American War, the island received its formal independence in 1902 on condition that the new constitution contained a clause, known as the Platt Amendment after the U.S. senator who proposed it, that gave the United States the unilateral right to intervene in Cuban affairs. This constitutional arrangement was accompanied by a treaty of reciprocity that structured economic relations between the two countries to the advantage of the United States. In these circumstances,

American capital quickly came to dominate the Cuban economy in general and the sugar industry in particular. Even if legally independent, the island was effectively a U.S. colony whose economy was overwhelmingly dominated by the production of sugar.[4]

Between 1895 and 1925, world production of sugar rose from 1 million to 25 million tons, and by the end of this period Cuba, with annual harvests of around 5 million tons, was the most important single producer.[5] In the second decade of the twentieth century, a speculative boom known as the "Dance of the Millions," largely financed by loans from U.S. banks, collapsed, and most of the Cuban sugar industry passed into American ownership when those banks foreclosed.[6] U.S. capital's control of the sugar industry throughout the early years of the republic ensured its domination of the wider economy.[7] Even though the Platt Amendment was abrogated in 1934, following an uprising against the dictatorial regime of Gerardo Machado, a new reciprocity treaty was signed the same year that was even less favorable than the first.[8] However, over the next twenty years the nature of the relationship between the two countries changed as U.S. capital moved away from direct ownership of sugar production into indirect control through banking, as well as making considerable profit from the control of utilities such as electricity and telephones. Nevertheless, by 1958, U.S. capital still owned 42 percent of the productive capacity of the Cuban sugar industry.[9] Between 1948 and 1955, $637 million in profits from sugar alone was repatriated to the United States, an important loss of capital that could otherwise have been used for internal economic development in Cuba.[10]

As the pattern of U.S. involvement in the economy changed, there was a parallel process of integration of the Cuban bourgeoisie into U.S. capitalism.[11] The Reciprocity Treaty of 1934 gave preferential access for Cuban sugar to the U.S. market, and in return U.S. manufactured products were subject to lower import duty, thereby impeding the development of a Cuban manufacturing industry. The Cuban non-sugar bourgeoisie tended to spread their interests between commercial and manufacturing undertakings. This contradiction prevented them adopting a unified class position on such matters as import/export or industrial development because, as importers, they opposed local production of anything that might compete with their imports, and as manufacturers they wanted protection for their own locally produced products. This prevented the adoption of a united position on protective tariffs, as each manufacturer argued for his individual advantage while having little material interest in supporting the claims of manufacturers of other products. Only the sugar bourgeoisie had a consistent position, one opposed to Cuban national industrialization because they wanted the maximum trade in Cuba's sugar. Sugar had dominated the Cuban economy for a very long time and had survived previous crises, so they saw no reason to diversify into other industries. Rather, they hoped to use their dominant position yet again to restore profitability, even if it was at the expense of the island's other economic interests. Additionally, agricultural employers gained an advantage from a high level of unemployment to ensure sufficient available cheap labor at harvest time, giving them another reason to oppose industrialization. Thus the most consistent business influence on government economic policy was in a direction that maintained Cuban dependence on sugar and was against any industrial development or diversification.[12]

Much of the rest of the economy was linked to sugar production, more or less directly. The major export traffic through the ports was sugar, and sugar played a dominant role in the development of the railway system.[13] Important sectors of manufacturing industry, such as rum and soft drinks, also required the availability of sugar as a raw material. The other major traditional industry, tobacco, had declined considerably, with exports down from 256 million cigars per year in 1906 to only 21 million in 1949, whereas cigarette imports had risen from 1.7 million packs in 1935 to 15.6 million in 1949.[14] The major utilities, telephones and electricity, were monopolies owned by U.S. capital. The large profits that these companies made in return for a poor service and how little of those profits were reinvested in Cuba had long been subject to criticism in the national press.[15] There were small textile and shoe industries, but these could not even supply internal needs. The position of the textile industry was made worse by the 1954 commercial treaty with Japan that allowed the Japanese to export cheap clothing to Cuba in return for a guaranteed import of Cuban sugar.[16] This deal provides another clear example of the dominant political influence of the sugar oligarchy. The non-sugar manufacturing bourgeoisie was organized in the Asociación

Nacional de Industriales de Cuba (ANIC, National Association of Cuban Industrialists), but it did not have sufficient political weight to push the government toward protectionist tariffs and industrial development policies, which were opposed by the Asociación Nacional de Hacendados de Cuba (ANHC, National Association of Cuban Landowners) representing the interests of the sugar oligarchy. A further complication that reduced the ANIC's ability to promote industrial development was the presence in its leadership of local representatives of U.S. business interests, most notably Colgate-Palmolive and Firestone tires, which had factories on the island. The parent companies of these U.S.-owned manufacturers had profitable links with the Cuban sugar industry. Nor was the Cuban non-sugar bourgeoisie itself independent of U.S. capital; however, they were linked more closely with U.S. finance capital, and the sugar oligarchy was linked to U.S. exporters of consumer goods. Although these factors meant that the manufacturing sector was unsuccessful in its attempts to pressure the government to adopt an effective industrial development policy, the ANIC and the ANHC were united in a belief that salary reductions were essential to make Cuban exports competitive.[17] Another source of disagreement between the two associations was the corruption endemic in Cuban political and economic life. ANIC members were largely excluded from this source of income and therefore protested loudly.[18]

A significant proportion of Cubans whose employment was not directly or indirectly involved with sugar worked in the top-heavy state bureaucracy, the service sector, or tourism. All three sectors were riddled with corruption, particularly in the case of tourism, which Enrique Cirules's *El imperio de La Habana* shows was heavily influenced by the U.S. Mafia.[19] Nearly all the government intervention aimed at developing the economy was directed to unproductive capital products, mainly in Havana, that did little or nothing to aid diversification.

With this high level of dependence on sugar, any change in either the price received for the sugar crop or the amount that could be sold had a huge effect on the island's economy. Therefore, when the political threat of a reduction in the amount purchased by the United States coincided with a heavy fall in the price on the world market, the Cuban economy as a whole faced a crisis.

## The International Sugar Market

Although Cuba originally produced almost exclusively for U.S. consumption, the growth of internal production of both beet and cane sugar in the United States had caused the American government to increase import tariffs, thereby causing the Cuban share of the U.S. market to decline as the price of Cuban sugar rose for U.S. consumers.[20] This in turn led Cuba to look elsewhere, and by the 1950s about half of the Cuban harvest was aimed at the rest of the world, so that the income from the "world market" developed a considerable significance in the island's economic affairs.[21] The heightened international tension at the time of the Korean War led to stockpiling of sugar, then considered an important strategic foodstuff, leading to considerable price inflation, so that from December 1951 when the world price of sugar was 4.84 cents a pound, it climbed to a brief high of 5.42 cents the following March.[22] This high price encouraged a vast increase in worldwide production, with new areas being turned over to both cane and beet farming, but, as there was not a comparable increase in consumption, the resulting crisis of overproduction led, within a year, to a collapse in the price to a mere 3.55 cents a pound.[23] At this time Cuba was producing 18 percent of the world total and thus the collapse in the market was disastrous for its economy. Cuban sugar farmers played their part in the general international scramble to grow more sugar and the 1952 *zafra* (sugar harvest) was the biggest in the island's history at over 7 million tons, compared to the previous record of 5.5 million tons the year before. Unfortunately for the Cuban producers, however, of that 7 million tons they were only able to sell 4.8 million, producing a general economic crisis for the entire island.[24]

In an attempt to cope with the immediate problems of the sugar industry, the government purchased 1.75 million tons of the 1952 *zafra* to be kept in reserve and off the open market, thus hoping to use Cuba's dominant position in the market to stabilize the price. Compensation was paid to the owners for this measure, which resulted in a budget deficit of $82.6 million.[25] The Cuban unilateral cutback in production was implemented by decree number 78, which ruled that the 1953 harvest would be restricted to 5 million tons by shortening the length of time in which cane could be cut.[26] The tactic of restricting the length of the sugar harvest was designed to increase profits for the owners of the sugar companies at the expense of their employees. The sugar workers were paid only during the actual cane-cutting period, and therefore if the harvest were of shorter duration the wage bill would be reduced. Should the restriction be successful in raising or at least stabilizing the price of sugar, this would maintain or increase the employers' income, or at least mitigate the fall in profit. Critics of the strategy of restricting production were clear at the time that only the sugar bourgeoisie could benefit from the policy of restriction, and it was widely portrayed as being against the national interest.[27] This illustrates the con-tradictions inherent in "economic nationalist" politics when the nation is divided into classes with divergent interests, and, in consequence, there is no single "national interest."

As many of its critics predicted, this unilateral action was a complete failure, as other producing countries took advantage of Cuba's volun-tary restriction to increase their output, and the price continued to fall. The total national income from sugar fell from $655.5 million in 1952 to $404.9 million in 1953, and the total wage bill for the industry fell from $411.5 million to $253.9 million.[28] Moreover, speculation, insider trading, and corruption were rampant, with those who ran the Instituto Cubano de Estabilización de Azúcar ( ICEA, Cuban Institute of Sugar Stabilization) enriching themselves scandalously.[29] The reduction in national sugar pro-duction was implemented by issuing production quotas to Cuban sugar companies, which were then able to trade these to their own immediate enrichment, while their employees faced being let go when their employer sold their quota. An example of this is the 1956 protest at the closure of *central* La Vizcaya in Matanzas when its quota went to La Chaparra in Oriente.[30] The UK government also profited from the unusually low price of sugar to end sugar rationing at home and buy a million extra tons from Cuba at less than 3 cents a pound.

Following the failure of Cuba's unilateral action to arrest the decline in the world price of sugar, an attempt was made to organize an international agreement to regulate the market. This approach had been tried before in the 1930s with the Chadbourne Plan, which had not been particularly successful because other countries, not members of the scheme, simply increased their production and undermined the scheme.[31] In 1953, how-ever, forty-four governments were present at the negotiations, and the

Cuban government, one of the most enthusiastic backers of the approach, had greater hopes that the sugar price on the world market might be stabilized.

The chaotic situation in the world sugar market prompted the intervention of the United Nations. In April 1953, the UN invited seventy-eight countries to send representatives to an International Sugar Conference in London, to take place in July of that year, with the intention of negotiating an International Sugar Agreement. The idea behind the agreement was to stabilize the price of sugar by allocating quotas to the different producing countries that would, in the words of the agreement, "regulate the world sugar market and reach an equilibrium between supply and demand that would allow the price to be maintained between the limits of 3.25 and 4.35 cents per pound."[32] The Cuban quota was designed to allow a *zafra* of 5 million tons. In the event of the price falling below 3.25 cents, quotas would be progressively cut by a maximum of 20 percent, and when that occurred no further action was envisaged. The final agreement was signed in August by only thirty-eight of the forty-four participating countries, while the rest of the sugar producing world, particularly Peru, Indonesia, Brazil, Formosa, and East Germany (an important sugar beet producer), was not bound by the treaty.[33] Not signing the agreement and increasing production was only an option for smaller producers whose economies were not so dependent on sugar. This may have been short sighted, but it represented an opportunity for growers in these smaller producing countries to gain an income they had not previously enjoyed. If Cuba were to have tried this approach, such was its importance in the world market that its withdrawal would have destroyed the agreement.

The partial nature of the International Sugar Agreement was to be its undoing, because those countries that did not sign the agreement could increase their production as much as they wished, while importing countries who were signatories were not obliged to buy exclusively from other member states. Furthermore, the agreement only restricted production in exporting countries and did not restrict internal production in participating importing countries, a particularly important loophole for European sugar beet producers. There were also two other important sugar regulation arrangements, the Commonwealth Preference and the United States' sugar quota schemes. The latter accounted for about half the Cuban production and would have an important effect on the situation as U.S. growers, eager to increase their own share of the domestic market, succeeded in their campaign to reduce the amount of sugar purchased from Cuba. This exacerbated the problem caused by the reduction in income from the rest of the world market. The Commonwealth scheme, designed to develop sugar production in the British Empire and guaranteeing an annual 2.5 million tons to Britain's colonies and ex-colonies, was an additional complication because it further reduced the potential market for Cuba.[34] Thus Cuba faced an unfortunate conjuncture, as falling prices due to overproduction coincided with a reduction in the American and British markets, where preference was given to internal U.S. and British Empire production. Meanwhile, some smaller producing countries took short-term advantage of the London Sugar Agreement's attempt to reduce the amount of sugar on the market and undermined the agreement by increasing their own production.

These defects were obvious from the beginning as the price dropped to 3.14 cents in November 1953, thus triggering a 15 percent drop in quotas as soon as the agreement came into force. The price continued to fall, and in May 1954 another 5 percent cut in quotas was decreed by the International Sugar Council, which had been set up under the agreement to manage the quota system. This intervention had little effect; in June, the price fell to 3.05 cents. The maximum cut in quota now having been reached, the agreement was powerless to act further, although the council did suggest a further voluntary cut.[35]

The failure of the London Sugar Agreement to achieve its objective of stabilizing the world market sugar price between 3.25 cents and 4.35 cents per pound was to have serious political repercussions in Cuba, where opponents of the regime, like the economist Oscar Pino Santos who wrote for the journal *Carteles*, criticized the agreement as an unpatriotic betrayal of Cuban national interests, which he predicted was doomed to failure in any case.[36] It is difficult to see how anything the government might have done would have stopped the fall in the price of sugar, but the fact that they tried and failed left them open to criticism. The critics' recommended approach, which amounted to little more than aggressively trying to sell more sugar on an unregulated market, risked a further catastrophic fall in the world price that could have bankrupted the country. Nevertheless, the fact that the weight of the measures adopted fell most heavily on the workers was to produce a strong reaction within the trade unions, a reaction exacerbated by changes in U.S. sugar-purchasing policy.

The United States had never been part of the international sugar market, having sufficient supplies from its own internal sources and client states such as Cuba and the Philippines. During the first decades of the twentieth century, Cuba supplied almost the entire U.S. market and then sold any excess on the world market, but the Jones-Costigan Act, passed by the U.S. Congress in May 1934, imposed a system of quotas that were not mutually negotiated but decided unilaterally by the U.S. secretary of agriculture.[37] This reduced the Cuban share of the U.S. market from 50 percent to 30 percent, and by the early 1950s the United States was buying only about half of the Cuban sugar crop. The U.S. quota system was further complicated by the fact that besides its commercial function it had a political dimension.[38] So, in May 1955, following an aggressive campaign led by Senator Allan Elender, the U.S. Senate passed a new "Sugar Law" that reduced Cuba's previously held right to 96 percent of any increase in U.S. consumption to 29.5 percent. This, according to Oscar Pino-Santos writing at the time, cost Cuba nearly 100,000 tons.[39] This additional threat to Cuban sugar production, which occurred despite a visit to Washington by a united delegation of Cuban employers and workers' leaders of all factions, served to increase anti-imperialist feeling among sugar workers.[40]

These feelings reinforced working-class nationalist politics and gave added credence to ideas of economic nationalism as a solution to poverty and insecurity. This in turn further undermined the credibility of the London Sugar Agreement, which was popularly seen as being a surrender to foreign interests.[41] It has been common since the 1960s to assume that opposition to foreign ownership was directed entirely against the United States. However, it should be remembered that European capital held a significant minority stake in the Cuban economy, and this was just as bitterly resented when it appeared to threaten the perceived Cuban national interest.

As the failure of the London Sugar Agreement to prevent the continuing decline in sugar prices was becoming increasingly obvious, the Cuban government's inability to think of an alternative strategy further reduced its standing. Peru and Indonesia had refused to join; Brazil and Formosa were unsatisfied with their quota and left; and many importers were never included. Moreover, the British Commonwealth received privileges that, given that London was the home of the agreement, served to further weaken the agreement's credibility. By early 1955, the price of sugar was 3.15 cents a pound, 10 points lower than the agreed minimum. Cuba appeared to be taking the majority of the restriction with a 30 percent reduction compared to the production levels of 1952, although the impact of that would be much worse if the U.S. quota were to be cut further, as now seemed likely. The London Sugar Agreement appears from these figures to be working against Cuba's interests, but remaining a party to the agreement maintained a level of profitability for the employers, even if this was at the expense of working-class employment and living standards. But living standards for agricultural workers were already appalling.[42] The figures contained in the 1957 report by a Cuban Jesuit association, the *Agrupación Católica Universitaria,* are graphic: 64 percent of rural dwellers with no proper sanitation, 43 percent illiterate, 91 percent undernourished—to give but a few examples.[43] Cuba's sugar workers therefore had little to lose by resisting, and though hardship does not necessarily generate militancy, when combined with a sense of injustice there is potential for industrial action.

These problems had already been foreseen by the International Bank for Reconstruction and Development (World Bank) in 1951 when, following the request of the Cuban government for a loan, an American economist, Francis Truslow, was commissioned to produce a report on the state of the Cuban economy.

### Productivity and Politics

The Truslow Report started from the position that international competition gave rise to the need to reduce sugar production costs and the recognition that mechanization must inevitably displace some labor. The problem was summed up as:

- employees strongly resist mechanization and cost-cutting methods;
- the discharge of employees for legitimate cause [is] made difficult or impossible;
- higher wages, coupled with opposition to methods for increasing

productivity, endanger the competitive position of the basic sugar industry itself.[44]

The opposition to productivity measures was rooted in the island's high levels of unemployment and underemployment, which explains the tenacity shown by Cuban workers in defending their jobs and the social clauses in the Cuban constitution that helped them to do so. The report recognizes that the high level of unemployment deeply affected the consciousness of those in work; job security was always an important concern of unionized workers.[45] Truslow sums up the situation as follows: "In Cuba it is usually easier, quicker and cheaper to divorce a wife than to fire a worker. Under prevailing conditions of chronic seasonal unemployment, it may also be easier to find a new wife than to find a new job."[46]

The report argued that increased productivity would attract investment, promote diversification, and thereby produce jobs, although it does recognize that the workers' reluctance to cooperate was based on their doubt that the money saved would be invested productively.[47] Underneath the call for greater cooperation between management and labor lay the concrete proposal to make dismissal of employees simpler, faster, and cheaper.[48] In the particular case of the sugar industry, the report called for mechanization, not of the planting and cultivating, but of the harvesting, which was the most labor-intensive part of production and would result in the redundancy of a very large number of workers.[49] The employers wished to extend the mechanization of the sugar industry beyond that recommended by Truslow to include modernization of the refining process in order to process the cane faster. This would not only save time and thereby reduce wages in the sugar refineries, it would also put pressure on the independent cane farmers, the *colonos*, to increase the pace of work of their harvesting crews to supply the same amount of cane in a shorter time. The sugar workers called this process *intensivismo*, replying with the demand that they be paid for *superproducción*; this expression meant that they wished to be paid the same total amount as they had been before the new machinery arrived.[50] Clearly this was not what the employers had in mind when they considered investing in new machinery.[51]

The Truslow Report was not merely concerned with the production of sugar, but also examined transport, which was an equally important part of the export procedure. The railway industry was close to bankruptcy and port labor was considered to be in need of reform to reduce its potential to disrupt loading. The report bemoans "the strategic position occupied by men who load and unload ships, in view of the big investment tied up in ships and merchandise, and the ease with which shipping companies can be subjected to important losses by sudden stoppages or delays."[52]

This "strategic position" has been used by dockers everywhere to enhance their wages, improve their working conditions, and maintain their manning levels. However, most employers would agree with Truslow in feeling that this obliged them to employ more workers than was strictly necessary, thereby reducing business efficiency. In particular, the report identified the main problem as the refusal to bulk-load sugar. The universal nature of maritime productivity disputes is underlined by the contacts established at this time between the dockworkers of Caibarién in northern Cuba, who were fighting bulk-loading and the workers in the port of Liverpool in England, who were in dispute over attempts to introduce the fork-lift truck.[53] The report further believed that wage levels were excessive, a factor that also exacerbated the precarious financial state of the railway industry: "With labor still making wage demands, it is believed that in many cases they have reached the limit that employers will tolerate."[54]

It should be noted that there is little mention of the question of inflation in the discussion of wage levels. In part this is as a result of the lack of reliable data. The U.S. embassy, noting that it was "impossible to do more than conjecture as to the actual expenditure of the working classes," concludes from their own observations that there was a considerable increase in the cost of living as a result of food price inflation.[55] This would have been another factor in stiffening labor resistance to wage cuts. Thus increased productivity was to be achieved by mechanization and longer hours of work, both policies that would reduce the need for the existing number of workers in circumstances of a chronically high level of unemployment and at a time when real wages were in any case falling as a result of food price inflation. To this was added the proposal for a cut or at least a freeze in money wages. There was therefore little prospect of workers voting for a party that intended to implement the Truslow Report.

In this context, the outlook for the 1952 general election looked unfavorable to the employers. Of the three candidates for president, Roberto Agramonte for the Ortodoxos, the recently founded anti-corruption party, was widely expected to beat rivals Fulgencio Batista, who had headed an earlier regime in the 1930s, and Carlos Hevia for the Auténticos, the current ruling party. The Ortodoxos were not a workers' party, but were relying on working-class votes for their expected victory. The main plank of their election platform was opposition to corruption allied to a vaguely expressed economic nationalism, which called for recovery of national wealth and promised to implement measures of social equality. Such was the popular revulsion with the level of corruption of the Auténtico administration that it was widely expected that the Ortodoxos were going to win the election handsomely, and that Batista seemed to be heading for a crushing defeat.[56] The Ortodoxos displayed no interest in implementing the Truslow Report and its concerns with productivity received no mention in their public statements. The Ortodoxos' platform spoke of the "Cubanization" of the economy, emancipating Cuba from foreign imperialism, nationalization of foreign-owned service industries and monopolies, and redistribution of arable land.[57] A study of U.S. diplomatic correspondence shows that this platform worried U.S. business interests and their allies among the Cuban bourgeoisie.[58] Eduardo Chibas, leader of the Ortodoxos until his suicide in 1951, would certainly have worried the First National Bank of Boston, which led a syndicate that loaned the Cuban government $200 million to build such projects as the tunnel under Havana Bay.[59] Chibas made it clear that if he was elected he would not repay the loan.[60]

When Batista and his associates in the armed forces staged a coup on March 10, 1952, it was quickly welcomed by the United States. There was in fact remarkably little internal opposition to the army takeover, such was the cynicism with politicians in general that developed over the first fifty years of the republic. The only social group to react strongly was the students.[61] The ousted president went quietly, partly for fear that an Ortodoxo election victory might have investigated and punished his corruption. Indeed, at the time some saw the main target of the coup as being the Ortodoxos rather than Carlos Prío.[62] There was then an unseemly scramble by the majority of professional politicians to reach an accommodation with the de facto government in the hope of retaining their lucrative privileges.[63] There are a variety of explanations for the success of the coup: the restoration of order, the corruption and inefficiency of the Auténticos, the desire of U.S. economic interests to restructure the Cuban economy, and the Cold War anti-communism of the U.S. government.[64] These factors all played a part, and it is not the intention here to propose a monocausal explanation. Nevertheless, given the lack of importance accorded elsewhere to the support given by business interests for the specifically anti-labor role played by the dictatorship, that particular aspect will be stressed, not with the intention of downplaying the importance of other factors, but of redressing the balance and bringing forward a neglected aspect of the history of the period.

The coup was, indeed, generally welcomed by capitalist interests, as it was felt that Batista would be more business-friendly than the alternatives. Within ten days of the coup, the major business associations had visited the presidential palace to offer their support: the Asociación de Hacendados, the Asociación de Bancos de Cuba, the Asociación Nacional de Comisionistas del Comercio Exterior, the Socios de la Bolsa de la Habana, the Asociación de Industriales de Cuba, and the Cámara de Comercio.[65] Meanwhile, the main pro-business daily paper, *Diario de la Marina,* which had supported Batista's election campaign enthusiastically,[66] contrasted the situation under the previous government, in which the "balance inclined monstrously toward the labor unions," with the statements of the new government, which were described as "serene and reasonable."[67]

In May 1952, the British ambassador wrote: "I am more and more convinced that the basic reason for the Armed Forces having staged the revolution was their utter disgust at the growing and unrestrained power of Labor."[68] Later that year he added: "The business community, industry and commerce have all welcomed the new regime. . . . If the coup d'état had to come, no better leader could in their view have been found and no more opportune moment chosen."[69]

The U.S. ambassador equally noted that businessmen were among the new regime's most enthusiastic supporters.[70] The role of the state as ultimate guarantor of the interests of the ruling class was to be clearly demonstrated in the period under Batista's rule.

## A Business-Friendly Coup

Attempting to influence the international market price of sugar was an important policy objective for the Cuban government, and the sheer size of the country's production seemed to offer the possibility of success in manipulating the market to maintain price levels. The government's attempts to achieve this, first by a unilateral cut in exports and then through participation in the International Sugar Agreement, ended in failure as the price of sugar continued to fall. This fall made the question of labor productivity more urgent. The level of profitability was a serious problem for nearly all sectors of the Cuban economy by the middle of the twentieth century, even without the fall in the world price of sugar. The Truslow Report identified the principal challenge facing the Cuban economy as low labor productivity, and the task of resolving this problem would be made much more difficult if the still-dominant sugar industry ceased to be profitable. To achieve this general increase in productivity, wages would have to fall and manning levels would have to be cut, and that in turn would require state action. The report foresaw that a dictatorship might result from this conflict of class interest.[71] Given the fear of most workers that the productivity measures proposed would be detrimental to their income and employment prospects, many employers thought that an authoritarian regime would be necessary to enforce the Truslow Report's proposals that, at least in the short-term, could only result in a considerable increase in the already chronic level of unemployment.

One of the reasons for the success of the coup of March 10, 1952, was support from the business community for a regime that could reduce the ability of Cuban workers to defend their wages and working conditions. Such a regime could push the balance of national income in favor of the employers. The new government sought to reduce opposition from organized labor by incorporating and corrupting the trade union bureaucracy, which would operate with the support of the Ministry of Labor and the police if necessary. Should that be unsuccessful, the regime had the army at its disposal to enforce its priorities. The year 1955 would bring this conflict to the fore.

## 3. THE EMPLOYERS' OFFENSIVE

T he year 1955 was a crucial turning point in the developing history of the Cuban Revolution. Up to this point, the Batista government had not tried very hard to enforce its productivity agenda, and the *mujalista* bureaucracy had generally maintained its control of the union structures, with few examples of serious industrial action. This all changed during 1955, with important disputes in several key industries. These would have long-term effects on the relationship between organized labor and the regime, as well as profoundly changing the balance of forces within the working-class movement.

At the end of 1954, the Batista government had two pressing industrial problems on its agenda. The falling price of sugar meant that the industry's employers were demanding wage and job cuts. They were particularly insistent as their demands for such cuts the previous year had been largely ignored pending the elections.[1] Additionally, financial problems in the U.S.-owned Ferrocarriles Consolidados (FFCC Consolidados), the railway company that operated the network in the eastern end of the island, meant that its owners also wished to cut their wage costs and staff numbers.[2] The government's confrontations with the workers in these two powerful industrial sectors, as well as with some other important groups of workers, made 1955 an important turning point in the history of labor mobilization in Cuba. The outcomes of these disputes were different in each industry, and the political trajectory of the leading protagonists was correspondingly different. The degree to which each group of workers were successful or not in their aims helped determine whether the politics of the PSP or the MR-26-7 would come to dominate the anti-Batista opposition in different industries and regions.

If the role of workers in the Cuban insurrection has been overlooked, the role of women workers has disappeared completely from view. When we speak of workers confronting the government and their employers, it is important to recognize that women frequently played an important role. The importance of working-class women in day-to-day labor struggles, and in the final triumph of the revolution, will be referred to frequently in this and succeeding chapters. An examination of contemporary sources, particularly photographs, demonstrates the significance of women both as workers themselves and as family members of workers in struggle: women railway office workers, bank workers, and shop assistants, as well as the solidarity provided by the wives and families of sugar and port workers. Two examples of this that are better documented, the office workers of Camagüey and the sugar workers of Delicias y Chaparra, serve as an illustration of women's wider involvement.

The account of the events of 1955 can be given sector by sector with only minimal disruption of the chronological sequence, because the government was careful to avoid a generalized confrontation and therefore engineered disputes in one industry at a time, beginning with the Cuban transport industry, continuing with the bank workers' dispute, then a number of single-enterprise strikes in industries such as brewing and textiles before getting to the sugar workers' strike. This sugar workers' strike not only involved half a million workers in the island's major industry, it also involved student activists, thus forming a link that would have a significant impact on the developing revolutionary situation. From this account, it emerges that the failure of these strikes at the hands of a repressive state and a corrupt trade union bureaucracy led a significant group of militant class-conscious workers to seek a different approach to the defense of their economic interests. To present a rounded picture, it is also necessary to address the apparent success of the port and tobacco workers in resisting the employers' offensive when, all around, their compatriots were suffering defeat after defeat. Reflecting on why the employers' productivity offensive was successful in some industries and not in others is key to understanding the later political development of different industrial sectors within the labor movement.

Batista planned his attack on working conditions carefully. He had reached an accommodation with the CTC but could not move too quickly because, if he undermined Mujal's base, that accommodation would be useless. Moreover, Mujal was accustomed to influencing government policy to a greater extent than would have suited Batista, and the new dictator took a little time to subordinate Mujal to his project. We shall see how Mujal's relationship with the government changed over time and how he became increasingly identified with the regime. Having established a good relationship with the CTC leadership, Batista adopted an approach that would be reprised thirty years later by the Thatcher government in Britain using an approach that became known as the Ridley Plan: an attempt to restore profitability by defeating workers sector by sector, making sure that the field of battle is always chosen by the government and that any chance of generalized and united industrial action is avoided.[3] Once the government had decided that the time was right to confront a particular group of workers, it acted with considerable brutality to overcome resistance. Nevertheless, the government did not always win, and particularities of each sector will be examined below along with the political conclusions each group of workers drew from their victory or defeat.

## Public Transport

The first significant confrontation between the Batista government and organized labor came in the transport industry. The Cuban railways were suffering from a particularly severe crisis as a result of years of underinvestment, though transport workers were well organized and had maintained a significant level of independence, particularly in Oriente Province at the eastern end of the island. The disputes in the transport industry in 1955 signify the first real defeat suffered by organized workers at the hands of the government and employers. The government managed the conflict so that the railway workers were not given reason to go on strike until after the sugar harvest was in, thereby denying them the opportunity to make common cause with the sugar workers, with whom they had traditional relationships of solidarity. The railway companies also had substantial holdings in the bus industry, which had led to links between the workers' organizations in both industries. It also meant that cost-saving measures would be applied on the buses as well the railway. It was in the bus industry that the new de facto government made its first attack on the labor movement, relatively quickly after the coup.

In July 1952, with no warning, one of Havana's two bus companies was placed under military control; the leader of the union, Marco Hirigoyen, was arrested; and 600 out of the company's 6,000 drivers were dismissed.[4] This served the double purpose of removing one of Mujal's internal enemies in the CTC and weakening one of the most militant groups of workers in the capital, thereby reinforcing Mujal's sense that his future lay with the regime.[5] Such decisive action by the government also served to impress upon both the business community and foreign observers that Batista was serious in his intention to confront organized labor.[6] The British ambassador, wrote that Autobuses Modernos, one of the two bus-operating companies in Havana, "had from the point of view of graft, rank inefficiency and financial loss become a crying scandal." He went on to "report this incident as an example of what can be achieved in Cuba by a strong man who is fearless of intimidation and is bent on cleansing public services of gangster and surplus elements. It is to be hoped that similar action, if required, will be taken at the appropriate moment to place the United Railways on an economic basis."[7]

The United Railways to which he refers, called Ferrocarriles Unidos (FFCC Unidos) in Cuba, was the railway company that operated services in the western half of the island. It had a majority of British shareholders and was practically bankrupt. The British owners had been trying to extract themselves and their remaining capital from the company for some time, a fact that gave the British embassy another reason to look kindly on the new Batista government: "The existence of a strong Government in Cuba greatly improves the chances of a settlement of the United Railways claim, which has been made more difficult by the attitude of organized labor in Cuba."[8]

Railways had developed early in Cuba, initially as a freight network that linked the sites of sugar production to ports on the coast; a passenger network uniting the major centers of population on the island was a later development. This association between sugar and railways was reflected in a history of solidarity between railway workers, dockers, and sugar workers that dates back to the beginning of the twentieth century.[9] The main railway trade union, the Hermandad Ferroviaria (Railway Brotherhood) had a socially conservative leadership that had close ties to the American Federation of Labor (AFL), but this attitude was far from universal within the organization and the local organizations, known as *delegaciones*, could be remarkably militant, particularly in the east of the island.[10] By the middle of the century, the network was divided between two companies, the British-owned Ferrocarriles Unidos which operated in the west of the country and the U.S.-owned Ferrocarriles Consolidados in the east. Both companies were in financial difficulties, but FFCC Unidos seemed to be in permanent decline.

The FFCC Unidos network infrastructure had badly deteriorated and was in need of massive capital investment. The report and accounts for 1948–49 painted a catastrophic picture of a bankrupt enterprise, operating under government supervision and kept alive by subsidies. The falling price of sugar, to which freight rates were linked, as well as the smaller crop led to revenue from sugar decreasing by over one million dollars. The chairman complained that "the principal difficulty has been the refusal of the labor unions . . . to permit the company to institute essential economies involving reduction of wages, dismissal of redundant staff and elimination of redundant services."[11] This led the writers of the Truslow Report to conclude that the wages and conditions of the workers could no longer be sustained at existing levels and were an obstacle to further investment.[12] In September 1949, FFCC Unidos finally managed to impose 800 job losses and had reduced wages to pre-1945 levels.[13] By means of this cut, and with the help of a government subsidy of $100,000 a month,[14] the company was able to stagger on until 1952 when, with mounting debts, it sought further layoffs and early retirements. The new Batista government approved a plan, known after its author Luis Chiappy, whereby the government took a 51 percent stake and negotiated a loan from the Bank of America and the Hanover Bank to settle accounts with the British stakeholders.[15] Gustavo Pellón, chairman of FFCC Consolidados, the U.S. railway company, was named as the *interventor* (government-appointed administrator) and thereby took control without any financial liability.

In addition to taking action aimed at resolving the company's immediate financial future, the government announced its intention of imposing the job losses outlined in the Chiappy Plan. The workers, having been disappointed by the response of their trade union in 1949, set up a rank-and-file–based *comité de lucha* (strike committee) that called a strike at the end of June 1953.[16] The government responded with military intervention and decreed that all who did not return to work immediately would be dismissed. Javier Bolaños, national president of the Hermandad Ferroviaria, ordered a return to work saying that he would do everything necessary to ensure that the reduction in staff would be "strictly limited to the numbers that the company required."[17] On July 26, an armed group led by Fidel Castro attacked the Moncada Barracks in Santiago and, under cover of the resulting repression, the authorities managed to enforce the return-to-work order and forced further layoffs in August. There is no surviving evidence of workers' reaction to the Moncada attack; we have already seen the hostile reaction of the PSP.[18] and it is likely that the outcome did not predispose the railway workers to support Castro. Its victory over the FFCC Unidos workers left the government free to deal with the problems of FFCC Consolidados. However, before doing so, Batista managed to improve his position through the elections he called for November 1954. Despite a high level of fraud and the withdrawal at the last minute of his only rival, these elections gave the government a certain level of legitimacy, at least in the eyes of international diplomacy, with the British ambassador describing Batista as "the type of president best suited to the country."[19] Once the 1954 elections were out of the way, the regime felt free to address the industrial issues confronting it, starting with the railways.

The financial problems of the Ferrocarriles Consolidados, though nowhere near as great as those of FFCC Unidos, were far from insignificant, with annual losses averaging $2.5 million. From the start of the economic downturn that resulted from the drop in sugar prices in 1953, the owners had been proposing wage cuts based on the government's decree number 1155, which gave the company the right to set wages according to the economic situation. The company was faced by a trade union organization with a long tradition of militancy and its proposals were met with an outcry from the workers, which forced a delay that was financed by a government loan.[20] Immediately following the November 1954 elections, FFCC Consolidados announced 1,550 redundancies and a 20 percent wage cut to be implemented from December 1, 1954.[21] The office workers in Camagüey, mainly women, were the first to receive the news as they would have to administer the cuts. They immediately walked out on strike. Some went down to the depot and the workshop, where their action was swiftly joined by the drivers and engineers. Others produced leaflets and posters and took to the streets of Camagüey in an impromptu demonstration, which received considerable support in a town that relied on the railway yards for much of its prosperity.[22] The wage cuts and redundancies were aimed mainly at the operating staff, and so the actions of the administrative workers demonstrate a high level of principled solidarity, although it is also likely that they would find family and friends among the workers under attack. As word spread, the action soon extended to the rest of the region, with a large street demonstration bringing the center of Guantánamo to a standstill.[23] The following day, the workers reported for work but initiated a *paso de jicotea*,[24] a work slowdown that caused widespread disruption to the service.[25] Taken aback by the level of resistance, the government declared a truce, suspended the cuts, set up a commission of inquiry with trade union and employer representation, and gave the company a further loan.[26]

FFCC Consolidados also owned four bus companies operating in Santiago de Cuba: La Cubana, La Cubanita, La Criolla, and La Mambisa. It tried to use the period of the truce to impose cost-saving measures by locking out the workers in these companies. Many of their colleagues in the other two bus companies in the city withdrew their labor in solidarity; the strike in La Oriental was solid, but only partial on Autobuses Modelos. The army started rounding up drivers and forcing them to take out their buses. In protest, a number of drivers occupied their local union offices and started a hunger strike but were soon evicted by the police. The police intervention was said to be at the request of Prisciliano Falcón, a leading *mujalista* official in Santiago. The hunger strike then moved to the offices of Delegación 12 of the railway union and continued for seventy-two hours, after which the company backed down, the lockout was suspended, and arrears of salary were paid.[27]

The company also used the railway truce for an extensive press campaign, which consisted of newspaper advertisements, press statements, and carefully placed interviews that argued that railway workers were being paid for hours they did not work and that wages had risen much faster than receipts.[28] One advertisement asserted that for every peso of income, the company expended one peso and 23 cents, of which 91 cents was in wage costs. In particular, the company complained that it was not benefiting from its modernization program, giving the example that it only took ten hours to get from Santa Clara to Santiago, but the crews were still paid for the twenty hours it had taken before the company had invested shareholders' money for infrastructure improvements.[29] In this last argument, we see encapsulated the employers' position on productivity: having invested money for technological improvements, they expected their wage bill to decrease. However, with little prospect of other jobs, the majority of the workers saw no reason why they should have their staffing levels or pay reduced in order to maintain or increase profit margins, a classic dispute about who should benefit from technological progress. There was little room for compromise between these two entrenched positions.

The railway workers were not idle during the truce period either, setting up a Comisión de Propaganda y Finanzas (Finance and Propaganda Committee) to coordinate the resistance. This body organized some short strikes in the Guantánamo region.[30] Having access to typewriters and duplicating machines, as well as the skills to use them, the women in the administration took a significant role in the production of propaganda material. When the truce ended on January 20, the company announced that it would withhold 35 to 40 percent of the workers' wages, suspend paid holidays, and make other similar economy measures.[31] As soon as the announcement was made, the Camagüey office workers again demonstrated, loudly proclaiming that they would not implement the cuts.[32] Despite government intervention to postpone the problem again, a move greeted as a victory by the CTC bureaucracy, the rail workers themselves did not trust the government and walked out on February 3.[33] The strike spread throughout the network, with many violent confrontations between the police, army, and striking workers, along with extensive solidarity actions by workers in other trades. *Carta Semanal* reports that in Morón, local bus and taxi drivers went on solidarity strike and a women's support group was set up in the town.[34] A large number of neighborhood support networks were set up by the female relatives of railwaymen, helped by the women from the offices, similar to the women's support groups of the British miners' strike of 1984–85. Women's groups would also be set up by the relatives of dockers and sugar workers during their own strikes later the same year. These actions by women were frequently a force for unity among workers of different trades as the women's groups were usually based in the areas where they lived and were able to use their positions in the neighborhood to build links of solidarity.

Many of the ports were also owned by the railway companies and dockers in Boquerón and Nuevitas struck in support of their railway colleagues, as a result of which 58,000 sacks of sugar lay idle on the dock.[35] Other port workers in Matanzas, Caimanera, and Manzanillo took advantage of the opportunity to publicly demonstrate both in support of the railway workers and to express their own opposition to bulk loading of sugar.[36] It should be remembered that the port workers had a very good practical reason for their solidarity as they recognized that they might need railway support later in their battle to reject a series of productivity measures with which their own industry was threatened. The most public demonstrations of solidarity took place in Camagüey where the CTC Federación Provincial (Provincial Federation) discussed the possibility of a general strike, while many workers independently took part in ten-minute solidarity strikes. All this activity resulted in numerous arrests, in response to which the women of Camagüey organized a demonstration demanding the release of all prisoners.[37]

With the *zafra* (sugar harvest) having only just started, following some difficult negotiations that had left many sugar workers deeply unhappy, Batista was concerned not to provide a pole of resistance that might have inspired disgruntled sugar workers in a movement that could have escaped the control of the trade union bureaucracy. The government therefore decreed another truce on February 8 while the Tribunal de Cuentas, the government accountancy service, investigated the situation of the company, this time for one hundred days. This new truce was funded with another 700,000 pesos.[38] The official union *comité conjunto* (joint committee), which had been set up by the CTC to oversee the action, ordered a return to work without consulting mass meetings in the depots. In Guantánamo, Delegación 11, the local organization of the Hermandad Ferroviaria covering the membership who worked for FFCC Consolidados, denounced the truce as a sell-out and continued the strike until the 11th, when, following Mujal's personal intervention, they were paid in cash, thereby overcoming the company's attempt to pay 70 percent in cash and the rest in scrip until the government subsidy arrived.[39] The line from Caibarien to Morón was reportedly still not working normally on February 17.[40] A special congress of the Federación Nacional Ferroviaria (the national federation of railway unions, including the Hermandad Ferroviaria and unions of office workers) was called to ratify the actions of the officials and, given that most of the delegations had not been elected by assemblies of the workers, such ratification was granted, although only after considerable bureaucratic manipulation from the chair.[41] Once assured that the official trade union machinery was back in control and further unofficial action was unlikely, the regime moved against some of the militants, with the Santa Clara courts condemning eighteen bus drivers and seventy-two railwaymen for *huelga ilícita* (illegal strike action).[42]

Following the end of the sugar harvest, the report of Tribunal de Cuentas recommended an 8 percent wage cut, forced retirements, scrapping the collective agreement, abolishing many bonuses, and lengthening the working day, as well as extensive service cuts.[43] Batista accepted the report and published decree number 1535 on June 7, the so-called "Laudo Ferroviario" (railway arbitration decision), which implemented the recommended measures and gave the company an annual subsidy of 600,000 pesos.[44] Within forty-eight hours Guantánamo was again out on strike, quickly followed by Camagüey and Santiago, 10,000 workers in all.[45] Now that the sugar harvest was safely gathered in, the full force of the state was moved against the workers, the army was mobilized, the Ministry of Labor denied the very existence of the strike, and the CTC leadership condemned it out of hand. The strikers replied by organizing *ciudades-muertas* or "dead towns" across the region, completely shutting down Camagüey, Guantánamo, Morón, Nuevitas, and Santiago. The tactic of *ciudad-muerta* was a form of civic general strike in which not only did the other workers in a town strike in sympathy but most business and commerce also closed their doors. The bus workers in Santiago who worked in companies owned by the FFCC Consolidados also walked out again and, on May 9, set up camp on the town hall patio in protest.[46] The CTC, realizing that the action was escaping its control, sent a committee to mediate but still failed to authorize the strike, although claiming to understand the grievance. Javier Balaños, leader of the Federación Nacional Ferroviaria, met the directors of FFCC Consolidados while appealing to the president to suspend the *laudo* for thirty days. Batista refused to meet union representatives as the police, army, and secret policemen started routing drivers and signalmen out of their houses and forcing them back to work at gunpoint.

We have already seen the importance of the women from the offices in launching the strike and that the solidarity actions of family members were of significance. Given that the army was rounding up train-operating and signaling staff, forcing them to work at gunpoint, it was difficult for these workers to publicly demonstrate and picket. In a pattern that was repeated in other industrial disputes of the time, this public role was often taken over by women, either railway office workers or the families of the strikers, who also played a leading role in setting up neighborhood solidarity committees. Though women made up only 10 percent of the Cuban workforce and many of them were in the notoriously difficult organizational territory of domestic service, the comparatively few trade-unionized women workers in the Cuba of the 1950s played a vital role in initiating and sustaining militant action out of all proportion to their numbers.

The *comité conjunto* capitulated after five days.[47] They ordered a return to work despite the continuing strength of the strike and growing solidarity from other workers. The final agreement was denounced by Gerrado Villariño and Jesús Robaina, leaders of the Hermandad Ferroviaria in Santiago and Camaguey, while the leading militants in Guantánamo went into hiding to avoid having to implement the order to return to work.[48] In return for a few minor concessions, the *comité conjunto* accepted an 8 percent wage cut, 600 layoffs, and signed a no-strike agreement, thereby placing the strikers outside the law.[49] This was the signal for the forces of repression to increase their physical attacks on the workers and, amid the demoralization caused by the perceived sellout, the strike was broken.[50] In the days that followed, many of the leading militants were dismissed.[51] This should not be seen as the end of the matter; we shall see the way in which the militants who led this dispute, particularly those from Guantánamo, would take stock of the defeat and produce new tactics for which they would soon develop a mass base.

However, the defeat of the workers in one of the oldest unionized sectors of the Cuban economy gave the government and the employers a considerable boost in confidence, so it was surprising how much difficulty they would have in dealing with another group that some did not even see as part of the working class.

## Banks

The next important industrial struggle to take place in 1955 was the dispute in the banking industry. This was significant for several reasons. Vicente Pérez, a communist trade union organizer at the time, said that he considered this to be a highly significant dispute as the bank workers were often thought to be part of the "aristocracy of labor" or even "middle class." They certainly had no history of industrial action, yet they fought an extremely determined struggle, using strikes, slowdowns, and other traditional forms of direct industrial action.[52] The essence of their dispute concerned the right to join a union. They finally went down to defeat after a bitter struggle that left many of their leaders victimized, in part because the employers were able to provoke the dispute after the railway workers had been defeated, thereby isolating their movement.

From the beginning of June 1955, the newly elected leader of the Havana bank workers, José Maria de la Aguilera, initiated a press campaign for a wage increase of 20 percent and against the existence of the so-called *Anexo A* (Appendix A).[53] This was a list of those who were considered to be "confidential employees" and who were forbidden to join a trade union. The demand for abolition of *Anexo A* was therefore a struggle for the right to organize.[54] The Ministry of Labor became involved and, on June 30, 1955, when they felt confident that they had broken the resistance on the railways, the government rejected the bank workers' demands and proposed a 5 percent increase.[55] At a mass meeting in Havana, Aguilera attacked the huge profits of the banks, contrasting the difference between those profits and bank workers' pay, after which he received a unanimous vote of support for his call for an immediate *paso de jicotea*.[56]

Meanwhile José Ignacio de la Cámara, president of the employers' association, counterattacking the new leadership of the union, maintained that the contract of employment was more appropriate for the bull market of the previous period and that the banks needed to build up their reserves. He claimed that, at a time when other industries were cutting wages, the banks were increasing the number of their employees, so therefore a wage freeze was the best they could offer. After Ministry of Labor mediation in the dispute, Aguilera told the government that the 5 percent offer was ridiculous, given the low wages in some parts of the country, and that it broke the constitutional right to a living wage for heads of families, and furthermore, senior employees had received much larger raises.[57] In fact, 1,300 of the 2,300 the bank employees in Havana were earning less than $200 per month and only 230 earned more than $300, even as bank profits were rising significantly. The full 20 percent claim would only amount to 9 percent of the banks' profits.[58]

Following a strike on the July 7, the employers started to victimize known militants. The CTC initially supported the industrial action, but Mujal's return from a trip to Washington changed the situation as he accused Aguilera of indiscipline. The Havana bank workers began a *huelga de brazos caídos*,[59] a form of action somewhere between a slowdown and a sit-in that involved the workers reporting for work but doing little or nothing while on the premises. At the end of July, this *movimiento de brazos caídos* was extended to all banks nationwide as the government issued a decree freezing wages in the sector and giving the strikers seventy-two hours to return to normal working hours, after which dismissals would be authorized.[60] The complete paralysis of the country's economy that had previously been predicted was avoided as senior staff managed to run a limited emergency service. Representatives of business and commerce fell in behind the banks and condemned the breach of the government decree, and on August 30 the Ministry of Labor used its powers of intervention to seize formal control of the Havana branch of the bank workers' union, an action solicited by Mujal with the support of the leadership of the national federation.[61]

The strike hardened as control of the union became an issue when the CTC executive voted to support government intervention. This gave the green light to police repression, with many arrests and violent attacks on striking workers.[62] Strikers, ejected from their own premises by the police, set up a new strike office in the premises of the Juventud Obrera Católica (JOC, Catholic Labor Youth), a Social-Christian organization, of which many bank workers were members and which was led by Padre Enrique Oslé, a friend of the bus workers' leader, Marco Hirigoyen.[63] This involvement of the Catholic Church provoked a ferocious debate between Mujal and Padre Oslé of the JOC, enabling Mujal to claim that he was defending secular trade union independence against Church interference.[64] There was considerable rank-and-file support for the bank workers within the CTC nationally, and the Communist Party newspaper, *Carta Semanal*, reported solidarity stoppages of ten to fifteen minutes in an impressive list of workplaces, but despite the concerns expressed by some of Mujal's internal rivals on the CTC executive, such as Angel Cofiño, the leader of the electrical workers' union, the CTC apparatus remained loyal to Mujal.[65]

On September 8, in a last-ditch attempt, a delegation of 500 strikers went to the Cardinal-Archbishop's palace and asked him to intervene, but this was construed as a mark of weakness by the employers, who refused the Church's offer of mediation. The *Diario de la Marina*, the main right-wing daily newspaper in Havana, was clear that, in order to win, the strikers needed to paralyze the economic life of the whole country and, having failed to do so, they went down to defeat.[66] The role of Mujal in orchestrating the return to work is significant, as he played a much more active and devious role than in the earlier railway dispute. On September 6, Mujal met both President Batista and José María de la Aguilera. Two places on the "intervention committee," set up to implement the seizure of the Havana branch of the union by the Ministry of Labor, were offered to the old executive as well as freedom for arrested strikers, ninety-eight men and two women, in return for normal workdays, with a promise that the government would study the wage claim.[67] Demoralized and undermined, the workers returned to normal work hours on September 12 and 13, while Mujal promised to work for the release of the detainees and the reinstatement of the 174 dismissed workers, which was to little effect in the case of the sackings with the announcement on September 15 that the dismissals would stand in the majority of cases.[68]

This incident is a good example of the *mujalista* method. In his report to the executive of the Federación Bancaria, Mujal spoke of the need to achieve a wage increase and that though he rejected all dismissals, there was an absolute need to stop all industrial action and to restore internal discipline by taking disciplinary action against the leaders in Havana who had "provoked the difficulty."[69] As may be expected, he expended much more energy on the question of internal discipline than on reversing the dismissals, which had to wait until the revolutionary victory in 1959.[70] On

October 31, the Ministry of Labor awarded a wage increase of 10 percent but greatly increased the number of workers on *Anexo A*, thereby indicating that the real issue at stake was not the employers' ability to pay an increase, but rather an attack on militant trade unionism.[71] Immediately following the dispute, Andrés Valdespino, writing in the weekly journal *Bohemia*, correctly argued that the attack on bank workers was part of an emerging pattern of wage cuts and mass redundancies.[72]

## Other Trades

The pattern of cuts Valdespino spoke of continued to be implemented sector by sector, with every effort made to prevent generalization of the resistance. An example of this is the dispute with the telegraph workers, which started over a government cut in seniority payments in the summer of 1955. Given the situation in the banking industry and fearing that they were in danger of fighting on two fronts, the government offered a compromise of a 4 percent cut for everyone. A partial strike at the beginning of July won a promise of continuation of the seniority payments, but, at the end of the month, these were much reduced. An apparently spontaneous strike broke out, and in response the authorities at first tried repression, with 205 arrests, 80 of them women, while the army took over the service. When it became clear that there was a danger of this dispute joining up with the bank workers, the CTC negotiated a compromise that would restore seniority payments in September.[73]

In 1955 there were many individual factory strikes, but the record is necessarily patchy and depends upon the presence of a reporter to write the story or whether the press had anything that was considered more important that week. A list of single-enterprise strikes taken from the pages of *Bohemia, Le Villereño,* and *Carta Semanal* for 1955 and displayed below in Table 3.1 gives some idea of the extent of the activity. The table indicates a high level of industrial action in a wide range of industries. What is noticeable is the militancy with which the actions were fought, with attempts to spread the action through demonstrations and symbolic occupations of public buildings. However, the government, in collaboration with the trade union bureaucracy, managed to isolate each action in its immediate locality, preventing a widening of solidarity. This permitted the police and army to crack down on the strikers in many cases without having to worry about the action becoming more generalized. Nevertheless, this did not always lead to defeat.

It is worth looking more closely at two of these strikes, the Tejaleros (textile workers) of the Havana suburb of Marianao and the workers from La Rayonera textile factory in Matanzas. These strikes had very different outcomes. The workers of La Rayonera suffered a wage cut, although they did manage to prevent redundancies, while the Marianao Tejaleros were ultimately successful in winning their demands. We shall see that these two different outcomes resulted in the workers concerned drawing different conclusions, with the Rayonera workers moving toward the politics of the MR-26-7 and the Marianao Tejaleros retaining their traditional support of the PSP.

There had already been a significant level of conflict in the Matanzas textile industry when, in September 1955, Gerado Fundora Nuñez, spokesman for the workers of La Rayonera textile factory, summed up his view of the situation as follows: "There is a campaign to convince the people and government of Cuba that industrial development requires the higher profits that result from wage cuts and changes to social legislation."[74]

Previously, in 1952, La Rayonera had tried to abrogate the collective agreement and impose redundancies on the grounds of unprofitability. This ended in a series of riots that were repressed by the police and army on October 2, during which the union local office was seriously damaged.[75] In February 1953, following a 20 percent wage cut, there was a 103-day strike by the province's sisal workers, which received considerable solidarity from the workers in La Rayonera, who went on to refuse to work fabric with less than 30 percent Cuban fibers.[76] The army again intervened in June 1954 to defeat a factory occupation at La Rayonera against proposed layoffs.[77] The situation finally came to a head in August 1955, when the end of a tax break led the company to go on a productivity offensive, claiming lack of financial viability. Management demanded 277 redundancies with the same level of production and eight hours' work instead of six for the same pay. They threatened otherwise to close the business in October, bringing troops into the factory to intimidate the workers; indeed it was an army officer who read the workers a list of names of those who would continue to work. The workers responded first with a slowdown and then with a rolling strike consisting of half an

## TABLE 3.1: Industrial Strikes during 1955

| Date | Place | Factory | Activity |
|------|-------|---------|----------|
| Jan. 26 | Havana | La Galleteria (bakers) | Strikers protest imposed contract; police intervene to declare "unlawful strike." |
| Feb. 9– Feb. 23 | Manzanillo | Zapateros (shoemakers) | 400 on strike against wage cuts and job losses; street and workplace collections; demonstrations: 80 arrests. |
| Feb. 9 | Havana | *Havana Post* (newspaper) | Newspaper is published only due to management strike breaking. |
| Apr. 6 | Luyanó, Havana | Hatuey (brewery) | *Pasao de jicotea* (work slowdown) against management abuse. |
| Apr. 27 | Pinar del Rio | Las Minas de Matahambre | 48-hour strike. |
| May 26, May 28 | Havana | La Tropical, La Polar, Modelo (breweries) | Brewers strike and occupy factory; police dislodge workers. Leaders arrested, charged with "unlawful strike." |
| – | Manzanillo | La Oriental (foodstuffs) | *Obreros de fideos* (workers) on strike against 52% wage cut; occupy town hall; 18 other factories strike in solidarity. |
| Jun. 15 | Manzanillo | La Oriental | Removed from town hall by police; action repeated. |
| Jul. 6 | Havana | La Ambrosia (brewery) | Strike. |
| Jul. 13 | Luyanó, Havana | Haguey (brewery) | *Pasao de jicotea* continues. |
| Jul. 27 | Manzanillo | Zapateros | Strike against CRIC (Regulatory Cttee. for Footwear Industry). Army occupies town, breaks down street barricades. |
| Aug. 16 | Guanbacoa, Havana | Zapateros | 500 demonstrate against CRIC. |
| Sep. 28– Nov. 2 | Matanzas | La Rayonera (textiles) | Concerted work slowdown. Strike ends after CTC intervenes; 300 layoffs suspended but pay cuts imposed. |
| Nov. 2– Dec. 14 | Marianao, Havana | Tejaleros (textile workers) | Strike against wage cuts; workers win after 51 days. |
| Nov. 23– Dec. 7, 14 | Cotorro, Havana | Hatuey | Strike starts after 4 weeks of agitation. Workers reject truce and retain CTC support. Finally sold out by CTC. |

hour on the first day, three-quarters of an hour the second, one hour the third, until the company locked them out and used the army to eject them from the factory.[78]

The workers set up a strike headquarters in the provincial CTC offices but the army and police expelled them from there as well. This led the movement to become generalized and escalated to a *cuidad muerta* in the city of Matanzas. The shop assistants in the Woolworth store in the city, almost entirely women, were among the leaders of this movement of solidarity, defying the army, which attempted to force them to reopen. The army organized strikebreaking and attempted to force shops to open while soldiers drove the buses.[79] However, repression failed to break the strike, and, with the situation getting out of hand, Batista called in Mujal and the two agreed to a truce to await the report of a commission of inquiry. This took the heat out of the situation and, more important, took the initiative away from the strikers, allowing the company to introduce pay cuts, although not the layoffs, in piecemeal fashion over the course of the next few months.

In most of the disputes discussed so far, the government and the employers were able to get most of what they wanted, but they did not have it all their own way, as can be seen from the dispute in the Havana suburb of Marianao between the textile workers and their employers. The dispute started in November 1955 against a management attempt to impose wage cuts. The action started as a *paso de jicotea* that soon escalated into an occupation. The army violently ejected the strikers from the factory and the employer locked them out. In response, the strikers occupied the local offices of the CTC *federación provincial*. The locally high profile provided by this occupation of the union offices enabled them to organize a demonstration of support by other workers and students, as a result of which the army occupied the neighborhood. The strikers elected a strike committee, and family members set up a women's group, Asociación de Mujeres y Familiares de los Tejaleros (Association of Textile Workers' Wives and Families), to organize solidarity. After four weeks, the Ministry of Labor threatened dismissal to all who did not return to work. The workers responded with demonstrations outside the *ayuntamiento* (town hall) and managed to win the support of the *alcalde* (mayor). The CTC leadership proposed a compromise of a reduced wage cut of 10 percent, but the workers rejected this. Finally after fifty-one days on strike, management capitulated and the strikers won.

It is hard to say why these workers were successful when so many others were not, but the factors in their success would have included the history of solidarity in the town, the presence of a large Communist Party branch capable of generating solidarity outside the immediate area, community involvement through the women's support group, and the approaching showdown with the sugar workers. Whatever the reasons, the political consequences of these two strikes present examples of an oft-repeated tendency: workers who manage to defend their conditions by traditional trade union practices, such as the Marianao textile workers, stayed loyal to the Communist Party and its policy of peaceful mass action, while those who were defeated turned toward the July 26 movement and its policy of violent confrontation with the forces of the state. Thus the textile workers of Matanzas led by Julián Alemán, who joined the MR-26-7 in September 1955, would provide one of the earliest working-class bases for the 26 July *sección obrera* (workers' section).[80]

## Students

Students are not workers, but nevertheless in Cuba they have a long history of making common cause with organized labor. Students commonly felt that their prospects would be improved by an economy run in the interests of local industry, which attracted them to revolutionary nationalist politics in considerable numbers. Given that many were educated in fields in which there was scant chance of employment, they shared the experience of economic insecurity with the sons and daughters of the workers and peasants, and this gave a material basis to the alliance between revolutionary nationalist students and class-conscious workers. Take, for example, the journal *Taína*, produced by the Asociación de Alumnos del Instituto de Segunda Enseñanza de Santiago de Cuba (Santiago Association of Secondary School Students) in the period 1954–56. Its politics spoke of the need to industrialize the country, called for patriotic Cubans to buy Cuban products, and expressed opposition to redundancies, to wage cuts, and to bulk loading of sugar.[81] This tradition of mutual aid between workers and students would be of particular importance in 1955.

Significant numbers of students had opposed the Batista regime from the outset with strikes, demonstrations, and riots. On April 6, 1952, the Federación Estudiantil Universitaria (FEU, Federation of University Students) in Havana symbolically buried the constitution and declared a strike until April 28. Indeed, the first martyr to the violent repression with which the regime met overt opposition was a student, Rubén Batista Rubio, who died as a result of injuries received during a student demonstration on January 15, 1953, called to protest the desecration of the monument to an earlier student leader, Julio Antonio Mella.[82] Cuban students proved themselves adept at using patriotic occasions for demonstrations against the regime, thereby giving themselves a cloak of nationalist legitimacy. Thus, in Santiago de Cuba, the first fights between students and police took place on December 7, 1952, as the students boycotted the official commemoration of independence war hero Antonio Maceo and organized an alternative event which was attacked by the forces of order.[83] This use of official events for unofficial demonstrations was also useful for joint events to build unity between students and workers. For example, on May Day 1953 there were two events in Santiago, the official Labor Day commemoration, where Guillermo Mestre of the electrical trades union, who represented the national leadership of the CTC, gave the address stressing the need to keep politics out of the unions, and an alternative meeting in the local premises of the Bacardi workers' union, the Sindicato de Licores. This was jointly organized with the federations representing university and secondary students and was addressed by the communist Juan Taquechel, leader of the Santiago dockers.[84] This relationship between workers and students would be strengthened by developments within student politics.

There was an ongoing political battle within the student federations between three principal tendencies: those students who wanted to get on with their studies and were not concerned with politics; those who felt there could be a political solution resulting from a compromise with Batista; and those who felt an uncompromising hostility to the dictatorship.[85] Elections were mainly won by the third group, although not always, as shown by the defeat of the Estudiantes Martianos in the Escuela Profesional de Comercio (Professional Commercial School) in Santiago by a slate dedicated to *"no más hablar de política"* (no more talk of politics).[86] Generally, the opposition performed better in the student elections, and young men and women who would later become important revolutionaries, such as Jorge Ibarra and Frank País, served as student union officers. The most significant election, however, was that of the openly revolutionary José Antonio Echeverría as national president of the FEU, which represented a distinct radicalization within the student milieu.[87] The election of Echeverría in early 1955 raised the stakes in the battle with the authorities. The first major student demonstration thereafter, in May in Matanzas to commemorate the murder of the nationalist leader Antonio Guiteras twenty years earlier, was viciously attacked by the police and Echeverría himself was hospitalized.[88] This was followed by a police raid, which destroyed the FEU offices in the university.[89] Julio García Olivares, a friend and political ally of Echeverría, writes that the 1953 Moncada attack and the subsequent murders had convinced Echeverría and his immediate circle that there was no possible compromise with Batista and that there was need for a bigger change than just a return to the situation before the coup.[90] There was a process of political development among the more radical students as the struggle progressed and by the end of 1955, Echeverría was openly talking of "*la Revolución Cubana.*"[91]

In parallel with these developments, the violence of the regime showed that traditional tactics of demonstration and strike were no longer sufficient in themselves. The repressive response to the election of Echeverría failed to intimidate the new student leadership but caused them to rethink their tactics, resulting in an open turn toward the organized working class while they formed a clandestine armed organization called the Directorio Revolucionario.[92] There were traditional bonds of solidarity between the students and militant workers, who frequently came to the university seeking support.[93] The police reaction to a student march in Santiago provided the opportunity to give the relationship a practical application.

On November 27, 1955, the students in Santiago celebrated their traditional event to commemorate the execution of a group of patriotic medical students by the Spanish authorities in 1871. At the same time, they also raised the issue of a colleague, Narciso Mártinez, who had disappeared the previous July and was commonly believed to have been murdered by the police. This infuriated the police, who attacked the demonstration. The students tried to barricade themselves in the town hall, but were ejected violently and three days of rioting ensued.[94] This spread to Havana on the

30th where the FEU executive called a seventy-two-hour strike in solidarity with Santiago. There was more violence in Santiago on December 7 when students tried to lay a wreath at the monument to the national hero Antonio Maceo, but this time photographs of the results of the police brutality appeared in the press.

Most of FEU national leaders were now in prison, so the December 10 executive meeting was composed mainly of deputies, one of whom, quoting the student–worker alliance of 1933, proposed a five-minute national strike on the 14th. Student organizers visited a large number of workplaces where they received a positive response from workers disillusioned with the performance of their official union leaders. The CTC officialdom, with the exception of the *gastronómicos* (hotel and catering workers), opposed the action, but nevertheless it was very well followed, particularly in transport, banks, docks, tobacco, shops, hotels, and restaurants, indicating a growing disillusion with both the official unions and the regime. The list of workplaces taking action in support of the students filled a whole page of *Carta Semanal*.[95] Dockers in the ports of Havana, Regla, Santiago, Cienfuegos, Nuevitas, Matanzas, and Manzanillo "simply refused to work for the rest of the day, causing chaos in busy ports."[96] It was widely reported that Mujal himself was kept waiting for five minutes for his coffee when the waiters refused to serve him in a café.[97] The success of the strike helped to raise political tensions, and Echeverría, on his release from prison, promised to return the solidarity.[98] Following a visit to the university by the Las Villas sugar workers' leader, Conrado Bécquer, he would shortly get the opportunity.

## Sugar

Although the government and employers had been relatively successful in their productivity drive up to this point, the real test would come in their battle with the sugar workers, which was widely recognized as being inevitable as the harvest season approached at the beginning of 1956. The nature of the Cuban economy meant that the sugar workers' union, the Federación Nacional de Trabajadores Azucareros (FNTA, National Federation of Sugar Workers), had always been the most important part of the Cuban labor movement and, because of this, defeating the sugar workers was vital to any attempt to force through productivity increases. A government failure to impose its will on the sugar workers would have given heart to other industrial sectors and undermined the employers' productivity drive. The fall in the international price of sugar in the early 1950s made this battle doubly important as there was a real crisis in the industry. From the point of view of the labor movement, this dispute is also significant as it was followed by the first major split in the trade union bureaucracy. The subsequent intervention of the Ministry of Labor in defense of Mujal's position in the union, following similar intervention in the earlier bank workers' dispute, shows the increased dependence of the mujalistas on state support as they lost influence among the rank and file. Faced with the collaborationist attitude of most of the official leadership, the workers displayed an ability to organize independently. All of these themes would recur in the following years leading up to the revolution.

We have seen how the government, as part of the strategy outlined by the London Sugar Agreement, had reduced the length of time that cane was harvested. This caused a reduction in the overall annual wage earned by the sugar workers. The failure of the London Sugar Agreement to stop the fall in prices meant that this reduction in their wage bill was still not enough for the employers to make profits. They therefore needed further cuts, which could now only be achieved by a cut in the actual rate of pay and a reduction in the numbers employed, with the remaining workers being expected to work harder. This dispute would leave the sugar workers defeated in their immediate gains, but at the cost for the government of alienating a significant number of workers and causing the first of several splits in the CTC bureaucracy. The employers were also dissatisfied by the outcome, as they were still expected to pay a bonus, albeit at a lower rate than the workers demanded. They had expected the government to destroy all resistance and the first signs of a cooling of business support for Batista became visible.

In 1953, as part of its attempts to stabilize the international price of sugar, the government had restricted the harvest to 4,750,000 tons and reduced wages.[99] A further reduction was under consideration for 1955.[100] In 1954, wages and conditions were frozen to 1953 levels, perhaps to avoid trouble before the elections, but the employers considered this to be economically unviable in view of the fall in prices.[101] As a result the employers proposed a *pro-rata* wage rate based on the price of sugar.[102] This produced an outcry, even from the moderate leader of the FNTA, José Luis Martínez.[103]

The FNTA in Oriente Province called for a twenty-four hour strike to demand the dismissal of the minister of labor.[104] The FNTA national conference in January 1955 supported Martínez's stand, with more militant elements agitating for an all-out strike.[105] Following a roundtable discussion with both the employers and the unions, the government decreed a harvest of 4,400,000 tons and a 7.31 percent wage cut, which would result in a saving for the employers of 23 million dollars, 15 percent of their wage bill.[106] The decree also authorized bulk sugar loading, a measure which would have led to thousands of job losses.[107] There was uproar in the FNTA conference, but Mujal persuaded the delegates to refer the strike call to a joint CTC/FNTA executive meeting. There, away from the pressure of the conference, Martínez and Mujal opposed a strike as impractical, saying that the FNTA was not prepared. The final vote was 53 to 19 against strike action.[108]

This conference is the first sign of a developing schism in the CTC bureaucracy and the emergence of a left-wing opposition centered around Conrado Rodriguez and Conrado Bécquer, known popularly as *los Dos Conrados*. Bécquer was deputy general secretary of the FNTA, and they were both Auténtico Party parliamentary deputies. They would go on to play significant roles in the Cuban Revolution. This conference was also the first report at national level of an intervention by David Salvador, a shop steward from a plantation sugar refinery, *central* Stewart,[109] near Ciego de Avila. He would soon become a founder member of the MR-26-7 and would lead the revolutionary CTC after the revolution.

Following the formal acceptance of the government decree, employers in the province of Las Villas started declaring mass layoffs. Conrado Rodriguez, the provincial FNTA leader, publicly accused Mujal and Martínez of betrayal,[110] an accusation that led Rodriguez and Martínez to fight a duel.[111] There was considerable disillusion at this retreat, both within the rank and file and among a minority of the FNTA leadership. Workers in *central* Mercedes, Matanzas Province, publicly burned effigies of Mujal and Martinez.[112] On the other side, the employers had been looking for a much greater cut in their wage bill.[113] The Ministry of Labor repaid the FNTA bureaucracy for their help in defusing the situation by delaying the scheduled union elections in which it was unlikely that any of the *mujalistas* on the executive could have retained their seats.[114] The scene was therefore set for a confrontation the following year, by which time, having defeated the railway workers and the bank clerks, the government would feel more confident. Meanwhile, both sides limbered up with a series of increasingly bitter skirmishes as can be seen in Table 3.2 (see next page) on sugar industry strikes during 1955, which details reports from *Carta Semanal, El Villareño,* and *Bohemia* during 1955.

Information on most of these local disputes is scarce, but considerable details have been unearthed about the strike at Delicias y Chaparra, in the region of Las Tunas.[115] This dispute shows the use of tactics that would become widespread in the national strike that would break out at the end of the year and highlights some of the problems faced by the employers and the government in their later full-scale onslaught on the sugar workers. It is also important because of the role of women who provided solidarity.

The strike started in October 1954 following an announcement by the company that there would be job cuts in the forthcoming harvest. A group of strikers occupied the town hall, but were quickly ejected by the Rural Guard. Women from the strikers' families, supported by the local branch of the communist women's organization, the Federación Democrática de Mujeres Cubanas (FDMC, Democratic Federation of Cuban Women), then retook the town hall and held it. They also managed to intimidate the Rural Guard into giving them the keys of the union local office, which they then kept open throughout the dispute. This is an example of the frequently seen phenomenon whereby agents of the state were prepared to use a high level of brutality against male strikers, but were reluctant to beat up women in the same way. Militant women were able to use this reluctance to the strikers' advantage. Most of the *mujalista* union officials had disappeared at the first sign of trouble, and the strikers organized themselves in the absence of their official leaders by holding daily mass meetings, despite the presence of Rural Guard on horseback with drawn sabres. Dockworkers in the local port of Juan Claro refused to load sugar for the duration of the strike, while women from dockworkers' families joined the women's support groups set up by the families of sugar workers. In confirmation of the role played by women in this dispute, a contemporary report

**TABLE 3.2: Sugar Industry Strikes during 1955**

| Date | Place | Factory | Activity |
|---|---|---|---|
| 3 Jan.[116] | Oriente | Delicias-Chaparra | Strike over job losses started previous October. 200 women prevent arrested workers being transported to Holguin by train, then prevent strike breakers entering workplace. Women's group goes to Tunas and to Holguin seeking solidarity. |
| 12 Jan. | | | Strike continues. |
| 23 Feb. | | | Harvest starts with no job losses but needs strike to get overtime pay. |
| 12 Jan. | Oriente | Central Carolina | 15-day strike against 4-day week: ¡Trabajamos semana completa o no trabajamos! (We work the whole week or not at all!)—successful. |
| 12 Jan. | Camagüey | Central Morón | Pasao de jicotea—army surrounds assembly. |
| 12 Jan. | Guantánamo | Ingenios Esperanza, Soldedad, Isabel | Management agrees to start of repairs on the same conditions as previous year and withdraws threat of wage cuts following threatened industrial action. |
| 16 Feb. | Camaguey | Central Florida | Strike against job losses. |
| 23 Feb. (20 Feb. in Bohemia) | Camagüey | Central Estrella | Threat of layoffs leads to strike; 60 workers arrested but released as strike continues and company gives way. Women active in solidarity. |
| | Matanzas | Central Dolores | Strike. |
| | | Central Tacahó | Strike. |
| 11 Feb. (El Villareño, Carta Semanal 23 Feb.) | Las Villas | Placetas | Police prevent FNTA plenaria provincial which was called to oppose job losses at centrales San José, Hormiguero, and San Isidro. |
| 1 March (El Villareño) | Las Villas | Central Hormiguero | Town of San Fernando cuidad muerta because of late start to harvest. Work starts again; arrested workers are released. |

**TABLE 3.2: Sugar Industry Strikes during 1955 (cont'd)**

| Date | Place | Factory | Activity |
|---|---|---|---|
| 20 March (Bohemia), 16 March *(El Villareño)* | Las Villas | Central Soledad | Sugar workers' wives and families occupy company offices but are dislodged by army. Conrado Bécquer arrested.[117] |
| 6 April | Havana | Central Hershey | 48-hour strike to defend *escalafón* (seniority agreement). |
| 14 Sept. (11 Sept. in Bohemia) 6 Nov. | Las Villas | Central Washington (owned by Batista) | Assembly held to discuss proposed 40 layoffs. Police attack and inflict 9 gunshot and 20 machete wounds. CTC equivocate. Strike threats in Las Villas. Sugar workers occupy site hospital and begin hunger strike. Families occupy school then occupy church and town hall. Solidarity strikes in the region. Company claims bankruptcy. Mujal washes his hands of the matter. *Los Dos Conrados* occupy church tower; intervention ordered. More army violence; intervener eventually concedes to workers and layoffs are withdrawn. |
| 23 Nov. (2 Nov. in El Villareño) | Sancti Spiritus | Central Amazonas | Demonstration in support of strike against firing of 84 workers. Town hall occupied. |

in *Carta Semanal* also tells us that 200 women managed to prevent police from taking arrested workers to Holguin by train and also stopped would-be strikebreakers from entering the workplace.[118] Further, it was reported that the women's group went to the nearby towns of Tunas and Holguin in order to seek solidarity. The fact that Delicias y Chaparra was owned by an American company gave the strike a nationalist twist and there was considerable public support and material solidarity from all over Cuba, with the strikers able to paint themselves as the true patriots. It was probably this patriotic solidarity that put sufficient pressure on the Ministry of Labor to rule in favor of the workers and give them a victory after an action that lasted 104 days.[119] This local victory had an important encouraging effect for the mass of sugar workers.

As the 1955 *tiempo muerto*[120] progressed, workers at local union meetings started formulating their demands, a process that the authorities tried to intimidate by the threat of violence up and down the country. The police attack on the workers of *central* Washington in Las Villas was one example of many, but received wider attention because it was owned by Batista himself. When the *central* Washington workers met in August 1955 to discuss the threat of forty redundancies, the police attacked the assembly, leaving twenty-nine workers hospitalized with gunshot and machete wounds.[121] The sugar workers responded by occupying the site hospital and beginning a hunger strike, while their female family members staged a sit-in, first of all in the school, then, after they had been ejected from there, occupying the church and the *ayuntamiento*. As solidarity strikes spread through the region, Bécquer and Rodriguez occupied the church tower.[122] As the confrontation escalated, the Ministry of Labor intervened, conceded to the workers, and the layoffs were withdrawn.

Feelings in the industry were further inflamed by reports of corruption in the sugar workers' pension fund involving both the government and the FNTA bureaucracy, and pressure increased when the American sugar import quota was threatened with reduction following protectionist pressure from U.S. sugar farmers.[123] In this atmosphere, the provincial union in Las Villas passed a resolution calling for opposition to their employers over the late start of repairs in the sugar-processing plants and the threat of 10,000 layoffs, while rejecting what they saw as a return to 1950 wage levels. The FNTA *plenaria nacional* (national plenary meeting) in November supported this approach and demanded a five-million-ton harvest, an end to wage cuts, and the restoration of the previous year's 7.31 percent cut, along with the reinstatement of all sacked workers, pay for *super-producción*,[124] and derogation of Clause 4 of decree 3164, which allowed employers to leave vacancies unfilled. They also raised the demand for full payment of the bonus known as the *"diferencial."*[125]

Before the start of each year's sugar harvest, it had been the agreement to pay the workers a *diferencial*, calculated on the increase in the cost of living in the United States. Though this might seem a bizarre reason for a bonus, it was based on the fact that a considerable proportion of the island's food was imported from North America. The *diferencial* also had a symbolic significance because it had been won by Jesus Menéndez, the legendary sugar workers' leader who, while traveling the country to organize a strike to defend the right to payment of the full *diferencial,* had been murdered by an army officer at the Manzanillo railroad station in 1948. No *diferencial* had been paid since 1951, but the idea captured the sugar workers' imagination in 1955.[126] Alfredo Menéndez, an economist in the Ministry of Sugar who was secretly a member of the PSP, used his access to the ministry's data to calculate that the *diferencial* should be 9 percent, although Conrado Rodriguez popularized the figure of 7.5 percent.[127] The fact that confrontation should erupt over the *diferencial* highlights the gulf that existed between employers and employed in the sugar industry. To the employers, the international price drop meant that they had a reduced ability to pay their wage bill and that a bonus dating back to better times was unacceptable. The majority of workers, on the other hand, already living in conditions of miserable poverty, felt that they were being made to bear the brunt of a crisis not of their making, and thus, the fight over the *diferencial* became hugely symbolic for both sides and a strike seemed unavoidable.[128]

The government refused to negotiate over the sugar workers' claim for payment of the *diferencial.*[129] Undeterred, starting on December 26 in Las Villas Province, but soon spreading nationwide, 500,000 sugar workers went on strike, and the union leadership, unable to stop the movement, tried to place themselves at its head. Then, following negotiations with Batista, the FNTA ordered a return to work on December 29, saying that the government had agreed to their demands. Bécquer and the opposition, calling themselves the Frente Azucarero de Acción Sindical (Sugar Workers' Trade Union Action Front), called for a continuation of the struggle as the government had decreed a *diferencial* of only 4.02 percent, which was calculated to be worth a total of only 6 million pesos to the workers, considerably short of the 18 million pesos that it would have cost to pay the full demand, which, it should be recalled, also included a demand for the reversal of the 7.31 percent wage cut from the previous year and compensation for *super-producción.*[130]

When faced with a level of repression  previously used only to attack militant students, the sugar workers turned to violence, setting up road blocks, burning cane fields, and occupying town halls and city centers, actions that resulted in hundreds arrested or wounded, with several strikers killed.[131] In addition to a complete stoppage of the sugar industry, there were solidarity strikes on the railways and on the docks. Despite the official instruction to return to work from the CTC, normal working was not fully resumed until the 4th or 5th of January.

To get a better idea of the extent of the strike, Table 3.3 records the reports to appear in the edition of *Carta Semanal* that immediately followed the end of the strike. This is only a partial account as it depended on the local presence of a PSP militant to file the report and we know from other sources that there were many other actions not reported here. Nevertheless, this table gives a picture of the strike that is rarely seen.

The picture that emerges from this account is of a widespread strike with extremely active and militant rank-and-file participation. The start of the strike in Las Villas Province is clearly the result of a decision of the local leadership based around Bécquer and Rodriguez. The speed with which the strike spread to the rest of the industry, despite the lack of any lead from the official union leadership, shows that there was a well-established network of militants capable of acting independently. The local industrial action during the previous year would have played a part in reinforcing existing links and establishing new ones. Once the strike started, the level of solidarity coming from other workers, particularly dock and railway workers, is impressive. Where normal peaceful picketing proved ineffective in the face of police and army aggression, there was no hesitation in resorting to sabotage, such as bridge burning and train derailment. Street demonstrations, road blocks, and the occupation of public buildings and town squares were also a common feature. Finally, where they were able, workers engaged in street fights with government forces, leaving many injured and several dead. It is hard to imagine what more the sugar workers could have done within the bounds of "normal" trade union activity; indeed, they had already pushed the boundaries of accepted trade union practice beyond its limits. Yet they were still defeated, and it must be seen as a defeat, despite assertions to the contrary in some quarters,[132] not just because they only got 4.02 percent rather than the 7.5 percent *diferencial* that they were demanding, but also, it must not be forgotten, because they did not succeed in restoring the 7.31 percent pay cut of the previous year, no *superproducción* was paid, the *zafra* was not extended to 5 million tons, and the full labor force was not reemployed. Conrado

## TABLE 3.3: Sugar Strike Reports from *Carta Semanal*, 11 Jan. 1956

### PINAR DEL RIO

| | |
|---|---|
| San Cristóbal, Mariel, Bahia Honda, San Diego del Valle | *Ciudad muerta.* |
| Pinar del Rio City | Solidarity strikes. |

### HAVANA PROVINCE

| | |
|---|---|
| Havana city | Solidarity strikes in the port, Hatuey brewery, and other factories. |
| Guanagay, Artemisa | Sugar workers occupy buildings. Solidarity strikes by tobacco, shoe, and bus workers. |
| Guines | All refineries stopped. Demonstrations; partial *ciudad muerta* (city-wide general strike). Army forces shops to open. Church occupied. |
| Palos | Demonstration attacked by police, one worker killed. |
| Melena del Sur | Sugar workers from *central* Merceditas demonstrate in town, traffic stopped and businesses close. |
| Madruga | Running battles between sugar workers and police/army; many arrests. |
| San Nicolas | Workers march into town from central Gímez Mena. Public meeting broken up by police. 500 workers occupy church and Union Club. |
| Central Hershey | Complete work stoppage. |
| Santa Cruz del Norte | *Ciudad muerta* demonstrations and road blocks. Workers occupy Yacht Club. 14 arrests, women's demonstration for their release. |
| Guanabacoa | Solidarity strikes by bus, shoe, and garment workers. |
| Marianao (suburb of Havana) | Solidarity from bus workers and staff of Tropicana nightclub, tile factory, and quarry. |
| Regla | Protest strike on bus routes 21 and 25. |

### MATANZAS PROVINCE

| | |
|---|---|
| Matanzas City | Solidarity strike by shop workers, printers, and La Rayonera and La Rex textile factories. |
| Colon | General strike and demonstration. |

## TABLE 3.3: Sugar Strike Reports (cont'd)

### MATANZAS PROVINCE cont'd

| | |
|---|---|
| Unión de Reyes | Workers from central Santo Domingo occupy town hall. |
| Coliseo | Joint demonstration by workers from 5 *centrales* with their families. |
| Pedro Betancourt | Workers from *centrales* Cuba and Dolores demonstrate and call on shops to shut. Army forces shops to open. Traffic brought to a standstill. |
| Cardenas | *Ciudad muerta.* Joint student/worker demonstration. Education institute occupied but evicted by army which patrols streets; many arrests. |
| Alacranes | Workers from central Conchita call the town to support them by ringing church bells; 1,000 people join demonstration. Workers from central España and central Tinguaro occupy Casino Español; evicted violently. |
| Las Villas (Cienfuegos, Sancti Spíritus, and Villa Clara) | *"En la provincia de Las Villas la casi totalidad de los municipios y las poblaciones azucareras se convirtieron en ciudades muertas."* [133] (In the province of Las Villas, there were general strikes in almost all the sugar towns and villages.) |
| Santa Clara | Strikers occupy the provincial CTC offices; ejected by force. Townspeople build roadblocks and stop traffic. |
| Santo Domingo | Strikers occupy church and town hall; evicted by the army. Protesters march around town; block the main road across the island, Carretera Central, and railway line by cutting down trees and burning trash. Locals forced by army to clear up at gun- and machete-point; many arrests. |
| La Esperanza | General strike. |
| Ranchuelo | Factory workers, tobacco, food, commerce, and construction strike in support. |
| Zulueta | *Cuidad muerta.* |
| Cruces | Sugar workers march in town. Businesses shut in solidarity. Police and army patrol town attacking passersby. |
| Cienfuegos city | Solidarity action by bus drivers, printers, port workers. Demonstration by students and workers in conflict with police and army, who try to force businesses to open, but massive demonstrations cause them to shut again. Stones thrown at police and army. |
| Hormiguero y Portugalete | Rural Guard evict strikers from their own union local. |

## TABLE 3.3: Sugar Strike Reports (cont'd)

| | |
|---|---|
| Palmira | Workers occupy the church, Colonia Espanola social center, and the Masonic lodge; evicted by force. |
| Aguada de Pasajeros | Workers from central Covadonga and Perseverancia and M. Victoria farms occupy town hall. Street demonstration in support. |
| Sancti Spiritus | Workers from *centrales* Tuinicó, Natividad, and Amazonas march into town. Workers in Compañia Nacional de Alimentos, tobacco and construction workers, taxi, and bus drivers join in solidarity strike. Commerce shuts down. Burning tires and trash block streets. |
| Quemados de Guines | *Ciudad muerta*. Electricity cut off. Tercio Táctico regiment from Sancti Spiritus reinforces local military post. Many workers injured, one killed. Imposing demonstration at the funeral of the dead worker. |
| Sagua la Grande | Town paralyzed. Church occupied and bells rung to attract support; protesters evicted at gunpoint. Train derailed to block the main road. Several injured, two seriously. Surrounding area also paralyzed. |
| Placetas, Cabaiguan, Guayos, Zaza del Medio, Trinidad | *Cuidades muertas* and demonstrations. |
| Fomento | *Cuidad muerta* . Army opens fire on demonstration; many wounded. |
| Yaguajay, Narcisa and Mayajigua | *Cuidades muertas* and demonstrations. |

| | |
|---|---|
| Camagüey City | Ten-minute strike stops city completely. |
| Moron | General strike, including bus and train crews, which cuts off town. Demonstrations and fights with police, many wounded and arrested. Strikebreaking bus burnt as are several railway bridges. |
| Florida | Joint strike committee from *centrales* Florida, Estrella, Céspedes, and Agramonte organize actions. Townspeople summoned by church bells; police and army open fire. Stones thrown. Many arrests but local military chief forced to parley with strikers. |
| Santa Cruz del Sur | Dockers refuse to load sugar; *ciudad muerta*. |

## TABLE 3.3: Sugar Strike Reports (cont'd)

### CAMAGÜEY PROVINCE (cont'd)

| | |
|---|---|
| Ciego de Avila | 5,000 demonstrate. Shops that had remained open are forcibly shut by mass action. Traffic stopped; students and workers occupy financial center and education institute; evicted by army at gunpoint. Children injured, one mother attacks soldiers with a knife. Roads to *centrales* Stewart, Baragúa, and Algodones blocked; railway blocked. |
| Esmeralda, Jaronu, Cunagua, Vertientes Francisco, Elia, Siboney, Najasa, Minas | Strike complete and all shops and businesses closed. |
| Nuevitas | *Mujalista* (pro-government union) officials order loading of sugar but railway workers refuse to transport it. |

### ORIENTE

| | |
|---|---|
| Santiago de Cuba | Solidarity meetings, particularly in port and Bacardi. |
| Guantánamo | Work stoppage complete; students join worker demonstration. Occupation of town hall and education institute. |
| Manzanillo | Work stoppage complete. Pilón dockers strike rather than load sugar. Sugar workers tour factories and a mass meeting agrees on a *ciudad muerta.* |
| Bayamo | Refineries in the region stop repairs. Marchers in the sugar villages of the area joined by other workers. |
| Puerto Padre | *Ciudad muerta. Centrales* Chaparra and Delicias stop work. Dock-workers in Cayo Juan Claro stop loading sugar. |
| Baguano y Tacajo | Work stoppage complete. Army tries to force dockers to load sugar at gunpoint but they resist and prevent further loading by derailing a train between the warehouse and the port. |
| Boston, Preston, Maceo, San German, Cacocum, Manati, Jobabo, Tanamo | Protesters stop repairs to machinery in preparation for the harvest. |

Bécquer was clear that they had not won and blamed Mujal for what he described as a sellout.[134]

The violence used by the state against strikers forged a bond of solidarity between workers and students as they realized they had a common enemy. The FEU repaid the solidarity they had received on December 14 by sending student organizers out into the sugar fields to help the strikers. In many towns students joined demonstrations in large numbers and occupied their colleges. The support they showed in the sugar strike gave the FEU enormous credibility among workers, and the revolutionary nationalist politics of the student activists gained a greater working-class following. When a section of the FNTA leadership tried to openly organize against what they saw as a betrayal, they were disciplined by the CTC bureaucracy and turned again to the FEU for help.

The looming split in the CTC became a reality when Bécquer and Rodriguez, along with some other officials who had supported the strike, were removed from the FNTA executive and some provincial leaders were expelled, with the CTC using the police to enforce the decision. New officials were imposed by the Ministry of Labor to replace those expelled, but in Las Villas and Camagüey no local sugar workers were available, so outsiders had to be used. Having been barred from their own building by the police, the anti-*mujalista* opposition in the FNTA met in the parliament building, using Conrado Rodriguez's position as congressional deputy to secure a meeting room. The meeting was attended by a clear majority of the FNTA executive. They declared themselves the real leadership of the union and proposed to go to court to establish it—a course of action that, unsurprisingly, came to nothing.[135] Attempts to form a breakaway sugar workers' union with the help of the FEU were equally unsuccessful as the Ministry of Labor and the *mujalista* trade union bureaucracy worked together using the intervention procedures to isolate the opposition.[136]

The news magazine *Bohemia* argued at the time that the *diferencial* represented much more than the money, but was rather a question of workers' rights and social justice.[137] Although it was several days before normal work was fully resumed, the final outcome was a success for the government, even though many employers did not see it that way, expecting the complete smashing of all resistance. Thus the Economist Intelligence Unit (EIU), having hoped in February 1955 that Batista "would override labor opposition," expressed disappointment in February of the following year saying: "A strike of 500,000 sugar and dockworkers was settled in the short term by a government decision in favor of the workers."[138] It is significant that the EIU included dockworkers in the strike because, completely unofficially, they involved themselves in the sugar dispute, taking advantage of an opportunity to use their solidarity action to further their campaign against bulk loading.

## Ports

The Truslow Report had recommended that sugar be bulk loaded by pouring the granular sugar directly into the ship's hold, a process known as *azúcar a granel*.[139] In Cuba at this time the sugar was placed in jute sacks at the refinery, shipped on trains to the port, then, still in sacks, manually loaded using cranes and conveyor belts into warehouses to await the equally labor-intensive transfer of the sacks into the holds of cargo ships. The technology had long been developed to mechanize this process so that the sugar could be poured directly into the bulk carrier ship's hold, but its use was highly controversial as it would have resulted in large-scale job losses. The economic importance of bulk loading can be seen from the estimation that manual loading normally proceeded at a rate of 800 tons per day, whereas direct bulk loading could increase that to 400 tons per hour, with half the number of stevedores employed.[140] The dockworkers were bitterly opposed to this measure, and, though the previous government of Carlos Prío had issued decree number 501 authorizing the loading of *azúcar a granel*, it had not dared to enforce it.[141] Batista confirmed the decree early in his rule, but then immediately deferred its application, allowing him to set the agenda for full implementation.

Having decided that its priority after winning the 1954 elections was the financial difficulties of the railway companies and the sugar industry, the government did not attempt to impose bulk loading on the dockworkers immediately, although it did start to prepare the ground. The dockers were under no illusions about the forthcoming attack, and as early as May 1954 *Carta Semanal* reported on mass meetings of dockers in Nuevitas, Santiago, Cienfuegos, and Matanzas, which mandated their delegates to the forthcoming national congress of their union, the Federación de Obreros Maritimos Nacional (FOMN, National Federation of Maritime Workers), to vote against accepting *azúcar a granel*.[142] When the conference actually opened at the end of January 1955, it became obvious to Gilberto Goliath, the *mujalista* general secretary of the FOMN, that despite having persuaded a significant number of delegates to ignore their mandate and to vote in favor of bulk loading, there was still a majority who would vote against.[143] Mujal, who chaired the conference personally, therefore postponed the decision until he was able to pack the hall with extra, unelected delegates.[144] Despite angry protests from the legitimately elected delegates opposed to the measure, it was passed by a clear majority.[145] As a result of this official acceptance, Batista issued a decree regulating loading and unloading of primary materials, but he was careful not to provoke the dockers further at this stage by specifying reductions in manning levels.[146] It was one thing to have a formal union policy that accepted bulk loading, it was another to enforce its acceptance at the local level and following an unofficial meeting, the opposition delegates returned to their ports committed to organizing resistance locally.[147]

When a local union organization appeared to be escaping from Mujal's control, the Ministry of Labor could "intervene," an expression meaning that they would take over the organization, at police gunpoint if necessary, and impose a safe bureaucrat to run it. This happened in Santiago in 1955, when the dockworkers, still under the leadership of the communist Juan Taquechel, started to organize against the threat of bulk loading and held some protest strikes.[148] The ministry intervened, although with only limited success as the dockers still managed to hold their mass meetings.[149]

Tension was raised further when, in January 1955, the British ambassador passed a note to the government demanding that, in future, all sugar exported to England be bulk loaded.[150] This was considered particularly provocative as Britain held large reserves and was not intending to buy its usual amount of Cuban sugar that year. Following the British demand, the port workers of Nuevitas set the lead in resisting *embarques a granel*, that is, refusing to bulk load the German ship *Parnas*, bound for England. Army strikebreakers were used to load instead.[151] Faced with this threat and the undemocratic nature of the official union's acceptance, seventy-eight local unions set up a *comité nacional contra los embarques a granel* (national committee against bulk loading) to organize opposition.[152]

However, the government had other, more immediate priorities and further delayed attempting to implement the decree.

Bulk loading of sugar finally reached 11 percent of exports by 1957, increasing to 25 percent by 1958.[153] However, this was still not mechanized bulk loading; sugar cargoes were ferried out on barges and then dumped out of sacks into the hold of a ship lying offshore.[154] The only advantage of this for the port employers was that they could thereby comply with the importing countries' requirements; apart from a small economy from the reuse of sacks, they saved no money at the Cuban end of the business. From the employers' point of view this was a disappointing retreat by the government, while the dockworkers emerged with their self-confidence enhanced and their manning and wage levels intact.

The first mechanized bulk sugar loading facilities were not established until the early 1970s with the inauguration of the new dock and warehousing arrangements in Guayabal and Matanzas, followed later by Cienfuegos.[155]

## Tobacco

The ports were not the only sector in which the Batista government's productivity offensive was less than successful; they were equally unable to force through mechanization of the home cigar market. In order to understand developments in the tobacco industry in 1955, it is necessary to return to the late 1940s.

Before the 1952 coup, the major cigar companies were unable to impose the mechanization of the internal market, despite the fact that Mujal and the Ministry of Labor had removed the traditional communist leadership from official control of the tobacco workers' trade union federation. It appeared that sterner measures of repression than those available to the Prío government would be necessary to defeat a determined and well-organized group of workers who commanded considerable popular support. Cuban cigar exports had fallen from 256 million per year in 1906 to only 21 million in 1949, and the Truslow Report argued that the only way to reverse this decline was by mechanization.[156] Such was the obvious crisis that trade unionists in the tobacco industry accepted the argument for mechanization for export, but were determined to resist mechanization of the greatly expanded internal market, as well as to demand financial compensation for those displaced by machinery. This policy was formally agreed at a conference of the Federación Tabacalera Nacional (FTN, National Federation of Tobacco Workers) in February 1948, and a campaign to defend hand rolling for domestic consumption was launched at a mass meeting in the Parque Central hotel in Havana, addressed by Lazaro Peña, the recently deposed communist ex-general secretary of the CTC, who had himself been a tobacco worker. Communists had a significant base in the tobacco industry and had strongly resisted intervention by the Ministry of Labor aimed at imposing *mujalista* officials. This had come to violence on many occasions, with gangsters linked to the Auténtico Party operating inside the factories with the consent of the owners and with the intention of intimidating and demoralizing the workers. Miguel Fernández Roig, union representative in the La Corona factory and an established leader of the Havana cigar makers, was murdered by an Auténtico gunman, who escaped with the aid of the police.[157] This campaign of violence was, however, only partly successful, and the tobacco industry was one of the sectors where the PSP was to maintain a significant presence throughout the 1950s. Later attempts to intervene in the tobacco unions in Las Villas and Oriente in 1956 would be met with a series of strikes.[158]

In November 1948, José Diaz Ortega, a member of congress from Pinar del Rio, proposed a motion in parliament that would have legalized the complete mechanization of cigar manufacture, both for export and for internal consumption. However, this was rejected following energetic lobbying by an alliance of tobacco workers and the owners of small factories who could not afford the investment required to mechanize.[159] Despite this rejection, in March 1950 the government of Carlos Prío, with the acquiescence of the national union leadership, now firmly in the hands of the *mujalistas*, issued decree number 1073, which authorized mechanization of cigar making for export and for 20 percent of the home market, along with compensation of 40 pesos per month for those workers who lost their jobs as a direct result of the measure.[160] Given the fact that over a third of Havana's cigar makers were already unemployed at this time and would therefore not have received the compensation, this last measure fell well short of the workers' demands.

Despite the purge of most of the tobacco workers' union organizations, the *unitarios*, as the communists and their allies in the workers' movement were known, still commanded considerable loyalty among rank-and-file tobacco workers and set about organizing a united front with the smaller employers, who stood to lose business to the large cigar companies as they could not afford the expensive new machinery.[161] Opposition was already strong in Las Villas, so a group of experienced *unitario* organizers went to Pinar del Rio to strengthen resistance there.[162] The newly imposed union leadership was forced to act, and in March 1951 a joint committee was set up to coordinate the struggle against decree 1073. By the end of June 1951, the joint committee had sufficient strength to call a strike for July 2. This became a general stoppage, with many towns in Las Villas organizing *ciudades-muertas*. In Cabaiguán, the town hall was occupied and there was a massive demonstration of support for the tobacco workers, despite considerable violent police activity. In the province of Las Villas the forces of order were in some danger of losing control of the situation, with the island's principal highway, the *Carretera Central*, and the main railway line blocked in many places. The mayors of thirty-one towns in Las Villas went to Havana to lobby President Prío and a forty-eight-hour truce was agreed. As a result of further negotiations, decree 2893 withdrew permission for mechanization of cigars aimed at the home market.[163]

Several points of interest emerge from this dispute. First, the Prío government's purges of the unions were not sufficient in themselves to ensure that productivity measures such as mechanization could be introduced. The new *mujalista* leadership was still vulnerable to pressure from the rank and file, particularly in areas where the traditional communist leaders and their allies retained support and respect despite being ousted from office. This lesson would not be lost on the Batista regime in the years following the coup, and the compulsory check off of union dues, the *cuota sindical obligatoria*, combined with greater police support for interventions, would reduce the bureaucracy's dependence on the rank and file. At this stage, the purges and "interventions" were only a partial success, because, as soon as halfway democratic elections were allowed, *unitarios* were frequently reelected. The success of the Communist Party's tactics, which took the form of an alliance between workers and businessmen who were opposed to the monopolizing tendencies of the bigger companies, ensured their continuing popularity among tobacco workers. Second, although there had been a certain amount of fighting between demonstrators and police on July 2, 1951, this had not intimidated the strikers and their allies. The Batista regime would attempt to remedy this by making sure that its use of repressive force would not stop at the bounds normally accepted in a democratic society, but would wound, kill, torture, and arbitrarily arrest where necessary, using the army to "aid the civil power" with fixed bayonets and live rounds.

Following the coup, the eight large companies that had already mechanized their export business sought to extend their use of the new machines to the home trade. The opening shots of the campaign were a short strike in Havana on May 18, 1953, and the setting up of a *comité de lucha contra la mecanización* (committee to fight mechanization) in Santa Clara. The government, in response to pressure from the larger companies, issued decree 895 which authorized the minister of agriculture to gauge the state of opinion on the subject of extending mechanization, which he was to do by consulting the official unions. Unfortunately for the supporters of mechanization, anti-*mujalista* forces in the union were still in place in Las Villas and, at the V Congreso Tabacalero Nacional (5th National Tobacco Workers' Congress) on June 20 and 21, 1953, they had enough delegates to sway the conference to opposition.[164] Indeed, Mujal was never able to exert the level of control over the FTN that he managed in most other organizations, in part because of the gross ineptitude and greed of those few leading tobacco trade unionists who supported his project, with the result that even anti-communist trade unionists were disgusted.[165]

The matter of mechanization then lay on the table until late 1955 when the large companies announced the setting up of a "persuasive" fund.[166] Two senators, Manuel Benítez and Ernesto Peréz Carrillo, as well as a congressman, José Luis Guerra Cabrera, independently proposed laws that would legalize mechanization, while the workers from H. Upmann and Partagas staged demonstrations outside the building. The matter was more complicated than most productivity arrangements for several reasons. Mechanization of the export trade had not increased sales or reduced prices, it merely increased profits for those firms that could afford the necessary capital outlay. Any extension of mechanization would not only bring redundancies to the mechanizing factories, but would be likely to result in a concentration of the industry into the hands of a few monopolies, mainly based in Havana, reducing employment opportunities in the provinces. The proposed compensation for displaced workers and ruined small businesses was to be a charge on the state, thereby using the public purse to effectively subsidize a few large companies.[167] This reactivated the alliance between the smaller producers and the *unitario* trade unionists in Las Villas, who relaunched the *comité de lucha contra la mecanización*. With the sugar workers' dispute now firmly on the horizon, the government had enough to deal with and the attempt to introduce mechanization was postponed. There was a halfhearted attempt to return to the matter in the new year of 1956, with Ministry of Labor interventions in some of the most intransigent local unions, which resulted in strikes, most notably in Zaza del Medion in February 1956, Bayamo in early March, and the entire province of Las Villas later that same month.[168]

A good example of the resistance to intervention can be seen in the reaction of the *unitario* leaders of the Sindicato de Torcedores de Cabaiguan (Cigar Rollers' Union of Cabaiguan), David Concepción and Miguel Reyes. At the first threat of intervention in January 1956, they issued a manifesto against intervention in the name of their own and several other local unions. This was followed by another manifesto in the name of all the Las Villas tobacco workers' organizations, the Comité Conjunto de Organizaciones Tabacaleras de Las Villas (Joint committee of tobacco workers' organizations of Las Villas). This clearly stated that the real reason for intervention was to facilitate the introduction of mechanical cigar rolling. Opposition to intervention was made the theme of the May Day rally that year. On a practical level, the *unitarios* removed all documentation from the union offices to prevent it from falling into the hands of the intervention committee. When the intervention committee finally arrived in Cabaiguan in November, they were met with a demonstration by workers from many different trades and 181 workers in the Bauzá factory signed a manifesto against intervention. Thereafter, the *unitario* tobacco workers in Cabaiguan organized under the name of the Comité Pro-Primero de Mayo (May Day Committee), ignoring the official structure and its imposed leadership.[169]

Given the less than successful attempt to intervene in the organizational base of the opposition to machine rolling, the matter, with the exception of a public meeting in the Teatro La Caridad in Santa Clara in 1957, where

Batista himself addressed interested parties to try to persuade them to accept *semi-mecanización*, was quietly dropped.[170]

## Reactions to Repression

The history of Cuba's port and tobacco workers' resistance to the government and employers' attempts to increase productivity poses a question: Why did the attempt to impose mechanization on both bulk loading of sugar and cigar production for the home market fail, when the government/employer productivity drive was relatively successful in most other industries? It is possible to use brute force and corruption to reduce the wage bill in industries such as sugar production, which rely largely on unskilled manual labor, or the railways, which were already mechanized. In both of these cases it was merely a question of intensifying workloads and paying lower wages. The problem with the docks was that the major productivity measure proposed by Truslow, bulk loading of sugar, required considerable investment in new machinery. Before employers were prepared to make such investments, they had be reasonably confident that they could make the workers use the new equipment. An earlier attempt to introduce bulk loading of cement had proved a costly failure.[171]

In 1950, the El Mariel cement company had paid $100,000 to install bulk unloading equipment in the port of Havana. The Havana dockers used their industrial muscle to force the company to employ as many stevedores on the bulk discharge as would have been required for manual unloading. The company dismantled the equipment and returned to the previous practice.[172] Given this experience, the port employers required a firm guarantee that their employees would operate any new equipment they installed for bulk loading of sugar. However, neither Batista nor Mujal could give such a guarantee. This structural difficulty for the employers was compounded by the dockers' own agency—their use of sympathy strikes.

Apparently disinterested solidarity action also serves as a warning to the sympathy strikers' employers of a general willingness to take industrial action. It also builds up a "debt of solidarity" that enables them to call for a return of solidarity in the future. An example of this occurred at the end of 1955, when thirty-four Santiago dockers were dismissed for "communism," and the Bacardí workers, themselves disputing attempts to mechanize rum production, held an assembly to protest and set up a committee to raise funds to support the sacked workers.[173] Such solidarity action can be used as a more or less open threat during negotiations and serves to intimidate the employer and thereby reduce its determination to proceed with measures that will clearly be unpopular. Cuban dockers were well aware of this and frequently stopped work in support of other workers.

Similarly, the failure to mechanize the domestic cigar market equally resulted from a combination of structure and agency. The problem of finding sufficient capital to purchase expensive new machinery was more acute in the cigar industry, and mechanization would inevitably lead to a few large monopolies dominating the market. This meant that the employers were divided on the measure. Such a split in the employers' ranks was then exploited by the tobacco workers, whose unofficial leaders, strongly influenced by Communist Party politics, found a group of employers that they could argue were "patriotic" and with whom they shared a common interest.

This all indicates that an authoritarian regime can be successful in forcing through cuts in wages and enforcing redundancies, but will find it much more difficult to impose the use of new machinery. The PSP, having given a successful lead in the docks and tobacco industry, would continue to maintain an influential position in these sectors, but the more militaristic approach of the MR-26-7 would start to have a greater appeal for those workers who had been defeated in the class struggles of 1955. Thus the success of the Marianao textile workers dispute, in which communist militants played a leading role, further convinced the PSP of the soundness of their strategy, which they defined by the slogans "Unity" and "Mass Struggle."

On the other hand, the workers of La Rayonera textile factory, whose dispute was described above, drew entirely different lessons from their dispute, which had demonstrated the collaborationist role of the official bureaucracy and their inability to resist state violence unaided. The provincial leader of the textile workers' union, Julián Alemán, was already a member of the recently formed *sección obrera* of the MR-26-7, and Aldo Santamaría, a member of the national leadership of the MR-26-7, was also employed in the industry in Matanzas. The MR-26-7 was able to recruit one of the earliest branches of its *sección obrera* in the factory, which would go on to provide significant support for the revolutionary process and to organize solidarity with the sugar workers during their strike.[174] Other strike leaders also joined the MR-26-7 after their disputes were defeated. For example, José María de la Aguilera of the Havana bank workers joined sometime during 1956 having been purged from the official structure of the bank workers' union by the process known as *intervención*.

Aguilera had been a member of the Ortodoxos and as such had always been considered an opponent by Mujal. The sugar workers' leader, Conrado Bécquer, on the other hand, represented a split in the CTC bureaucracy. Having come from the Auténtico Party, he had originally been part of the *mujalista* machine, but as the situation developed and became more polarized, he had to choose between the bureaucracy and the rank and file. He chose the latter and also joined the MR-26-7, although it is difficult to be precise because he operated aboveground for as long as possible. Thus, the emerging leadership of the 26th July Movement's *sección obrera* came from different backgrounds but were all products of the defeats their sectors suffered in 1955–56. Of all these disputes, the sugar workers' is obviously the most significant. As the most important sector of the economy, winning the battle in the sugar industry was crucial to the government's productivity offensive, and the relative success heartened Batista and his supporters. However, their celebrations were premature as many sugar workers considered that they may have lost a battle but not the war.

These confrontations destroyed many illusions and convinced a significant minority of workers that there was no longer any reformist solution to their problems.[175] The year 1955 marked an important shift in the balance of power and economic advantage in Cuba. Previously, despite the corrupt leadership of the trade unions, the majority of workers had seen their wages and conditions remain more or less stable and had not felt particularly troubled by the close relationship between their official leaders and the government; indeed, many probably welcomed it, as such arrangements with previous governments had become the norm in trade union practice. The employers' productivity offensive that followed the fraudulent 1954 elections marked a turning point. The trade union bureaucracy now proved to be an obstacle, rather than a support, as the government moved to implement the philosophy behind the Truslow Report.

It would have been difficult to implement the Truslow Report under a democratic regime. This is partly because, as the workers started to feel betrayed by their leadership, it became increasingly necessary for the Ministry of Labor to intervene in order to prevent the ousting of the *mujalista* officials, which undoubtedly would have happened if democratic elections had been permitted. When workers attempted to fight despite their official leaders, they were confronted by the full force of the state.

On December 30, 1955, the train crews on the Ciego de Avila to Morón line were on strike in solidarity with the sugar workers. The army, with fixed bayonets, surrounded the workshop in Morón and an officer said, "Either the engines go out or there will be a bloodbath!"[176] This broke the strike.[177] Unarmed workers, whose trade unions were doing all they could to obstruct any generalization of solidarity, could not fight such a threat using traditional trade union methods. There were, however, small groups of militants who emerged from all of these defeated strikes who looked for new methods of defending their interests, the most energetic of which were some railwaymen from Guantánamo.

## 4. WORKERS TAKE STOCK

There are two sorts of defeats workers can suffer. There are defeats like that which followed the 1848 revolution, the Paris Commune, the taking of power by Hitler in Germany, or the Pinochet coup in Chile. These set the workers' movement back years, or even decades, and when it reemerges it has to start virtually from scratch.

There are other defeats which are best seen as interludes between battles. These are particularly prevalent after a period of working-class advance which has lost momentum. Then the employing class goes on to the offensive against one section of the class after another, trying to wrest back what it lost not so long before.

—CHRIS HARMAN

The defeats of the workers in the majority of the class struggles of 1955–56 are much closer to "interludes between battles"; the workers' movement did not have to "start virtually from scratch."[1] Rather, there was a pause for reassessment during which new tactics emerged to deal with the dictatorship and its allies in the trade union bureaucracy. There were two very different responses to the challenges facing the working-class opposition movement: on the one hand, the approach of the July 26th Movement aimed at instigating an armed insurrection and, on the other hand, the Popular Socialist Party's attempts to generate mass action. The July 26th Movement in Guantánamo merits close examination, as the railway workers in this area not only had the most militant tradition in Cuba, but would go on to make an important contribution to the revolution as they developed the concept of "*movimiento obrero beligerante*" (trade unionism on a war footing). This was the combination of mass action with sabotage, an approach that led telephone workers to cut phone lines, sugar workers to burn fields, and railway workers to derail strikebreaking trains during strikes. In order to achieve this in conditions imposed by a dictatorship, they also pioneered a clandestine cell structure that would later be extended nationwide to form the basic organizational model of the MR-26-7 *sección obrera*.

The PSP national leadership profoundly disagreed with the approach of the MR-26-7, which they criticized as being inimical to "*la lucha de masas*" (mass struggle), by which they meant widespread strike action, combined with demonstrations and other protests. In PSP terminology, the tactic of "mass struggle" was counterposed to armed resistance and sabotage, which was decried as "putschism" or "individual terrorism." In practical terms, the communists' approach was to build their front organization, the Comité Nacional de Defensa de las Demandas Obreras y por la Democratización de la CTC (CNDDO, National Committee for the Defense of Workers' Demands and for the Democratization of the CTC) and to argue for a general strike to bring down Batista in the same manner as the August 1933 strike had removed President Gerardo Machado. However, despite their criticism of the MR-26-7, the PSP leadership had to recognize its growing influence.

One particular aspect of the class struggle during 1956 and early 1957 assumed increasing importance—the growing involvement of the state in the internal affairs of the unions. The "intervention" procedures used by Mujal and the Ministry of Labor became a significant arena of industrial tension and raised the question of control of the unions. The continued necessity for such external intervention in the trade unions at local and national level shows the increasing difficulty faced by the *mujalistas* in the battle to win the hearts and minds of the organized working class. There were three major political tendencies in the Cuban labor movement: MR-26-7, the PSP, and *mujalismo*. The necessity for more government intervention is an indication of a shift in the balance of forces away from the bureaucracy.

For many people, the history of the insurrection starts with the landing of Fidel Castro in the *Granma* at the end of 1956. This approach tends to neglect the role of the underground resistance on the island, which had already established a network capable of sustaining the newly arrived nucleus of the rebel army, as well as conducting armed actions and sabotage. As part of this underground, the MR-26-7 *sección obrera* in Guantánamo was able to produce significant strike action in support of the armed uprising in Santiago at the time of Fidel Castro's arrival in the *Granma* at the end of 1956. By this time, communists in Santiago had a much closer relationship with the local *fidelistas* than with the national leadership of their own party. This would lead to the Santiago PSP calling strikes in support of the MR-26-7 armed action in defiance of direct instructions from their leadership in Havana, an example of the regional differences that play such an important role in understanding the course of the insurrection. It also shows that the political convergence between the PSP and the MR-26-7, which would culminate in the formation of the Partido Comunista de Cuba (PCC, Communist Party of Cuba) in 1965, had its roots in the working-class movement in eastern Cuba.

Following the period of intense activity in 1955, there was a relative lull in industrial action, during which the various forces within organized labor regrouped and reorganized. The MR-26-7 started the work of building their *sección obrera,* and the PSP began building the CDDOs and the union bureaucracy, attempting to shore up its position with the support of the state. These developments are important in gaining an understanding of how organized labor responded to the next major turning point in the history of the Cuban insurrection, the *Granma* landing.

### Guantánamo and the 26th July Movement

The city of Guantánamo and its surrounding region produced some outstanding workers' leaders who would go on to assume an important role in the Cuban Revolution. Following the defeats of the bank, railway, and sugar workers' strikes of 1955, a group of railwaymen, who had many years of experience in industrial struggles, were attracted to the MR-26-7 because they felt the need for armed support when faced with the failure of conventional trade union tactics in the face of a brutal dictatorship. This group would develop new tactics and methods of organization that were more suitable to the context in which they found themselves, and their approach would go on to be adopted by the MR-26-7 nationally following their important contribution to the uprising of November 30, 1956.

Upon his release from prison in May 1955 following an extensive amnesty campaign, Fidel Castro founded the Movimiento Revolucionario 26 de Julio (MR-26-7), named after the date of the attack on the Moncada Barracks. This was a formalization and restructuring of a relatively extensive existing network of anti-Batista individuals and small groups, some of whom had been loosely cooperating since 1953.[2] Finding himself unable to operate in Cuba because of government surveillance as well as being the target of government death squads, Castro almost immediately left for Mexico to prepare for the armed rebellion. He left Frank País, leader of one of the preexisting constituent groups, the Santiago-based Acción Nacional Revolucionaria (ANR, National Revolutionary Action), to coordinate support for his return. As *jefe de acción* (action chief) for the province of Oriente, Frank Pais's work consisted of gathering and storing arms, searching for possible landing sites for the return, producing propaganda material, and building the organization.[3] Shortly after the defeat of the FFCC Consolidados strike in September 1955, País visited Guantánamo with a view to extending the organization to this important center of working-class militancy. For those railwaymen in Guantánamo who wished to reorganize after their recent defeat, MR-26-7's approach had great appeal in that it placed the general strike at the very center of its tactics, while also seeing the need to combine that strike with an armed insurrection.[4] Frank País was introduced by a local student, Enrique Soto, to Octavio Louit, a railwayman, who agreed to form a branch of the revolutionary organization in the city, an endeavor to which he quickly recruited another railway worker, Ñico Torres.[5]

It will always be difficult for historians to write about successful clandestine opposition to a dictatorial regime, as one of the prerequisites for such success is to leave as few traces as possible. Thus, for example, the only contemporary public reference to Ñico Torres from this period that has so far come to light is one report in the Guantánamo local paper that Torres and two others had been arrested by the SIM, the regime's military intelligence arm, and charged with *actividades comunistas* (communist activity).[6] Guantánamo is off the beaten track and, even today, a difficult journey from Havana; most foreigners have only heard of the town in relation to the neighboring U.S. naval establishment.[7] However, it was a city with strong working-class traditions that centered on the railway yards.

At the time, the railway was the only practical land link with the rest of the island, and this gave the railway workers a sense of their own power, which they frequently exercised, not only for the betterment of their own economic position, but also in support of their wider political demands and in solidarity with other workers. They had built equally strong links with local students and peasants. In the latter case these links can be traced back to the epic battles of Realengo 18 in the 1930s, and in the former, examples of joint action between students and railway workers can be found in the demonstrations organized in opposition to the March 10 coup d'état and the Canal Via Cuba, the U.S. sponsored bid to build a canal that would have cut the island in half.[8] It is therefore no accident that Frank País's first call to organize a revolutionary organization should be to the railwaymen.

In order to trace the development of the MR-26-7 in Guantánamo, it is useful to return to some of the specific details of the 1954–55 railway conflict in that locality. In 1954, as soon as the financial situation of FFCC Consolidados became public knowledge and a strike appeared to be inevitable, Delegación 11, the local branch of the railway workers' union, set up a *comisión de propaganda* (propaganda committee), which distributed 12,000 leaflets during the course of the dispute. Once the strike started, many workers felt that the strike committee based on the official leadership was too passive, and a mass meeting elected a second strike committee, which was then ratified by a meeting of departmental representatives.[9] This ability to react quickly and collectively to changing situations was to prove crucial as the situation developed. In another move that prefigured their activities during the later stages of the insurrection against the dictatorship, striking workers derailed the train to the U.S. base that was being driven by strikebreaking managers, an early example of *movimiento obrero beligerante* (trade unionism on a war footing).[10] After the strike, in order to oppose the *mujalista* bureaucracy from the inside of the trade union movement, a Comité Central de Acción Ferroviaria (Railway Workers' Central Action Committee) was set up.[11] However, the defeat of a well-organized strike by an economically powerful group of workers with considerable experience in industrial activity made some Guantánamo militants go a stage further. They concluded that, unless the Batista regime could be militarily defeated, they would no longer be able to defend and advance their conditions and wages, nor would they be able to regain control of their own trade union while Mujal and his associates had the support of the state. The MR-26-7 appeared to offer a solution to their problems. In return, they would contribute their considerable industrial experience, which would contribute enormously to the building of the underground resistance.[12]

By the end of 1955, the Guantánamo group of the MR-26-7 had a stable leadership composed of:

| | |
|---|---|
| Coordination and Propaganda: | *Enrique Soto* |
| Deputy for Propaganda: | *Samuel Rodiles* |
| Chief of Action and Sabotage: | *Julio Camacho* |
| Workers' section: | *Octavio Louit* |
| Deputy for workers' section: | *Ñico Torres* |
| Other committee members: | *Amancio Floirán* |
| | *Margot Hernández* |
| | *Demetrio Monseny* |
| | *Gustavo Fraga* |
| | *Luia Lara* |
| | *Juan Bécquer* |
| | *Aristides Iturralde* |

Initially, the work of the group mainly consisted of recruiting and building a clandestine workplace-based cell structure, each cell composed of a member responsible for coordination, one for sabotage, one for fund raising, one for propaganda, and one for mass action such as strikes and demonstrations. Each cell member, apart from the coordinator, recruited up to ten others to help with the work. The coordinator was the only member who had any contact with other members outside the cell. There was a flexibility in the structure of the cells of the *sección obrera*, with the organizations following the industrial and union structures in each trade.[13]

In order to grow, there was a need for propaganda to spread word of the organization's existence. In part, this was a question of distributing national material such as Fidel Castro's courtroom speech, subsequently known as "History Will Absolve Me," and nationally produced manifestos.

The recruitment of several cells among the town's students gave access to the hand-operated printing facilities of the Instituto de Segunda Enseñanza (Institute of Secondary Education) and the teacher-training college, which enabled the production of more specific and locally targeted leaflets. Further publicity was achieved by extensive wall-daubing of slogans, often simply writing "*26 de Julio*" in a public place. This was combined with ingenious publicity stunts such as releasing a horse in the town center with placards denouncing the dictatorship tied to its back, causing the police to look ridiculous as they rushed about trying to catch the terrified animal.[14]

Throughout the insurrectionary period the propaganda produced by the MR-26-7 was very strong in its denunciation of the iniquities of the regime and its allies, but much less specific about the proposed solutions, concerned mainly with a general appeal to rebellion and revolution. In this, there is a notable contrast with the printed material produced by the Communist Party, which contains detailed proposals. This is because the MR-26-7 did not see itself as a political party, but as a movement that could unite all patriotic Cubans who believed in democracy and social justice. Given the cross–class alliance that the organization represented, any attempt to be specific about the concrete meaning of these terms would have risked a split, which all sides of the movement wished to avoid.

In a manner that is common to effective militant rank-and-file working-class organization everywhere, it was necessary to undermine the influence of the trade union bureaucracy.[15] To this end, MR-26-7 cells started to organize short strikes and slowdowns over any issue that came to hand. On the railway, this policy was often implemented by stoppages of only five or ten minutes, which nevertheless proved extremely disruptive to the railway timetable while minimizing the possibility for victimization. For example, the strike to defend the right to paid sick leave in July 1956 is evidence that the railway workers were still in a combative mood despite their defeat on the major issue a year earlier.[16] As a result of this muscle-flexing during 1956, the MR-26-7 *sección obrera* was able to extend its organization to other industries in the Guantánamo region, with sections among the workers in the U.S. naval base at Guantánamo Bay, the sugar workers, shop workers, tobacco workers, bakers, electrical workers, telephonists, civil aviation, and bus and taxi drivers.[17]

While building the organization in the workplaces in Guantánamo, the newly recruited militants also started to prepare themselves for the forthcoming armed struggle. Some small arms were procured from the U.S. base, purchased illegally from U.S. military personnel, and over 200 volunteers spent time in remote rural areas familiarizing themselves with their use. Gustavo Fraga, a worker at the U.S. base, set up an explosives workshop that produced 600 grenades that Octavio Louit transported to Santiago using his position on the railway. Sugar workers in the workshops of *central* Ermita also constructed improvised explosive devices (IEDs). However, these early explosives were unreliable, and it took some time and experimentation before effective IEDs would be produced. It is easy for amateurs to underestimate the difficulties involved in clandestine armed activity, and there would be many casualties and arrests before the organization gained the necessary experience and structure to pose a military threat to the regime.

There was a similar problem with the early sabotage operations. Cane-burning has a long history in Cuba, and sugar workers had the necessary skills and experience. For instance, they would soak a rat in petrol, set it alight and let it run through the cane fields spreading the conflagration.[18] However, most other industries did not have this experience, and the early sabotage in the electricity industry was carried out with more enthusiasm than efficiency. This exposed the entire organization to danger and it was quickly resolved to tighten the level of discipline in the selection of targets for sabotage. A major responsibility of the person in each cell charged with organizing sabotage was to coordinate activity with the regional leadership to ensure organizational security. Once this approach was established, the number of sabotage actions was reduced, but their growing effectiveness helped to increase the atmosphere of crisis that undermined the regime's credibility.[19]

There was a clear intention to use explosives to cause material damage and to avoid injury to passersby, although it is the nature of explosives, particularly in untrained hands, that they will often kill and injure innocent bystanders as well as killing the saboteurs themselves when they explode prematurely.[20] This attempt to avoid "collateral damage" did not spare the MR-26-7 the accusations of the Partido Socialista Popular that they were terrorists. However, given that many of the *guantanameros* were ex-Trotskyists, there was also a legacy of sectarian bitterness to add to the tactical differences with the PSP and such accusations had little influence on them. Thus we see the MR-26-7 and the PSP drawing different conclusions from the defeats of 1955 and reorganizing to face the next period in a very different fashion.

*Partido Socialista Popular and Mass Action*

The Communist Party's intervention in the sugar workers' dispute at the end of 1955 appears to have been successful, and the detailed local strike reports in *Carta Semanal* indicate widespread party involvement in the action.[21] This success and the disappointing results of its participation in the electoral politics at the end of 1954 led the party to turn to the working class. This would bring them into closer contact with the MR-26-7, as well as more direct competition. The resulting interaction would begin the process of convergence between the two organizations, although agreement at anything but the local level was still a long way off. The public criticisms of Conrado Bécquer in *Carta Semanal*, discussed in greater detail below, added personal antagonism to political differences.

The Comités de Defensa de las Demandas Obreras (CDDOs) had been active in the sugar industry since the end of 1954 with national leaflets issued in the name of the Comité en Defensa de los Demandas de la Zafra de 1955 (Committee for the Defense of the Demands for the 1955 Sugar Harvest), along with more local propaganda referring to specific problems or demands.[22] The Havana CDDO felt strong enough to call for a demonstration outside the FNTA plenary that resulted in a group of militants staging a protest on the roof of the CTC headquarters, the Palacio de los Trabajadores (Workers' Palace).[23] CDDO propaganda among sugar workers continued through 1955, as well as during and immediately after the strike itself. Moreover, the government policy of blaming communists for the strike served to raise their standing among workers and, given the popular support for the strike, in some wider sections of the community as well.

Following a successful launch at a conference in April 1956, the national organization, the Comité Nacional de Defensa de las Demandas Obreras y por la Democratización de la CTC (CNDDO), held monthly meetings that discussed detailed interventions in industrial disputes.[24] For example, a copy of the report of the October 1956 national meeting has survived.

This meeting discussed the elections in the FNTA, provided data to show
that profits in the sugar industry were rising considerably, which justified
a 15 percent wage claim, reported on a victorious three-week strike against
victimization at the Once-Once textile factory, as well as continuing industrial action on the Havana buses. It finished with a discussion of progress
in forming regional CDDOs.[25] Throughout 1955 and 1956, there are
records of provincial CDDOs being formed in Havana, Matanzas, Las
Villas, and Oriente, and the pages of *Carta Semanal* regularly contained
reports of activity by local CDDO groups.[26] A document from the archives
of the *Instituto de Historia de Cuba* lists sixty-one CDDOs for the province of Havana by industry (see Figure 4.1). There is also a report that
sixty workers attended the founding meeting of the CDDO for one of the
Havana bus companies, Omnibus Aliados (Allied Omnibus). This group
went on to issue a professionally printed four-page manifesto, accompanied by an equally professionally printed pamphlet, with a cover price of 5
cents, titled *¿Qué es un comité de defensa de las demandas obreras?* (What
is a committee for the defense of workers' demands?), which explained the
strategy in some detail.[27] This bus workers' leaflet gives valuable insight
into the methodology behind the approach to industrial organization
taken by the PSP. The leaflet starts with a statement that the intention is
not to divide or form a faction, but rather to unite all bus workers within
the union with the intention of turning it into a fighting organization that
will defend and advance the workers' wages and conditions. The eighteen-
point program starts with a pay demand for a 30 percent increase and
then goes on to list a series of specific grievances concerning Christmas
bonuses, sick pay, pension contributions, etc. The program continues with
a series of measures to restore the democratic functioning of the union
and calls for CDDO groups to be formed on each bus route. Significantly,
the leaflet is signed by thirty-two drivers. There are no overtly "political"
demands.[28] This would fit in with the PSP's general line of fighting for
"immediate demands" as a means of advancing "*la lucha de masas.*"

From the surviving evidence, it is hard to discern the extent to which the
composition of the CDDO groups extended beyond the PSP membership
and its immediate periphery, but there is sufficient detail to make it seem
likely that, at least in some areas, they were able to intervene effectively
in the labor movement at the local level. Thus an account of the October

14 meeting of the local sugar workers' CDDO in Las Villas, the Comité de las Demandas Azucareras de Las Villas (Las Villas Committee for Sugar Workers' Demands), records a discussion of a number of interventions in local disputes as well as organizing a hunger march, all in a way that any serious working-class militant would recognize.[29] Be this as it may, the development of the CDDO strategy was sufficiently encouraging for the Communist Party leadership to believe that their general political orientation was correct. It has become custom-

**TABLE 4.1: Committees for the Defense of Workers' Demands (CDDO) in Havana Province**

| | |
|---|---|
| Azucareros (sugar) | 12 |
| Familiares azucareros (sugar workers' families) | 7 |
| Tabacaleros (tobacco) | 6 |
| Zapateros (shoes) | 14 |
| Textiles (clothing) | 4 |
| O. Aliados (public transport) | 6 |
| Metalurgicos (metallurgy) | 4 |
| Portuarios (dockworkers) | 2 |
| Carpinteros (carpenters) | 1 |
| Otros Comités (others) | 5 |
| | 61 |

List of CDDO in Havana Province, from IHC 1/8: 13A1/7.1/1-6 CNDDO *Rehorrir* (no date).

ary to belittle the part played by PSP members in the insurrectionary phase of the Cuban Revolution, but this ignores the immense contribution they made to sustaining levels of working-class discontent in areas where they had influence.[30] However, the PSP's success in embedding itself in the labor movement had been accompanied by a growing political inertia and resistance to change.

Nevertheless, with the notable exceptions of the ports and the tobacco industry, in nearly every case of industrial action in 1955 and early 1956, a combination of trade union corruption and government violence had proved too much for the unarmed workers, who saw themselves defeated sector by sector.[31] This situation required an explanation, and the PSP drew the conclusion that the reason for the defeat was the lack of trade union unity, which could be restored by the CDDOs. This tactic was also seen as the way to overcome the class treason of Mujal and his associates, among whom they included sugar workers' leader Conrado Bécquer.[32]

The relationship between the PSP and the purged sugar workers' leaders was strained, as can be seen by the tone of the reports in *Carta Semanal*. The communist newspaper formally supported Conrado Bécquer and his colleagues and opposed their removal from office. However, it was clear that they thought that Bécquer had only acted under mass pressure rather than from any political conviction. Bécquer and Rodriguez were also criticized for not challenging the anti-communist attitudes of Mujal and Martinez.[33] Later, in February 1956, the PSP went further and denounced Los Dos Conrados in the same terms as Martinez.[34] In October of the same year, the CNDDO published an open letter to Bécquer and Rodriguez, denouncing them for trying to sneak back into the official union structure.[35] The PSP did not to know that Conrado Bécquer had secretly joined the 26th July Movement at the end of the strike and that he was striving to conceal this from the authorities in order to retain the advantage of his limited parliamentary immunity. Thus, for example, he was able to appear on television with Conrado Rodriguez in the lead-up to the 1957 *zafra*, gaining a platform to call for a strike if the previous year's *diferencial* were not paid promptly as well as demanding that previous years' wage cuts be restored, which caused the U.S. embassy to give Bécquer the credit for forcing the government's hand in the 6 percent sugar workers' wage increase of the following March.[36] Such accusations would not make future relationships between the MR-26-7 and the PSP any easier and serve as a demonstration of the difficulties experienced by public figures joining clandestine revolutionary organizations.

Although the PSP had taken part in the campaign for the amnesty that had finally secured the release of the surviving Moncada veterans, it was slow to realize that the MR-26-7 was a potential ally.[37] Nevertheless, the two organizations did not completely ignore each other. During Fidel Castro's stay in Mexico, he was in contact with several exiled Cuban communists, including Lazaro Peña, who had been General Secretary of the CTC before the 1947–48 *mujalista* takeover, when the PSP was the dominant force in the federation.[38] It is hard to know whether these contacts were sanctioned by, or even occurred with the knowledge of, the Communist Party leadership, for though the PSP was far from monolithic and contained the factions and personal differences that are inevitable in any party, it was remarkably disciplined and nearly always presented a common front to the outside world. These contacts produced no agreement, but reflect an increasing realization in some sections of the PSP that the MR-26-7 was a force with which to be reckoned. Thus we see, on

August 15, 1956, when commenting on one of Fidel Castro's statements, the PSP introduced the concept of armed insurrection as a possibility, all the while continuing to stress the necessity to link this with mass action.[39]

The practical implications of the different positions held by the MR-26-7 and the PSP can be discerned in their different interpretations of an earlier period in Cuban revolutionary struggle, the uprising against Machado in August 1933, and the subsequent general strike in 1935. In August 1956, the PSP began referring back to these events to argue for a mass general strike to bring down the government, a tactic that became central to their propaganda for the next period.[40] However, their version of this history was only partially correct; they concentrated on the successful strikes of 1933 and ignored the failure of the 1935 strike. The massive general strike in 1933 was combined with an army mutiny, ironically led by Batista himself. A general strike always poses the question of state power and the balance of armed force, but on this occasion, army involvement meant that the question of state repressive violence was not at issue. The MR-26-7, on the other hand, concentrated on explaining the failure of the 1935 general strike, which the army mobilized to smash, in terms of the failure to combine a general strike with armed insurrection.[41] The latter approach appeared increasingly relevant to many working-class militants, as the Ministry of Labor used state power to shore up Mujal's hold on the trade union machine through the process known as "*intervención*," thereby making it increasingly difficult to operate within the official union movement.

### Mujalista Interventions

If the MR-26-7 and the PSP used 1956 to consolidate and expand their strength in the labor movement, the *mujalista* bureaucracy was pushed onto the defensive and had to rely more and more on the support of the state. During the course of 1956 and 1957, intervention in the internal affairs of the CTC's constituent federations and local unions became one of the principal sources of friction in Cuba's industrial relations. With each attempt the methods used became increasingly draconian and demonstrated the developing reliance of Mujal on the Ministry of Labor as his base in the unions withered. This close relationship with the state enabled the *mujalistas* to maintain their grip on the machinery of the CTC, but it also increasingly bound their fate to the successes and failures of the Batista regime. The *mujalista* tactics included interference in union elections, removal from office of elected officials, expulsions of troublesome officials from the unions, and discrediting individual leaders by false or exaggerated accusations of communism, Peronism, racism, and the like. To these internal means of control should be added the direct intervention of the state, which ranged from the Ministry of Labor postponing or annulling elections to the presence of armed soldiers intimidating those who dared attend union meetings that might vote to defy the leadership. This process led to greater worker discontent and alienated previously loyal sections of the bureaucracy. This discontent and alienation resulted in the necessity for ever-increased use of the state to maintain Mujal's position, which in turn gave those opposed to the regime an argument that the return to trade union democracy required the overthrow of the regime.

The anti-communist purges of the CTC had begun in the late 1940s, when the PSP was removed from its leadership positions as part of the *mujalista* takeover.[42] The first major use of the procedure against non-communist union officials occurred in the immediate aftermath of the 1955 bank workers' dispute. The purged officials were allowed to stand for reelection in the next set of elections and they won, only to be removed from office on a technicality.[43] Learning from this incident, when the FNTA was purged following the sugar workers' strike, the elections were rigged to prevent the purged officials gaining reelection. This proved counterproductive from Mujal's point of view, and thereafter officials were appointed with little or no pretense of democracy. I shall discuss these two cases in some detail to better understand the developing internal politics of the CTC and then examine a surprising turn of events in the electrical workers' federation, where Mujal needed to request ministry intervention to secure his control of this previously docile trade union. This is an indication of the extent of disaffection among the Cuban working class at the time of Fidel Castro's return from his Mexican exile.

When the bank workers' revolt was defeated in the middle of 1955, an "intervention committee" took control of the Havana branch of the trade union and a large number of militants were dismissed from their employment. Nevertheless, the strike leader José María de la Aguilera and some of his comrades stood for office in the March 1956 national elections for the Federación Bancaria (Bank Workers' Federation) and, much to the surprise of the *mujalista* faction in the union, they won handsomely at national level as well as the provincial elections in Havana, Las Villas, and Oriente. The Ministry of Labor was equally surprised; it had allowed the rebel faction to stand because it was felt they had no chance of success. The ministry now acted in a manner that would undermine the legitimacy of the *mujalistas* by disqualifying Aguilera's faction on the grounds that they did not work in the industry, having been dismissed at the end of the strike. This approach effectively gave an employer the right of veto in trade union elections, as they could dismiss candidates from employment and thereby disqualify them, and Conrado Bécquer was quick to point out that Mujal had never been a worker in his life.[44] Apart from a brief notice of his arrest in October 1956, there is little further trace of Aguilera in the public record until he emerges as one of the leaders of the MR-26-7 *Sección obrera* in January 1959.[45] We know, however, that he was one of the principal underground leaders of the MR-26-7 in Havana. His hand can be seen in the recruitment of the local MR-26-7 *secciones obreras*, which, in almost every case for which there is a surviving record, at least one bank worker is in a leadership position. It should also be noted that, if militant workers were learning new approaches to organization, so too were the *mujalistas*, who did not make the mistake of allowing a free election again.

The next union to suffer intervention at the hands of the CTC was the sugar workers' federation, the FNTA. This trade union contained a significant group of leading officials who, while being members of the Auténtico Party, were not supporters of Mujal. Their differences had come to a head over the sugar workers' strike at the end of 1955 and they publicly expressed their opposition. The way in which Mujal dealt with this problem relied more heavily on the state than previously, in part because this represented the first real split in the CTC bureaucracy.

On January 4, 1956, immediately after the strike, Eusebio Mujal and FNTA general secretary José Luis Martinez were given a direct instruction from Batista to purge the opposition, receiving the full support of the police in so doing. The police surrounded the Palacio de los Trabajadores, the main building of the CTC in Havana where the FNTA also had its headquarters, and refused admission to Conrado Bécquer, Conrado Rodriguez, and their associates. At the same time, Martinez issued a press statement saying that they had been expelled.[46] Three of the expelled sugar workers, Bécquer, Rodriquez, and Jorge Cruz, were parliamentary deputies and they drew considerable media attention to the expulsions by staging a hunger strike in the capitol building.[47] Meanwhile Mujal accused Bécquer of being a communist. As with the report of the arrest of Ñico Torres on a similar charge referred to above, these are examples of the way in which Cold War anti-communism was used as a cover for attacks on any militant worker, even those such as Bécquer and Torres with a long history of political disagreements with the PSP. In the case of Mujal's attack on Bécquer, the use made of "guilt by association" is particularly striking as Mujal's evidence for the accusation was that he had seen photographs of Bécquer talking to known "reds." Bécquer's reply was that he had seen pictures of President Eisenhower talking to known communist leaders such as Molotov at the United Nations and went on to ask if the FBI were investigating the U.S. president on the same basis.[48]

Mujal and Martinez's actions were endorsed by the CTC executive, although it was necessary to again surround the building with police to exclude those members of the executive who might oppose the intervention.[49] The only mildly contrary voice came from Angel Cofiño of the electricity workers' union, the Federación de Plantas Eléctricas, who was concerned at the extent of the interventions rather than the principle. Mujal explained that the intervention committee had been obliged to seek police and army support because of threats of violence from some of his opponents.

There was considerable opposition to the interventions among the union rank and file, with strikes and demonstrations in Yaguajay, Sagua la Grande, Morón, Ciego de Avila, and Florida. While the workers at *central* Narcisa in Yaguajay were alone in staying out on strike against the interventions for nearly two weeks, workers in many other workplaces refused to work with the newly imposed "official" union representatives. In many cases the employers quietly asked them to leave in order to ensure that the harvest went ahead. The authorities matched this resistance from the workers by arrests leading to prison sentences, which ranged from ninety days for eleven workers in Madruga to a year in a reform school for a seventeen-year-old communist, Oscar Bengochea from Sancti Spiritus. An electrical worker, whose case was reported nationally when it was discovered that he was a personal friend of Angel Cofiño, was also imprisoned for a year for sabotage committed in solidarity with the strike; he had plunged the city of Cienfuegos into darkness. Even more generalized were the victimizations of known militants, with mass sackings of fifty or more workers not uncommon. The level of state support for the interventions can also be seen from the use of troops to seize control of the union offices in *central* Trinidad, which was Bécquer's home base. The Federación Regional Obrera (Regional Workers' Federation) of Sagua la Grande, of which Conrado Rodriguez was the general secretary, was dissolved completely for organizing a general strike in the region it covered as a protest to the interventions.[50]

The FNTA elections, scheduled for February 1956, were postponed by the Ministry of Labor in the aftermath of the recently defeated sugar workers' strike and eventually took place on August 26, 1956. In order to achieve the desired result, decree 1559 introduced the idea of a *sello de buen cotizante,* a stamp to indicate that its holder was a member in good standing.[51] When Bécquer condemned the failure to distribute these in areas where the opposition had support, Mujal replied in a radio broadcast that must have shocked even some of his own supporters: "What do they want? The stamps are not for sharing among those who oppose us . . . If our enemies decide on violence on Election Day, blood will flow, not ours, but theirs."[52]

Some stamps finally arrived, although so did the Rural Guard, and, though Bécquer was allowed to stand for local office in *central* Trinidad and Rodriguez in Sagua la Grande, Mujal later used their victories to claim that this proved that the elections were fair. The PSP did not appreciate the stand taken by Bécquer and Rodriguez, and the CNDDO attacked the pair for writing an open letter to the new executive of the FNTA, criticizing them for failing to recognize that the new executive was as bad as the old and accusing them of trying to sneak back.[53] In most places the elections were openly corrupt; for example, in *central* Dolores, out of over 500 workers, only 32 were allowed to vote in an election supervised by a platoon of soldiers. On the eve of the FNTA congress, which took place a month later, Conrado Rodriguez placed proof of Mujal's corrupt misuse of the compulsory check off before the court. Nothing came of this, but Mujal was spurred to issue an angry and unconvincing rebuttal to the press. Fearing for their safety, *Los Dos Conrados* arrived at the congress armed with pistols, but were forcibly disarmed at the door. When Bécquer spoke from the rostrum, he was booed and jeered by Mujal's supporters, which resulted in a fistfight.[54]

These elections were obviously intended to give a measure of legitimacy to the *mujalista* faction, but in order to win they had to run the election in such an openly corrupt fashion that, if anything, their claims to legitimacy were reduced still further. Furthermore, the fact that they had to allow some opposition election victories meant that Bécquer and Rodriguez were able to cause a scandal at the congress. From Mujal's perspective, however, there was one positive outcome: José Luis Martinez, who had been blatantly embezzling FNTA funds, was replaced by Prisciliano Falcón.[55] Falcón had been the provincial secretary of the CTC in Oriente and had proved his loyalty to Mujal in Camagüey by assuming control of the sugar workers' union there following the 1956 purges, when no local candidate could be found.[56] He would prove to be much more malleable than the unreliable and greedy Martinez.

This election marked the end of Mujal's flirtation with democracy. The bank workers had proved that he could not retain control in the face of a genuine election, and a rigged election did nothing to enhance his reputation and could be used by his opponents to undermine his position. Intervention in *central* Trinidad and the final removal of Bécquer from all elected office, which took place in March of 1957, marked the end of any pretense of democracy within the CTC, which thereafter openly operated as Mujal's personal fiefdom. This meant that any trade unionist who seriously wanted to defend wages and working conditions had to align with the opposition. There were still some honest, but not particularly radical union officials who had gone along with Mujal up to this point, but the contradictions proved too much for a number of these, who left the Cuban labor movement entirely, further reducing Mujal's legitimacy. Samuel Powell of the sugar workers' union is probably the most prominent of these and left to become general secretary of the plantation workers' section of the International Confederation of Free Trade Unions.[57]

The personal rule of Mujal within the CTC threatened even the "loyal opposition" based around Angel Cofiño, leader of the electricity workers' union. The final split came over the government's decree 538, published on March 13, 1957. This decree forbade the employment of "communists" in public service and was warmly welcomed by Mujal. There was considerable opposition to the wide-ranging nature of this decree, which was summed up by a *Bohemia* columnist, Andres Valdespino, as giving the employers, who he described as the most reactionary in the world, the right to denounce anyone who disagreed with the current economic order as a communist.[58] The U.S. embassy recognized that Mujal could use control of the screening panel to whittle away at Cofiño's base in the electrical workers' union.[59] Cofiño saw this as both a threat to his independence and, given the general political turmoil over the decree, an opportunity to gain independence from Mujal's tutelage for the Federación Eléctrica. The two men's relationship, never good, had deteriorated further when, in February 1957, Mujal had maneuvered to replace Cofiño with Oscar Samalea as president of the Retirement Fund of the Electrical, Gas and Water Workers.[60] Reacting to this situation, the executive of the Federación Eléctrica called a referendum among its membership on the proposition that the electrical workers leave the CTC on the grounds that decree 538 threatened the independence of the federation. The Ministry of Labor proved them correct by using another decree to justify intervention and the executive of the Federación Eléctrica were suspended for two years. The telephone workers' union executives, often seen as allies of Cofiño, were silenced by the threat of a similar fate if they supported the electricians.

The reaction of the workers in the electrical industry surprised everyone, as they had no tradition of militancy and were considered by many to be part of the "aristocracy of labor." Workers in Pinar del Rio occupied the company office until they were ejected by the police. The same thing happened in Santa Clara, but here they retreated to the union office and barricaded themselves in. The response in Santiago was a *paso de jicotea*, and Camagüey reacted with a half-day strike. However, Havana was the center of resistance to the intervention, led by the women who worked in the offices. Despite Cofiño's attempts to reach a compromise to save his position, the dispute took on a life of its own. There were a series of demonstrations and walkouts that continued until late May, when the women from the head office of the electricity company used Mother's Day as an excuse for a pro-Cofiño rally.[61] Even the baseball matches at the sports clubs of bank, telephone, and electrical workers became scenes of demonstrations for trade union democracy. Sabotage of the street lighting circuits started to occur and small bombs went off in electricity substations. Mujal claimed that this proved that communists were involved; and the head of the national police offered a reward of 5,000 pesos for information on the saboteurs. Decree 1045, issued on May 14, reinflamed the situation by declaring whole layers of workers "confidential employees" who could not join the union.

The women from the offices staged a demonstration outside the union building, the police opened fire with birdshot, and thirty were arrested. Cofiño, now in hiding, called for a slowdown that quickly spread to Oriente, Las Villas, and Camagüey. On May 16, the telephone workers stopped work for fifteen minutes in solidarity, and, though Mujal was publicly denying the effects of the movement, the intervention committee felt obliged to declare another eighty expulsions from the union. All of this reminded the bank workers of their recent difficulties, and, despite the best efforts of the imposed *mujalista* leadership, these workers struck for fifteen minutes on May 21.

The government appointed a "military intervention officer" over the electrical workers' union, who, working with the intervention committee, directed a strikebreaking operation. This had limited effect because of the skilled nature of many of the jobs in the industry. The army presence did, however, cause many workers to walk out entirely. The army gave the striking workers until the 23rd to return to normal working hours, and by this date most had gone back. Soldiers occupied the electrical plants, making notes of absences and slow or deliberately careless work, and many rank-and-file leaders, many of them women, were arrested. Press reports suggested that both the company and the ministry had tried to put pressure on Mujal to diffuse the situation but he refused to back down, perhaps because he realized that if he were to be seen to give in in the face of mass pressure, his hold on the apparatus of the CTC could quickly crumble.[62]

An interesting side issue in the electrical workers' dispute is the question of racism. In the public dispute between Mujal and Cofiño, one of the accusations that Mujal raised was that of racism in the electrical workers' union, which, he points out, had only recently withdrawn its support for a color bar on employment in the profession and was still overwhelmingly white.[63] The fact that this accusation could be used as part of a justification for intervention implies a low level of racism within the Cuban working class. It is reasonable to suppose that there was little politically significant racism between workers, for otherwise Mujal, not known for taking up unpopular issues of principle, would not have raised the matter. This denunciation of racism coincided with a large public anti-racist rally, which was organized by the main organization representing Afro-Cubans, the Federación de Sociedades Cubanas (Federation of Cuban Societies). This meeting took place in the CTC headquarters with Mujal and his close associates playing a leading role and denouncing racial discrimination in very strident terms.[64]

The increasingly heavy-handed approach taken by Mujal and the Ministry of Labor in their use of the intervention procedures is clear evidence of the growing levels of disenchantment among the general union membership. This would provide fertile ground for the growth of the July 26th *sección obrera*, which would have its first serious test at the end of 1956 with the return of Fidel Castro.

## Granma *and the Workers*

Fidel Castro and his comrades planned to return to Cuba in the motor launch *Granma* at the end of November 1956. In Santiago, Frank País had the responsibility of organizing an armed uprising to cover the landing. The plan also required supporting activity in Guantánamo. The actions in Santiago and Guantánamo were significant in several ways. They demonstrate a growing rapprochement between some elements in the PSP and the MR-26-7 and the strength of the organization in Guantánamo, and were first real test of the concept of *movimiento obrero beligerante*. On the other hand, the military inexperience of the militants was clear and weaknesses that would need to be addressed in the future became apparent.

On the morning of November 30, 1956, a group of men, dressed in olive green uniforms with red and black armbands marked "*26 Julio*" and carrying machine guns and M-1 rifles, attacked the customs office in Santiago, quickly managing to set it alight with Molotov cocktails. As soldiers arrived to reinforce those in the customs house, the rebels spread out through the city, attacking numerous other targets. In the chaos, a military Jeep collided with a jam delivery truck and the frustrated soldiers shot the driver and his assistant. By 9 a.m., the army and police, unaware of the strength of their opponents, had retreated to their barracks, leaving the rebels in command of the streets. It was several hours before the authorities could regain control of the island's second city, following the arrival of 400 reinforcements under the command of Colonel Barrera Pérez, who would be appointed military commander of Santiago, following the humiliation of his predecessor.[65] The actions of the MR-26-7 in Santiago were largely successful in their primary objective, which was to draw attention away from the arrival of the nucleus of the rebel army on the coast near Manzanillo, although they did result in important losses of life among the rebels. The national leadership of the PSP was aware of the impending *Granma* landing, but believed that the whole scheme was adventurist and wanted no part of it. However, the local PSP organization in Santiago had cordial relations with the Movimiento Revolucionario 26 de Julio and took a different view. As a result, the military actions of the MR-26-7 on November 30, 1956, received the support of the Santiago communists led by Ladislao Carvajal, provincial secretary of the PSP, in defiance of a direct order from Havana.[66] This cordial relationship was particularly important in the port, where the cooperation extended to help with distributing each other's clandestine propaganda to reduce the risk of police detection.[67] So, on the morning of November 30, Juan Taquechel successfully pulled the Santiago docks out on strike in support of the insurrectionary activities organized by the MR-26-7.[68] As a result, Taquechel, Sergio Valiente, and three other dockers' leaders were suspended from office and then dismissed from their employment by the Ministry of Labor in January 1957.[69]

Frank País had previously requested the MR-26-7 branch in Guantánamo to aid the actions in Santiago in two ways: first by impeding the progress of reinforcements from Guantánamo to Santiago and second by forcing the military in the Guantánamo region to remain on a war footing, thereby distracting them from both the uprising in Santiago and Fidel Castro's landing near Manzanillo. Command of the MR-26-7 actions was divided between Julio Camacho, Octavio Louit, and Ñico Torres. Comancho's responsibility was to lead an attack on the barracks in *central* Ermita, while in the town itself Louit organized sharpshooters to open fire on the post office, the police station, and the barracks of the Guardia Rural. Torres had the responsibility of organizing a general strike in the area and to prepare a group of guerrillas to start another front in the Sierra Canasta. The attack at Ermita, carried out by workers from the refinery, was relatively successful because of the element of surprise. Following this attack, the group managed to block the road out of town and shut down the railway access to Santiago by holding up a train at gunpoint and disabling it. Some of those involved later returned to work believing they had not been recognized, but they were mistaken and they were arrested. On the other hand, the armed actions in town failed because the cartridges had become damp and would not fire.[70]

Torres's group started by cutting the telephone connections with the outside world and set fire to several railway bridges. However, there was confusion around the start of the strike as the signal to walk out was to have been the shots fired in the attack on the police station. Given the problem with the damp cartridges, the signal could not be given and the strike did not start until the following morning. Once the word was passed successfully, the strike was fully observed and the town shut down completely. Government forces obliged some stores to open at gunpoint, but they quickly shut again when the soldiers had passed on. Soldiers also drove some buses, but these were boycotted by the townsfolk. Having achieved their objective of assisting the uprising in Santiago, the majority of workplaces returned to work on December 3, while the railway workers stayed out until the 6th. Both Louit and Torres state, in later interviews, that the Guantánamo PSP helped with the strike action, but insist that the action was clearly led by and under the control of the MR-26-7.[71] We should recognize the organizational achievement represented by a five-day railway strike in solidarity with an armed revolt that posed no economic or political demands. There have been few parallels in history; perhaps the only comparable example is the French general strike of August 1944 at the time of the liberation of Paris from Nazi occupation, where the lead was also taken by railway workers.[72]

### Temporary Lull

The government must still have appeared to be in a strong position at the beginning of 1957, an assessment shared by the British ambassador who reported that the government "has the backing of the Army, big business and the United States."[73] The clandestine preparations made by both the

July 26th Movement and the PSP, even if they had been detected, cannot at this stage have appeared to pose any great threat to the stability of the situation, while the events surrounding the *Granma* landing must have seemed like a storm in a teacup. The greatly reduced number of strikes since the defeat of the sugar workers would have reinforced the backing the government received from big business and the United States, with those few strikes that did break out being quickly isolated and defeated. It was unlikely that the growth of the CDDOs would have seemed very impressive to the government, as the CTC remained firmly in the hands of Mujal and his associates. The interventions and purges in the trade unions would have appeared to be successful in removing the few remaining troublemakers. Most important, profits were increasing, and wages were falling behind price increases on basic goods.

This would prove to be the last period of relative tranquility for Batista and his government, for the industrial peace proved to be only a temporary lull. The growing concern and confusion in U.S. embassy reports indicate the general surprise at the militancy of the electrical industry workers' response to the purging of Angel Cofiño.[74] It can be seen as a symptom of a new atmosphere of discontent and a recovery in working-class confidence. The MR-26-7 in Guantánamo showed the important role that organized labor could play in an insurrectionary situation and, though this approach was still limited to a small area in the far eastern end of the island, its successes did not go unnoticed in parts of the MR-26-7 leadership. Meanwhile, the PSP continued to fan the flames of discontent.

Yet an examination of the politics of the PSP during 1956 shows the hope that mass struggle for immediate economic demands would grow into more generalized action, which would lead to the end of the Batista regime by relatively peaceful means, based on the PSP's interpretation of the August 1933 strike, which, in their analysis, led to the end of the Machado dictatorship. They conveniently ignored the role of the army in the removal of Machado. This contrasts with the developing politics of the MR-26-7, which drew the lesson from the failed 1935 general strike that such a strike needed to be combined with an armed insurrection in order to succeed.

## 5. RESPONSES TO STATE TERROR

The British embassy's assessment of the situation in Cuba at the beginning of 1957 was that "recent events drawing attention to anti-Batista feelings in the island should not blind us to the government's basic strength."[1] The ambassador was not alone in failing to recognize the threat that Fidel Castro and his forces might present to the regime, for the early days in the Sierra Maestra were extremely difficult for the rebels. However, as the year progressed and the rebel force grew in size and effectiveness, the diplomatic reports became increasingly concerned that "as long as the Cuban government handles affairs as badly as they have done up to now, there is little prospect of an improvement." The ambassador recognized the counterproductive nature of police brutality, nevertheless understanding that "when terrorism is rampant it is not easy to stop the police using unlawful methods."[2]

As the year 1957 progressed, the opposition reacted to these "unlawful methods" with protest strikes and a number of women's demonstrations, as well as an increase in armed actions and sabotage. These different tactics for handling violent state repression represent the tactical divergence between the PSP and MR-26-7, with the Communist Party insisting on *la lucha de masas*, whereas the rebels led by Fidel Castro were advocating a more military approach. However, merely examining the pronouncements of the leaderships of these two groups, without consideration of the practical activity of ordinary members, fails to examine the interaction between the rank-and-file activists of the two organizations. The realities of clandestine labor organization often forced militants of different tendencies to cooperate in workplace situations, frequently without the knowledge or approval of their leaders.[3]

The response of the Batista government to the *Granma* landing and the start of rebel military operations in the Sierra Maestra represents a fundamental turning point in the history of the Cuban Revolution. Up to this point, police action had been kept within certain limits. In the main, the security forces had used clubs, the flats of their machetes, or fire hoses to repress dissent. From the start of 1957 we see increased use of firearms, resulting in many more deaths and serious injuries. There was also the start of a systematic use of torture and semi-official death squads. During the period from December 1956 through April 1958, the two principal opposition tendencies with influence among the working class, the PSP and MR-26-7, pursued different strategies in the face of this increased repression. Both organizations learned from their experiences, and, by the beginning of the summer of 1958, there was sufficient convergence for them to discuss joint work, arguably the next important turning point in the history of the insurrection.

The activities of the various components of the working-class movement during this period can be seen through their clandestine publications, which show the changing state of the class struggle and the escalating government reign of terror. The nature of clandestine publication and distribution inevitably means that there is an unevenness in the archival record—to be caught with an opposition leaflet could have been a death sentence. Nevertheless, there is more than sufficient material in the archives to paint a rich picture of the lively political discussion that must have taken place in the workplaces and poorer neighborhoods in this period of flux between December 1956 and April 1958. Although the dramatic events in the Sierra overshadowed the day-to-day class struggle, some sectors of the working class showed clear signs of a recovery in confidence during 1957. This recovery caused an exasperated government to respond by including militant workers' representatives among its targets for repression, which, in turn, led to a surprising amount of workplace activity aimed at combating state violence. The failure of these workers to fully defend themselves by traditional trade union action put pressure on both the PSP and the MR-26-7.

In particular, there was a debate over the best way to respond to the increasing government repression both between the PSP and the MR-26-7 and internally within these organizations. The ferocity of the government response to any opposition began to move the Communist Party leadership to reconsider their attitude to armed action and their analysis of the nature of the July 26th Movement. This reconsideration was spurred on by the growing political significance of the rebels and their popularity among sections of the Communist Party, particularly the youth wing.[4] The growing acceptance among labor activists of the need for an armed response to state violence resulted in a change in the balance of forces, with the 26th July Movement increasing its presence in the working class.

## Class Struggle

The year 1957 started with a wave of demands for large wage increases, with a 20 percent increase and a $90 minimum monthly wage the common demand. Though many workers were fearful of the consequences of traditional strike action over economic demands, they still raised those demands in a form that unnerved their employers. The picture is uneven, but it would appear that some groups of workers were better placed to defend their interests than others and that this affected the political conclusions they reached. Yet as the level of state violence increased the major concern of most workers shifted from economic to political questions, leading to a series of strikes in protest at repressive government violence. However, before considering these developments, it is useful to examine reactions to a wave of management attempts to dismiss militant union activists, starting in mid-1956; these victimizations show that working-class confidence had been maintained in some industrial sectors.

Following the defeat of the sugar workers in January 1956 there was a brief downturn in the number of reported strikes, but the first signs of a revival appeared in mid-1956 when there were some significant disputes against the dismissal of union delegates and threats of closure in the textile industry. The first such strike broke out in July 1956 in the Fábrica Las Vegas in Santiago de las Vegas. There is no record of the outcome, but a dispute later the same month in the Once-Once textile factory, which was situated in the Havana suburbs, has left better records. In this case, three shop stewards were dismissed following two weeks of industrial action, which took the form of a *huelga de brazos caídos* (slowdown). The mainly women workers responded to this victimization by occupying the factory, but were soon expelled by the police. They continued their action outside the gates. After three weeks on strike, with growing local solidarity from workers in other textile factories, the management reinstated the stewards.[5] At the same time, there was a week-long strike in the Marianao textile factory of Damián y Hmos., which resulted in a wage raise. This was followed by a lockout in the Betroma SA factory in Matanzas, which management were threatening to close, unsuccessfully as it turns out, there being later references to other disputes at this workplace.[6] There are also reports of a demonstration against the threatened closure of La Ribon textile factory in Marianao in January 1957. This was followed by protests against the threat by the management of La Rayonera that they would cut 300 jobs for "lack of markets."[7] The fiercest struggle, however, took place in La Concordia Textil SA in Guanabacoa, where the workers resisted a three-month lockout aimed at imposing wage cuts. The factory reopened in February, but there is a surviving leaflet in the Cuban National Archive calling the workers to a mass meeting on April 10 in order to resist further threats and a potential betrayal by the national union federation.[8] Much of the trouble in the textile industry at this time was as a result of competition from cheaper foreign textiles. The government had originally promised a subsidy to assist the local industry, but management claimed that this was no longer forthcoming and was attempting to force through job cuts and threatening to close factories.[9] This industrial action provided useful recruits for the MR-26-7 *sección obrera*, because the accusations of "dumping" cheap foreign textiles gave increased relevance to their politics of revolutionary nationalism. Indeed, under the leadership of Julián Alemán and Joaquín Torres, the Matanzas provincial office of the textile workers' federation, the FPTT, became a local organizing center for clandestine revolutionary activity.[10]

Another example of resistance to victimization can be seen in the railway workshops of the FFCC Unidos in Luyanó, a working-class suburb of Havana. On Friday, November 16, 1956, at 10:40 a.m., Eladio Cid, president of Delegación 2 of the Hermandad Ferroviaria, came to the railway workshop and told workers that they must work on weekends because the company was in financial difficulties. At midday, 200 workers out of the 300 employed in the workshops assembled for an impromptu mass meeting and refused to accept the new arrangements. The workers clocked off

and went home, chanting *!Para trabajo extra, pago extra!* (Extra work,
extra pay!). On the following Monday, at 10 a.m., a worker called Gabriel
Canut was suspended without pay because of the speech he had made at
the meeting on the previous Friday. All 300 workers rushed to the office
shouting that they would not work until he was reinstated. The police
were called, but by the time they arrived the workers had left the workshop and gone down to the train terminal, where they persuaded the train
crews to stop working. Just before 11:00 that evening, Canut was reinstated and weekend working without pay abandoned subject to future
discussion.[11] There was another strike in the same workshop against
more attempted victimizations in January, but with management unable
to force through the dismissals five workers were arrested by the police.[12]
Management finally succeeded in dismissing twenty workers in February
1957 with the help of the police, although unpaid weekend working was
never imposed.[13]

The events in the textile and railway industries described above were
essentially defensive, but they show a recovery in confidence. A more
offensive approach was displayed by the Caibarién dockworkers in the
early part of 1957, when they felt strong enough to take action in order to
enforce the agreed manning levels. In this particular case, they struck the
port for several days to ensure that the full complement of workers were
employed loading the sugar freighter *Aida*; management had employed
one fewer than the contract specified. It is clear from the way this strike is
reported that both sides realized that more was at stake than just one man's
job; the breaking of the agreed contract was viewed by the dockers as the
tip of the iceberg.[14] This is perhaps untypical for the general feeling of the
time, but it is evidence that a few groups of workers had managed to survive the bruising struggles of 1955–56 with their confidence intact. More
significant, however, was the return to militant activity by the bus drivers
of Havana, who had been uncharacteristically quiet during the early part
of the Batista era.

During the summer of 1956, the Havana bus drivers raised the demand
for paid meal breaks and stopped work over a demand for the reinstatement of sixty scheduled workdays on the rota (a fixed order of rotation
of personnel), which had been cut four years previously.[15] At the start of
1957, management of the two Havana bus companies refused to pay a

traditional bonus that gave bus drivers an extra month's pay at New Year. The drivers in the depot of Autobuses Modernos that operated routes 23, 24, and 25 were the first to react by going on strike. The strike quickly spread until it affected 90 percent of the fleet, by which time management backed down and agreed to pay half immediately and the remainder on January 5. Threatened with a similar response from the drivers of the other company, Omnibus Aliados, this company's management offered a payment of $50 in cash.[16] It should be stressed that, similarly to the Caibarién dockers, this was seen by the bus workers as protecting their traditional rights from erosion; the original agreement for an extra month's salary at Christmas was negotiated as a form of savings scheme to enable workers to have extra money to celebrate with their families. On the other hand, the employers clearly felt that they were paying a month's wages for nothing, and it became an obvious target for economies in strained economic circumstances. Rather like the dispute over the sugar workers' *diferencial* at the end of 1955, this is another example of the gulf of understanding that existed between workers and their employers in such matters.

This renewed militancy continued in March 1957 with a partial strike on routes 30 and 57, operated by Omnibus Aliados, in protest at a cut of eighteen duties. This was followed by a general refusal of all Havana drivers to operate the newly purchased larger forty-five-seat buses, as this would have enabled the same number of passengers to be carried by fewer drivers, thus potentially reducing the number of drivers employed.[17] Another strike broke out on route 79 in April to protest the arrest of two bus drivers, followed by a similar incident on route 19 in May. In these last two strikes, strikebreaking soldiers drove buses, which would have contributed to the bad feeling that led to a half-hour strike on routes 21 and 22 in November against the arrest of a colleague who had refused to pick up a soldier between stops.[18] The Omnibus Aliados workers were also numbered among the union groups supporting the PSP's 1957 wage campaign, discussed below, linking a 20 percent wage claim with the demand for compensation for driving the new, larger buses.

The Havana bus workers had a long and militant history. Their strike had started the anti-Machado rebellion in 1933 and they were among the few sectors who had struck both in support of Lazaro Peña during the 1947 anti-communist purges of the CTC and in protest at Batista's coup in 1952. However, they had been quiet ever since the arrest of the union leader Marco Hirigoyen and the dismissal of 600 drivers in July 1952.[19] This return to form by Havana bus workers, perhaps influenced by the activity of the sectoral CDDO, is symptomatic of a more general discontent, characterized by increased pressure for wage increases.[20]

Sometime in the summer of 1956, sensing a change in mood, the PSP decided to conduct a campaign for a 20 percent increase and a $90 per month minimum wage for all workers. The report of the October national meeting of the CNDDO contains a detailed argument about sugar workers' wages. It argued that the forthcoming *zafra* would be 5 million tons and that the price had held up because of the poor harvest in Europe. This had resulted in large profits for the employers, for example, the Vertientes Camagüey Sugar Company, whose profits rose from $392,900 in 1953 to $485,000 in 1954, and $794,200 in 1955. Salary reductions for the workers caused by wage cuts and shorter *zafras* compared to 1952 resulted in considerably lower wage bills for the employers: for 1953 a total reduction of $157 million, for 1954 the wage bill was $160 million less, for 1955 the reduction was $186 million. The year 1956 saw a slight recovery, but the total was still $181 million less than 1952. *Intensivismo* (intensification of work patterns) and mechanization had produced a situation where a *zafra* of 5 million tons, which would have taken 145 days in 1925, could be gathered in a mere 88 days in 1957. All this led *Carta Semanal* to the conclusion that the claim should be for a 20 percent increase, accompanied by the demand for full payment of the *diferencial* and a prompt start to the pre-harvest repairs.[21] The PSP's intervention in the sugar workers' wage debate was implemented by large numbers of leaflets, both nationally and locally produced, aimed at propagating the policy.[22]

The campaign for a 20 percent increase appears to have struck a chord with workers across a range of sectors, as illustrated in Table 5.1 (see next page) below listing wage claims submitted in the first half of 1957. These reports come from *Carta Semanal*, but there is some independent verification in the mainstream press. For example, *El Mundo* records the fact that the Havana bus drivers were demanding a 20 percent raise.[23] The U.S. embassy also reports "Mounting Pressure for Wage and Salary Increases."[24]

**TABLE 5.1: Wage Claims Submitted in the First Half of 1957**

| Date | Place | Factory | Activity |
|------|-------|---------|----------|
| 9 Jan. | Havana | Omnibus Aliados | Demand 20% wage increase. |
| 13 Feb. & 27 Mar. | Matanzas | Henequeneros | Demand equal pay in the whole of agriculture based on parity with the highest paid. Management threatens lockout. |
| 13 Feb. | Havana | Omnibus Aliados | Demand 20% wage increase to compensate for larger, 45-seat buses. |
| 20 Feb. | Federación Nacional de Comercio | | Demand 20% wage increase. |
| 27 Feb. | Havana | Gastronomicos | Demand $90 minimum monthly wage and 20% wage increase. |
| 6 Mar. | Federación Nacional de Calzado | | Demand wage increase. |
| 6 Mar. | Havana | Five-and-Dime (Woolworth) | Demand $90 minimum monthly wage and 20% wage increase. |
| 6 Mar. | Luyamo | Metalúrgicos | Metalworkers demand wage increase. |
| 20 Mar. | Havana | Sindicato de Laboratorios | Mass meeting demands 20% wage increase. |
| 20 Mar. | Havana | Tuberias santiarias | Demand 20% wage increase. |
| 20 Mar. | Las Villas | Banks | Demand 20% wage increase. |
| 27 Mar. | Havana | Hotel Sevilla | Demand 20% wage increase. |
| 27 Mar. | Havana | Fabrica Larrañaga | Demand 20% wage increase. |
| 27 Mar. | Havana | Hotel Sevilla | Demand 20% wage increase. |
| 27 Mar. | Provincia de la Habana | Central Portugalete | Two short strikes win a 10% wage increase. |
| 27 Mar. | Havana | Hotel Sevilla | Demand 20% wage increase. |
| 3 Apr. | Havana | Hotels | Hotels Vedado, Comodoro, and Nacional demand 20% and $90 min. monthly wage. |

**TABLE 5.1: Wage Claims Submitted in the First Half of 1957 (cont'd)**

| Date | Place | Factory | Activity |
|------|-------|---------|----------|
| 17 Apr. | Havana | Federación bancaria | Demand 30% wage increase. |
| 29 May | Caibarién | Dockworkers | Mass meetings protest high cost of living. |
| 5 June | Havana | Brewery workers | Assembly demands 20% wage increase. |
| 5 June | Santiago | Bacardi | Assembly demands 20% wage increase. |
| 12 June | | Goodyear | Newly elected union committee presents list of demands including 30% wage increase. |
| 12 June | San José de las Lajas | Metalworkers | Publishes a manifesto demanding 20% wage increase and expresses solidarity with Concordia textil. |
| 12 June | | Textil La Sedentia | Assembly demands 20% wage increase. |
| 19 June | Caibarién | Stevedores | Motion to FOMN demanding 20% increase. |

Source: Compiled by author.

Some official bodies such as the Federacion Nacional Gastronómica, which represented workers in the tourist industry, took up the demand and set up *comités de lucha*. However, these official committees were organized in such a way as to make sure they did not escape bureaucratic control, thus representing a token response to a popular demand. They were not given the authority to initiate action. Nevertheless, the fact that the bureaucracy felt the need for such a gesture is testimony to the popularity of the wage demands.[25] By February 1957, similar pressure from below had also forced the Federación Nacional de Comercio (shop workers) and the Federación Nacional de Calzado (footwear) to formally raise the demand for 20 percent.[26] These wage demands were rarely pursued by official industrial action because of a mixture of bureaucratic inertia within the official structure and fear of state violence among the rank and file. The widespread popularity of such wage claims indicates that many workers did not feel they were sharing in the prosperity so often mentioned by supporters of the regime.[27] Moreover, these demands would have worried many employers who must have hoped that, by now, their employees would be sufficiently cowed to enable further advances in productivity without undue difficulty.

The tightened censorship meant there was little useful reportage in the mainstream press after March 1957. We therefore have to rely today on reports in *Carta Semanal*. The PSP had a political interest in playing up the number of strikes, but though there appears to be a measure of effervescence in terms of demands, protest meetings, etc., very little of this develops into strikes or public demonstrations. Given the level of repression, particularly the increased use of government death squads, this is hardly surprising. Nevertheless, the defensive strikes and the agitation over wages described above lends weight to the argument that the repressive activity of the Batista regime had not succeeded in its aim to create a "more disciplined and docile workforce."[28] Rather, the focus for working-class activity shifted as many militants sought ways of restoring their bargaining position by taking action against state repression.

## *Reign of Terror*

If there was not much direct industrial action over wages in this period, there was a surprisingly militant response to the spate of beatings, murders, and disappearances with which the government greeted the start of the armed rebellion in the Sierra Maestra. This government violence was not merely aimed at supporters of the rebels in the Sierra, but was equally used to remove troublesome workers' leaders irrespective of their political persuasion.

The government responded furiously to the outbreak of armed rebellion in Oriente. Following the events of November 30, 1956, there were forty arrests, seventeen from Guantánamo city and twenty-three from the Ermita sugar refinery. One of the arrested, Luis Raposo, was tortured to death, while Arnaldo García González was not even arrested, simply murdered by a government death squad on December 9. Most of the arrested were later released, but six received sentences of between three and six years in the Isle of Pines. Many others, including Julio Comacho, Octavio Louit, and Ñico Torres, had to leave their jobs and go underground.

The murder of members of the opposition was not confined to the Guantánamo region. The most notorious case was the so-called *pascuas sangrientas* (bloody Christmas holiday) in which, on Christmas Day 1956, twenty-four people from the Holguin district were killed by soldiers of Regiment number 8 and police of the 7th Division under the command of Colonel Firmin Cowley. Some were shot while others were hanged from trees near their homes. At the same time, two more oppositionists were shot in Santiago. Among the dead were members of all opposition parties, including several members of the PSP. The PSP formally denounced Colonel Cowley to the Supreme Court—unsurprisingly to no avail.[29] This incident would be the start of a government policy of using death squads to eliminate suspected rank-and-file workers' leaders in the aftermath of confrontations with rebel fighters. Inevitably, many of the victims were not politically active, merely in the wrong place at the wrong time.[30] This heightened level of semi-official repression was combined with the suspension of constitutional guarantees and the formal introduction of press censorship.[31]

Despite these killings, the British ambassador felt that "one is far from having the feeling of living in a police state" and that Batista "appears to have the real interests of his country at heart."[32] The restrictions, which by most standards would merit the description "police state," were reported by the embassy as follows:

- The right of assembly and procession is limited.
- Freedom of speech and writing is limited. Newspapers and periodicals are subject to pre-censorship before issue.
- Private correspondence, private documents and telephonic, telegraphic and cable communications are subject to censoring and monitoring.
- Free entry into, exit from and movement within the national frontiers is subject to control.
- No plea of habeas corpus may be made in respect of detained persons.
- The clause laying down that detained persons may only be tried or condemned by a competent tribunal is suspended.

• The clauses of the penal procedure code establishing that an accused
  person must be considered innocent until his guilt is proved, that he
  may not be held incommunicado, and that persons accused of political offenses should be kept separate from those accused of common
  crime, are all suspended.[33]

Relaxed at the beginning of March 1957, these restrictions were soon
reimposed following an attack on the presidential palace on March 13,
1957, by militants of the Directorio Revolucionario (Revolutionary
Directorate, a largely student-based anti-Batista organization led by José
Antonio Echeverría who had previously been president of the FEU).
Thereafter, for most of the rest of the period of dictatorship, researchers
are reliant almost entirely on clandestine publications for historical information on opposition activity, as the legally published press is silent on
practically all matters that do not reflect to the credit of the government.

The army, Rural Guard, and police were clearly profiting from the situation to remove some troublesome workers' leaders. For example, in an
incident at *central* Delicias, not only were two PSP members murdered,
but the secretary of the local union was only saved from abduction by the
Rural Guard by the prompt actions of his daughters, who created enough
of a commotion that the neighborhood was alerted and the would-be
abductors driven off.[34]

This government policy of employing death squads can be seen developing in early 1957, with the Santiago newspapers containing frequent
stories of the discovery of the dead bodies of young people who had been
shot after being beaten and tortured.[35] It was common for a Jeep full of
plainclothes police or off-duty soldiers to arrive outside the house of an
opponent of the regime and shoot him in front of his family and neighbors. *Carta Semanal* contains numerous reports of communists being
killed in this period, with a common method being the reported release
of the victim following a period of incarceration and then his body being
subsequently found hanged from a tree near his home, with the official
verdict being suicide.[36]

The most public demonstration in response to these assassinations
occurred in Santiago following the discovery of the bodies of five young
men, all tortured before being shot.[37] Over a thousand women, led by

relatives of the slain, attempted to hold a protest but were dispersed by the police. This caused a stir in the press and contributed to the restoration of censorship following a brief relaxation of it.[38]

It has already been noted that the police normally proved less likely to use the same level of violence against women than they showed toward men. When this proved not to be the case, the maltreatment of women roused greater indignation, as can be seen by the shocked reaction of the newly appointed U.S. ambassador when women were attacked by police using fire hoses while they were attempting to give him a protest letter during a visit to Santiago.[39]

Despite the censorship, which meant that many of the protests against state violence in 1957 have gone unreported, there is a record of a number of short strikes, sometimes only lasting five or ten minutes, in Havana in April and in Layunó, Caibarién, Cabaiguin, and Remedios later in the year.[40] There is also a record of some short strikes against violence in the railway workshops of FFCC Consolidados.[41] An incident in the Ciénaga workshop serves as an example that was repeated in many other workplaces. José Ramirez Casamayor, a PSP militant, had recently returned to work after a period of imprisonment for his political activities, when a security guard on the gate of the workshop calmly shot him dead in front of his workmates. There was a short work stoppage and a demonstration at his funeral, but the killings continued.[42] It may be assumed that some of the workers in Ciénaga decided that sterner measures were necessary, as a group of railway workers led by veteran militants Ricardo Rodríguez and Emilio Delachaux began using the workshop facilities to prepare explosive devices.[43]

An example of the new realities for organized workers can be found in the Santiago docks, where a MR-26-7 cell had been established by Santiago Casacó, a long-standing and well-established activist. The police tried to clean up the port by means of arrests, vandalizing the local union offices, and similar acts of repression. In reply, in January 1958, person or persons unknown shot and killed Filipe Navea, a well-known pro-government official of the FOMN, the dockworkers' union, in the port of Santiago. Colonel Río Chaviano, military governor of the town, responded by killing five dockers in their homes, and the dockers, in turn, replied with increased sabotage, such as the burning of a sugar warehouse in February

1958.[44] Such tit-for-tat violence continued, albeit on a lower scale, up to the end of 1958.

While strikes and demonstrations were important for the developing mood of resistance to an increasingly brutal and dictatorial regime, in themselves they were insufficient to defeat the government or even to force meaningful change in government policy. Many rank-and-file PSP members were coming to recognize the inadequacy of the tactic that the party referred to as "*la lucha de masas*" (mass struggle) The year 1957 saw the increasing popularity of the MR-26-7 among many rank-and-file PSP members and a willingness to engage in joint action. Take the example of the city of Manzanillo, where the most successful mass action in the early part of 1957 took the form of a town-wide general strike on January 28, 1957, to protest against police and army brutality. This was supported by partial action in Santiago and Contramaestre.[45] Manzanillo had always been a Communist Party stronghold; it was, after all, the hometown of the party leader Blas Roca, and was now the nearest town of any size to the rebels in the Sierra Maestra. There was a personal relationship between many local militants of the PSP and the MR-26-7 in Manzanillo, and local communists, particularly members of the party's youth wing, *Juventud Socialista*, often helped in the support networks for the rebel army, although how much of this was known by the leadership in Havana is uncertain.[46] When *Carta Semanal* refers to the activity of a *frente unico de oposición* (united opposition front) in opposition to a pro-government rally in Manzanillo, they are careful to speak of the support of "members of the 26th July Movement" rather than of the organization itself.[47] The importance of personal relationships in neighborhoods and workplaces is often underestimated when considering the development of resistance to authoritarian regimes, where the success of any clandestine activity will depend to a large extent on personal trust, which is frequently more important than political differences.

Though there is evidence of cooperation at the local level in Manzanillo, there was still considerable distance between the manners in which the two organizations were organizing against the government's campaign of terror. The PSP's response in its stronghold of Manzanillo was a simple withdrawal of labor. In contrast, the day the dead body of Rafael Orejón, leader of the MR-26-7 cell in Nicaro, was returned to his family in

Guantánamo, the workers in the electrical plant sabotaged the machinery and plunged the town into darkness for the whole night.[48]

Strikes, such as the one that took place in January in Manzanillo, are the normal first reaction of workers when confronted with repression. However the ever-increasing level of violence with which the state responded was easily able to overwhelm the unarmed workers. This lent weight to the arguments of the July 26th Movement in favor of the armed struggle. The situation was extremely complex, one in which rank-and-file militants were grappling with competing strategies. The success or failure in winning support for either *la lucha de masas* or *la lucha armada* (the armed struggle) among the uncommitted would have encouraged or discouraged the proponents of that approach at the leadership level. We have no record of such local discussions, but a careful reading of the leaflets, pamphlets, and periodicals produced by opponents of the regime suggests that there were impassioned debates between advocates of the alternative positions. While such discussions would have been held behind closed doors, the written sources provide an indication of the kind of issues that were raised. I would argue that the ability of ordinary workers to influence the decisions of their leaders is frequently underestimated, and that this is particularly true in circumstances when two organized political tendencies are competing for influence in a particular arena.

## Competition and Collaboration

The surviving clandestine propaganda material available in the archives gives us a valuable glimpse of the ways in which the competing strategies for overthrowing the regime were argued out. They are a useful guide to the relationship between supporters of the Communist Party and supporters of the July 26th rebels, not only at the leadership level, but also at the grass roots. Increased state terror, particularly where this was directed against working-class organizations, makes the question of collaboration between different opposition organizations a matter of urgency. Therefore, the relationship between the MR-26-7 and the PSP starts to take on greater significance. As the 26th July Movement extended its political and organizational reach, the two organizations came into increased contact, thus raising the question of how their relationship functioned on a practical level, despite their ideological and tactical differences. While they were in competition for membership and influence, they were also confronted with making decisions about possible cooperation. The printed statements of both organizations enable us to assess their formal political positions and then to examine the daily practical application of these positions. A pattern can be seen emerging as the politics of the PSP and the MR-26-7 started to converge and the first signs of growing practical collaboration appear. This convergence was most pronounced in the milieu of the workplace, where attitudes toward collaborative activity were particularly relevant, both because of the pressures for joint action imposed by everyday industrial relations problems and because militant workers were most likely to suffer the same dangers from the increased state terror.

In July 1957, the MR-26-7 launched an underground newspaper, aimed at labor, under the name of *Vanguardia Obrera*. This paper was an extension to the national level of the previously existing paper from Guantánamo, *Línea Obrera*.[49] Early editions of *Vanguardia Obrera* were amateurishly produced, using Roneo duplicators, and a more professionally printed version is not seen until mid-1958. The main reason for the difference in appearance between the *Vanguardia Obrera* and *Carta Semanal* is the relatively well-established position of the latter. When the preexisting PSP newspaper *Hoy* was banned in 1953, it had not been difficult to establish a distribution network for its underground replacement among a party membership with a tradition of selling papers to their workmates. Indeed, *Hoy* had been briefly closed down in 1951, and the first volume of *Carta Semanal,* produced for a few months in that year, had served as a dry run for the more serious, clandestine, conditions prevailing under the dictatorship.[50] The MR-26-7 had no such previous experience on which to base its practice. *Carta Semanal* also had an established political line, as well as a network of militants used to reporting local disputes. *Vanguardia Obrera*, on the other hand, was attempting to represent the ideas of a much more politically diverse organization whose working-class members rarely had the experience of being "worker correspondents." Therefore, the MR-26-7 paper was more prone to general exhortations to revolution without specifying the nature of that revolution.

Moreover, the MR-26-7 leadership had not yet learned the lesson of the sugar strike, which had shown the importance of the economic struggles in radicalizing workers, and thus ignored the PSP's insistence on the importance of raising "immediate demands."[51] The MR-26-7 was a cross-class organization whose founding leaders had little understanding of the day-to-day practicalities of organizing in the workplace. Even among those who had a militant trade union background there was a tendency to ignore matters that might cause splits between supporters with different class interests and to concentrate on the politics of national unity and opposition to tyranny. This allowed everyone to interpret the politics of the organization according to their own beliefs and interests. Such was the hatred of Batista in the ranks of the rebel movement that his removal was the foremost priority, and until the overthrow of the dictatorship had been achieved the discussion of other matters could be postponed. Most of the leaders of the MR-26-7 *sección obrera* had joined because the traditional trade union methods of securing their class interests had proved inadequate in the face of government repression; their main concern was the defeat of that repressive machine and the restoration of democratic control of the unions. They clearly believed that they could defend and advance their wages and conditions if the restraints inherent in the dictatorship were removed. This explains why organizational unity seemed so important, why there was a desire not to alienate middle-class supporters of the movement, and why "immediate economic demands" could be left to a future date. Later, *Vanguardia Obrera* would become more responsive to working-class economic concerns, a change that would, in part, result from closer contact with PSP activists at the local level.

Local groupings of both organizations also produced simpler material, such as extracts taken from longer articles in the main newspaper, leaflets and bulletins commenting on local issues or disputes, and small flyers for distribution at random from passing cars. A number of such leaflets have survived, with a particularly important set having been produced by the local PSP branch in Luyanó. These, mainly dated around the end of 1957 and the beginning of 1958, give us an insight into the political debates and forms of organization in this Havana suburb. They are hand-typed and duplicated, but set out with considerable care. Among the surviving examples are bulletins aimed at the workers in the mineral water factory El Copey, the Aldesa food distribution depot, the Hatuey Brewery, and the railway workshops, as well as more general leaflets aimed at particular trades such as truck drivers and woodworkers.[52] The survival of leaflets from over fifty years ago must be a matter of chance, and we can assume that Luyanó was far from the only place where such initiatives were undertaken. These leaflets appear to have been issued outside the workplace, but are clearly based on detailed information from within. In addition to the commentary on matters of immediate concern to the particular group of workers addressed, there are some common themes: the need for unity, the fight against state repression, the betrayals of the *mujalista* bureaucracy, and the superiority of the old CTC under the leadership of Lazaro Peña.

A series of leaflets, titled *Bolos* and aimed at the woodworking industry, show the political dilemma faced by the PSP. On the one hand, they wished to push their line of "mass action" and opposition to what they saw as terrorism, and on the other, in order to campaign against the arrest and murder of their militants, they needed to work together with groups that they defined as "terrorist," most particularly the MR-26-7.[53] In Luyanó this was accomplished by setting up the Comité Revolucionario de Luyanó (Luyano Revolutionary Committee), which spoke jointly in the name of the PSP and the MR-26-7, along with the local CDDO and other revolutionary organizations. A leaflet produced by this committee calls for a strike of five to ten minutes on Friday, October 25, 1957.[54] As well as conventional leaflets, the Luyanó committee produced smaller flyers that were typed four to a page, which was then quartered. These were designed to be scattered from the windows of a speeding car.[55] The success of such initiatives can be seen from the report in *Carta Semanal* that records that the strike in Luyanó was observed in ten factories and that similar five- or ten-minute strikes took place in Caibarién, Cabaiguin, and Remedios, crediting the local united front committees for organizing the action.[56]

A larger leaflet, issued to call the strike in Luyanó, is interesting in a number of ways. It specifically refers to the differences in program and conception of revolution held by the constituent organizations, but states that by uniting forces the dictatorship can be overthrown. Moreover, the form taken is of an open letter, calling for unity, addressed to the national leaderships of the constituent organizations and others such as the students' union (FEU) and the Directorio Revolucionario: "We think that this strike, which will surely be widely followed in Luyanó, could be spread to the whole of Havana if all of the organizations that we are addressing, either jointly or individually, would call publicly for this strike of 5 minutes and if their leaders and members will work together to make it a reality."[57]

There is also evidence of the existence of a Comité de Frente Unico de Trabajadores de la Roselia (Roselia Workers' United Front Committee) and a Comité Obrero Revolucionario de San Miguel del Padrón (San Miguel del Padrón Revolutionary Workers' Committee), both of which address themselves to the leaderships of all revolutionary opposition groupings in a similar way to the Luyanó committee. A leaflet from Roselia finishes by saying:

- Build a United Front in your workplace, under the national flag. Think of our homeland in this hour of her greatest difficulty in all our history!
- Long live the unity of the working class!
- Forward comrades, Unity and Struggle![58]

The nationalism of the MR-26-7 is side by side with the PSP's slogan of "*¡Union y Lucha!*" (Unity and Struggle!). Similarly, a leaflet from the San Miguel committee dated March 1958 is particularly interesting in that, on the one hand, it uses the PSP formula "*por un gobierno representativo de amplia coalición democrática*" (for a government representing a broad democratic coalition), and on the other hand, salutes the heroic guerrillas in the mountains using language reminiscent of the MR-26-7.[59] We have no way of knowing the extent to which sections of the leadership of either the MR-26-7 and the PSP encouraged these local united fronts, but they coincided with the first negotiations between the two organizations, which began when the veteran communist sugar worker Ursinio Rojas arrived in the Sierra Maestra for discussions with Fidel Castro, sometime in October 1957.[60] Clearly, the leaders of the PSP now recognized the political importance of the MR-26-7 or were well aware that they were competing with them for influence in a working class that the communists had previously thought of as their private constituency.

Toward the end of 1957, the MR-26-7 *sección obrera* also came to be referred to as the Frente Obrero Nacional (FON).[61] This name change was portrayed by the 26th July Movement as an opening out to other political tendencies, but at this stage it was little more than a rebranding exercise, albeit a successful one as the MR-26-7 grew in numbers and influence within organized labor. As a result, it came into greater contact with the PSP, which concretely posed the question of their practical relationship. An abstract call for "unity" is easy to make, but the practical application of the slogan is much more difficult. In December 1957 *Vanguardia Obrera* asked the question "*¿Unidad con quiénes?*" (Unity with whom?). This is only answered in the vaguest of terms, completely sidestepping the relationships with the communists. It seems likely that this ambiguity was deliberate to enable the July 26th Movement the maximum freedom to maneuver. Later in the same edition, another article calls upon all other revolutionary organizations to help build the FON from the base, as the organization that would have responsibility for launching a revolutionary general strike to overthrow the dictatorship.[62] Thus we see that MR-26-7 clearly saw itself as the directing organization of the revolution and that other oppositionists had to accept their lead. "Unity" was to be on their terms. Such an approach was a practical possibility for those in a leadership position charged with producing editorial content for a national paper. However, those militants at the local level who had the task of implementing the party line found themselves having to take a more nuanced approach.

A long-established unofficial network of MR-26-7, Communist Party, and independent militants operated in Oriente Province, a good example being the way in which employees of the FFCC Consolidados railway network were able to coordinate their militant activities.[63] The MR-26-7 had established its influence on the FFCC Consolidados at a relatively early stage in its development, partly because of the work of the Guantánamo group, but also through Pepito Tey, who was an express messenger between Camagüey and Santiago.[64] In an interview recorded in 1978,[65] Armando Yuñuz, a Santiago railway worker and MR-26-7 militant, recalls that by June 1955 there was already a sabotage cell of twelve railwaymen in the city and that, by the time of the November strike, they had thirty-three train crew, nine express agents, five in track maintenance, seven in the workshop, five in the cafeteria, and two porters. Of these, Gerardo Poll and Efraín Palencia are listed as collaborating PSP members.[66] Similarly, in another oral testimony given in 1984, Rogelio Arógestegui of the MR-26-7 and Alvaro Vázquez Galago of the PSP speak of working together on the railways in Camagüey, although they say that this occurred against the wishes of the middle-class local leadership of the MR-26-7, commenting that the workers had a different attitude to other social classes. They also criticize the PSP leadership for being slow to recognize the 26th July Movement as a potential ally.[67] We know of similar collaboration between working-class militants of the two organizations in Vázquez, near Puerto Padre in Las Tunas, northern Oriente Province.[68] Equally, in the Bacardí factory in Santiago de Cuba, a *comité del frente único* (united front committee) had existed since 1954 when a group of Auténticos and Ortodoxos, later to form the July 26th *sección obrera* in the factory, joined with their PSP colleagues to protest at the official CTC refusal to allow Juan Taquechel the right to speak at the May Day rally.[69] The effectiveness of this joint work is confirmed by the repeated mutual support between the Santiago dockers, led by communists and the Bacardí workers, the majority of whose leadership were supporters of the MR-26-7.

It is clear from the study of the propaganda material of the period that there was a political flux as the leaderships wrestled with the problems of their chosen strategies. We also get a glimpse of the ways in which politics at the local level developed and affected the official party line of both organizations. However, despite the increasing talk of "unity," it must never be forgotten that, despite the political convergence between them, the communists and the rebels were both maneuvering for leadership of the resistance to Batista.

## A Time of Transition

The *Granma* landing in December 1956 represents a qualitative change in working-class involvement in the revolutionary process in Cuba. Before this time, class-conscious workers had attempted to defend their interests by the more or less traditional means of strikes and demonstrations, and the government had, with some notable exceptions, successfully defeated them with the help of a corrupt trade union bureaucracy. The police and security forces had freely used clubs and fire hoses, only occasionally opening fire, but generally kept their use of force within bounds. From the beginning of 1957 there was an escalation in the level of state violence against civilians, particularly in the east. This intimidation significantly reduced the number of strikes, although it does not seem to have reconciled workers to accepting their lot. They may have been weakened, but they had not been broken and there is clear evidence of a search for an alternative strategy to defend their rights and livelihoods.

The strikes in textiles, the railways, and on the Havana buses were essentially defensive, seeking to preserve traditional bonuses, to prevent the victimization of local union activists, or stop threatened redundancies or closures. Unofficial industrial action can be very effective in defending the status quo; it is much less so when offensive action is required, for instance in the case of wage claims, which are most successful when there is organization extending beyond the individual workplace. This requires either the support of the trade union bureaucracy or a well-established and widespread unofficial network. Thus, although the PSP's campaign for a 20 percent wage increase received widespread support, the CTC official structures were not going to organize the industrial action required, and the PSP itself did not have the capability of setting strikes in motion unofficially in the face of escalating state terror.

A closer look at the list of those workers supporting the 20 percent claim shows them to be largely Havana-based. However, by 1957, workers in the east of the island were becoming more concerned with government repression, which was much fiercer in Oriente and Camagüey, as well as being increasingly accompanied by torture and death squads. The mounting repression during 1957 and early 1958 affected both organizations equally, with frequent reports of PSP militants joining the MR-26-7 members among the missing, murdered, arrested, or tortured.[70] The ability of the MR-26-7 to offer a possible solution to the problem of government-organized violence accounts for the spread of its *sección obrera* network in the east and its increasing attractiveness to ordinary communist workers.

# 6. TWO STRIKES

In the period from the end of 1956 to the beginning of May 1958 two important mass strikes took place in Cuba. The first, starting in Santiago de Cuba at the beginning of August 1957, was a great success; the second, called for April 9, 1958, was an abject failure. An analysis of these events is crucial in gaining an understanding of the developing tactics of the communists and the July 26th Movement. The strikes can be used as a lens through which the issues can be examined. It is also possible to assess the growth of the rebel clandestine labor organization by examining the extent of each strike. Finally, the lessons learned by the rebels from the failure of the April strike resulted in far-reaching organizational and political changes, arguably ensuring the final victory of the revolutionary forces.

As 1957 progressed, the predominant political and social question became the continued existence of the dictatorship.[1] This change in priorities from the economic to the political, combined with the growing realization that small-scale industrial action was becoming impractical in the face of repression, resulted in increased workplace sabotage and clandestine aid to the rebels, while the frequency of local or sector-based strikes decreased through 1957 and early 1958. As part of this process, the MR-26-7 set up a committee, chaired by Ñico Torres, to organize the spread of clandestine revolutionary working-class organizations from Guantánamo and Santiago to the rest of the island, and at the same time building a support network for the rebels in the hills. It is, of course, always difficult to trace the activities of successful clandestine movements; police and newspaper accounts only describe the failures. Nevertheless, there is evidence, in addition to leaflets and underground newspapers found in the archives and personal collections, as well as the recollections of participants, which can guide an attempt to reconstruct the previously untold history of the spread of the influence of the revolutionary workers' underground.[2] This leads to a reassessment of the role of clandestine organization in the successful general strike in Oriente Province, which was sparked by the death of Frank País, a popular national leader of the MR-26-7 urban underground, who was murdered by the police in Santiago in August 1957. This strike is commonly characterized as "spontaneous," but a more nuanced explanation is needed that considers the relationship between spontaneity and organization.

Following this strike, both the PSP and MR-26-7 stepped up their propaganda for a general strike to overthrow the regime. However, the leaders of these organizations drew very different conclusions from the strike, each using the experience to reinforce an entrenched position. Nevertheless, starting in October 1957, the PSP and rebel army leaderships began talking to each other on a relatively formal basis. However, discussions with the PSP had not advanced greatly by the time the MR-26-7 called a general strike on April 9, 1958. This strike, which received almost no working-class support in Havana, cost the lives of many of the movement's best underground activists. The subsequent repression was particularly severe, with Batista's chief of police issuing the instruction: "No wounded. No prisoners."[3]

In the aftermath, both the PSP and the MR-26-7 took stock in May 1958. The changes in the practice that resulted from these internal debates and the lessons drawn by both organizations led to a convergence in the tactics they advocated for the overthrow of the dictatorship. The PSP accepted the need for armed opposition to the dictatorship and the MR-26-7 took a more open approach to working-class organization. This paved the way for practical joint activity and a new phase in the revolutionary process that marked another turning point in the history of the Cuban insurrection.

### A Clandestine Network

Frank País, national leader of the July 26th urban underground, was one of the first among the organization's leadership to see the potential importance of a revolutionary labor movement. He was killed before he could implement his ideas, but the seeds he planted flourished as the networks of militants he encouraged spread from their origins in Guantánamo.

Frank País was arrested in March 1957 as part of the government crackdown following the November 30 assault on Santiago and an attack on the presidential palace by the Directorio Revolucionario on March 13. Along with over a hundred other MR-26-7 defendants, he was released in May, when Judge Manuel Urrutia defied pressure from the government and ruled that they were exercising their constitutional right to rebel in the face of tyranny. Upon his release, País immediately set about reorganizing the MR-26-7 underground movement. As part of this process, he decided that much greater attention was to be paid to recruiting and organizing workers. As a result of the success of the strike in Guantánamo in support of the *Granma* landing, Ñico Torres, now a wanted man, was made coordinator of a committee charged with rolling out the workplace cell structure and spreading the Guantánamo example nationwide. He spent the next year criss crossing the island with this objective. However, while Frank País was certainly in the forefront of those in the movement who saw the importance of labor support for the revolution, he still had an incomplete understanding of the need to organize workers around their specific class-based interests.

Of the senior figures in the organization with a labor movement background, other than those from Guantánamo, José Maria de la Aguilera had led only a single strike in a white collar industry, while David Salvador's experience was limited to local activity in the sugar mill at *central* Stewart near the town of Ciego de Avila in the rural center of the island. Conrado Bécquer was still leading a double life, attempting to maintain a precarious legality, and Julian Alemán was deeply involved in the ongoing troubles of the Matanzas textile industry and did not yet have effective lines of communication with Santiago. From the beginning, the 26th July Movement had a perspective of organizing workers, but their role had been seen principally as providing financial and logistical support for the rebels in the mountains, as well as engaging in sabotage. The success of the Guantánamo strikes in early December 1956 had impressed Frank País enormously with their power and potential, but he seems not to have realized the years of previous work that had been necessary to create the solid foundations that his MR-26-7 *compañeros* in that city had been able to draw upon.[4]

The PSP was continually urging the importance of "immediate demands" in the process of organizing workers to resist the dictatorship, but the MR-26-7 leadership would not come to realize this until later, after they had suffered a severe setback in April of the following year. Thus, the MR-26-7 propaganda aimed at the working class at this stage of the movement's development was extremely general, concentrating on appeals to patriotism and rejection of corruption and tyranny. There was some mention of the defense of wages and conditions, demands for trade union democracy, and vague promises of social justice, but the lack of familiarity with the working-class political milieu is clearly evident in surviving leaflets and newspapers.[5]

Nevertheless, when Frank País was released from prison, he wrote a report calling for serious attempts to be made to recruit workers saying that the movement had forgotten the importance of the workers, who, if well organized and led, could overthrow the regime. He urged the creation of a disciplined and educated leadership that could lead small-scale general strikes to gain experience, in the way that had already been done in Guantánamo, where he described efforts made to organize the workers as formidable and which had shown in practice what could be done.[6] However, according to the memoirs of Armando Hart, one of the leaders of the MR-26-7 in Santiago, during these early months of 1957, Frank País's main priorities were to support and supply the rebel guerrillas in the Sierra Maestra and to win over the *conjunto de instituciones cívicas* (civic institutions) to supporting an armed insurrection.[7] This organization, led by the president of the Cuban Medical Association, was a loose association of nearly two hundred professional and religious organizations ranging from the Freemasons to the Catholic Teachers' League and the Havana Bar Association. It had come to represent the more liberal elements of the Cuban middle class, who were becoming increasingly alienated from the regime as the violence worsened and the economy deteriorated.[8] As part of the process of attracting support from the *instituciones cívicas*, a meeting of the 26 de Julio leadership in the Sierra Maestra in February 1957 decided to set up the Movimiento de Resistencia Cívica (MRC). This organization, while being firmly controlled by MR-26-7 members, was nominally independent and acted as a bridge between the rebels and the civic institutions.[9] It is clear from the memoirs of participants such as Armando Hart that the MRC received a much higher priority than did building the MR-26-7 *sección obrera*.[10] The Guantánamo militants, having received the blessing of the national leadership, would be given a free hand in building their organization and spreading the ideas of *movimiento obrero beligerante*.

To this end, Frank País asked Ñico Torres to write a report describing their organization in Guantánamo. Frank País gave this report to Armando Hart, who in turn sought the advice of friends in the PSP and other Santiago trade unionists with whom he was in contact, such as a Bacardi delivery driver, Ramón Alvarez. This process led to Torres being appointed head of a national committee charged with organizing the movement's work in the labor movement. The committee consisted of Torres, a sugar worker called Asterio Hernández, a telephone engineer, José de la Nuez, and a bank worker, Jorge Gómez. It was in pursuit of this task that Ñico Torres began to tour the country in order to generalize the experience from Guantánamo, while Octavio Louit and Ramón Alvarez moved to become provincial workers' organizers for Las Villas and the central region of the island. It is hard to trace the progress of this work because its secret nature precluded the keeping of records and its success required that the activities of the group did not come to the attention of the authorities. Nevertheless, we can piece together the general lines of the organizing drive from later interviews.

For example, we know from the investigations of Delio Orozco, City Historian of Manzanillo, that Torres and Gomez were in the town of Manzanillo in May 1957. Gomez knew another bank worker, Nardi Iglesias, who had already started building four-person cells in his own industry. From this base, the Manzanillo *sección obrera* grew and formed cells in the unions representing electrical workers, transport, telephones, pharmaceuticals, bakers, shop workers, shoemakers, and coffee roasters. The Manzanillo electrical workers specialized in sabotage, teaching workers in other trades the use of explosives, while the bus drivers of the El Paraíso company brought propaganda material from Santiago. Given the proximity to the rebels in the Sierra, raising money and supplies for the rebels was of considerable importance and the Manzanillo *sección obrera* sold bonds known as *bonos*, which served as propaganda fliers as well as fund-raisers.[11] Torres and his committee were not the only MR-26-7 activists organizing among the working class. In Matanzas, recruiting out of the disputes in their industry, the textile workers became the backbone of their regional *sección obrera*. The struggles of the textile workers from 1952 onward, the sacrifice of the Cuban textile industry to the interests of the sugar oligarchy in the 1954 commercial treaty with Japan, and the anti-union attitude of the Hedges family, American owners of two factories, La Rayonera and Textilera de Ariguanabo, all served to increase nationalist sentiment and provided fertile grounds for the MR-26-7 to recruit members. The local offices of the textile workers' union became the organizing center for the 26th July Movement in the province, which also adopted an approach, similar to the Guantánamo militants described above, of combining sabotage and strike action.[12]

There is no surviving record of anyone from Guantánamo visiting Matanzas, and it seems likely that textile workers of the province independently developed similar tactics to meet a similar problem. They were coordinated by Julián Alemán, regional secretary of the Federación Nacional de Trabajadores Textiles (FNTT). Julián Alemán was also national vice general secretary of the union, but he had managed to conceal his links with the MR-26-7 and, along with Conrad Bequér and Conrado Rodriguez, was one of only three senior trade union officials to break with Mujal and join the rebels. He was succeeded in his role as coordinator of action in Matanzas by Joaquín Torres, who worked for La Rayona, when he was forced to leave the area to escape the attention of the police after helping to organize a strike at the end of July 1957 following the murder of Frank País in Santiago.[13]

### "Spontaneous" Strike?

In the summer of 1957, Frank País, now MR-26-7 National Coordinator of Action, was based in Santiago, where he was working both to promote the movement's clandestine operations and to organize support for the guerrillas in the nearby Sierra Maestra. His murder at the end of July 1957 by a local police chief provoked a general strike in Oriente, which was probably the biggest public demonstration of opposition during the

entire Batista dictatorship.[14] The August '57 strike is normally characterized as "spontaneous," though spontaneity is confused with lack of
organization and political direction. This betrays a failure to understand
that a far greater level of organization is required to produce a "spontaneous" strike than one formally called by the bureaucracy. Statements by
militants involved in the strike paint a more complex picture and lend
weight to Daniel Guérin's assertion that spontaneity and organization are
always intertwined. As he argues, "There is always someone pushing for
spontaneity."[15] Therefore it is probably fair to say that, though the demonstrations and strikes at the time of Frank País's murder and funeral
were spontaneous in the sense that no organization had planned them
in advance, the speed with which the strikes spread suggest a high level
of clandestine organization that was able to react quickly and seize an
opportunity without requiring orders to do so.

Frank País was caught in a police roundup on July 30. He was identified by a police informer and shot dead on the spot by Colonel José Maria
Salas Cañizares.[16] This was part of a reign of terror that the colonel had
imposed on the city of Santiago de Cuba in the period following the events
of November 30, 1956. Frank País's funeral was the occasion for a massive show of opposition, not just to his murder, but in protest against the
general level of brutality being visited on the city.[17] Miguel Angel Yero, an
activist in the MR-26-7 *sección obrera*, describes how he and his comrades
went to the funeral with the idea of initiating some action, if at all possible.
Seeing a large turnout, combined with the fact that very many Santiagueros
shared their anger, they started to shout for a strike. The call was taken
up, and the 60,000 people at the funeral marched through the town, calling workers out of their factories, offices, and shops until the town was
paralyzed in a strike that lasted five days. Contemporary photographs and
accounts of the funeral confirm the prominent part played by women in
the demonstrations following the funeral.[18] The July 26th Movement had
recently been working to organize the shopworkers in Santiago, and these
workers, predominantly women, played an important role in forcing their
employers to close the city's commercial enterprises as well as picketing
out other groups of workers.[19] Many of these women attempted to present
a letter to U.S. ambassador Earl Smith and were attacked by the police
using fire hoses. This shocked the newly appointed ambassador whose

mission thereby did not start well.[20] The vehemence of the popular reaction startled the police and army, which, after a few skirmishes, retreated to their barracks where they were besieged for the rest of the day.

The strike spread quickly in Oriente, *Carta Semanal* reporting complete shutdowns of Palma Soriano, Contramaestre, Bayamo, Manzanillo, Guantánamo, Campechuela, and Jiguaní.[21] In Manzanillo, the situation was considerably aggravated when two soldiers opened fire on a group of passersby who were jeering at them and, in the process, killed two little boys, aged five and eight, the Cordové brothers. The strike in Manzanillo lasted several days following this outrage.[22]

An MR-26-7 militant from Guantánamo, Demetrio Monseny Villa, was in Santiago as the strike started and carried news of the events back home. The leadership of the MR-26-7 in Guantánamo had been taken by another ex-Trotskyist, Gustavo Fraga, who worked on the U.S. naval base. A strike committee was formed, and, starting with the railways, the town and surrounding country went on strike the following morning, August 1. Frank País was well known and respected in the area and the strike was completely solid the railway, the electrical plant, the aerodrome, the banks and buses, along with most shops and businesses, shutting down. To accompany this industrial action, strikers bombed some bridges and power lines as well as taking part in armed skirmishes with the police and rural guard. Here as well, the brutal behavior of the forces of order helped spread the strike, as the army broke open closed shops and threw their merchandise into the street, thereby giving a propaganda coup to the rebels, who ensured that the soldiers were the only ones engaged in looting.

Fraga, as well as being in overall charge of the 26th July intervention in the strike in Guantánamo, was also running the explosives factory in a garage in the city. On August 4, there was an explosion that killed Fraga and several other members of the movement. The explosion in the bomb factory was a blow to the movement, as they not only lost some important militants, but also a considerable stock of weapons. However, it served to prolong the strike and deepen bitterness against the regime as the first act of the police on arrival at the scene was to shoot dead two neighbors who were not involved with the MR-26-7 but were merely trying to put out the flames and stop the fire spreading to the rest of the neighborhood. Such acts of random brutality against uninvolved bystanders, similar to the killing of the Cordové boys in Manzanillo, are a common feature of the times that did much to increase opposition to the regime. But with Guantánamo the only city remaining on strike by August 9, the national leadership of the MR-26-7 ordered a return to work, fearing the army was planning to make an example of the town.[23]

Octavio Louit, now a clandestine organizer for the 26th July Movement, was in Santiago for consultations with the national leadership when Frank País was killed. He returned to Camagüey to spread the strike, while Torres continued on to Havana to see what could be done in the capital. In Camagüey, there was a positive response from the rail workers, the intercity bus drivers, the banks, and the airport. However, it did not prove possible to produce a similar result in Las Villas, where the army had rounded up as many militants as they could and succeeded in intimidating most of the workforce, with bus and truck drivers being forced to return to work at gunpoint. There were considerably more stoppages in Pinar del Rio Province, most notably the town of Artemisia.[24]

Both sides saw Havana as key to the situation, and the government concentrated its efforts here. The action did not spread to Havana immediately and the Havana strike committee called for the action to start on August 5. There was little response, although there was some action from bus drivers and construction workers, along with stoppages in the Coca-Cola factory and by the tobacco workers employed by the Partagas and H. Upmann companies. Little or nothing occurred in the suburbs or the rest of Havana Province. The Matanzas textile industry saw some partial strike action and token stoppages, but Julián Alemán's base in La Jarcia was the only factory where the workers walked out completely.[25] Once the strike had failed to get off the ground in Havana, it quickly petered out in the east.[26]

Although it is difficult to trace the organization of a clandestine movement, this strike gives us a snapshot of the development of the workers' underground in the summer of 1957. There was clearly an established organization in most of Oriente Province, given the speed with which the strike spread to other towns, such as Bayamo. The response from Camagüey suggests a well-rooted network there as well. It is probably significant that Octavio Louit, speaking twenty years later, used the expression "*núcleos obreros combativos*" (combative workers' cells) for the organizations in Ciega de Avila, Jatibonico, Florida, and other parts of the central zone, while talking of *"compañeros muy valerosos"* (very brave comrades) in Las Villas, thereby implying a real network in the former case, but more isolated individuals in the second.[27] We know that the MR-26-7 *sección obrera* in Las Villas was based on the sugar workers around Conrado Bécquer. Bécquer was still operating legally at this stage and may not have prioritized building the underground network outside his traditional base. It may also be assumed that the Las Villas *sección obrera* was not yet organized to reflect the Guantánamo experience with its principles of *movimiento obrero beligerante*, but was concentrating on support and supply for the guerrillas. Finally, Bécquer had sour relations with the Communist Party, as witnessed by the mutual public recrimination and accusations.[28]

Generally speaking, areas where the August strike was most effective were those where there was established cooperation between the MR-26-7 and the PSP, a point made indirectly by *Carta Semanal* in its analysis, which was printed in the following weeks. The Communist newspaper blames the failure to convince the majority of the Havana workers to join the strike on government repression and Mujal's "treason," but spends the most time expressing the opinion that these could have been overcome had there been unity in the opposition. Indeed it goes further and, without presenting any evidence, accuses the "bourgeois opposition" of undermining the strike and being more interested in not offending the U.S. ambassador. The MR-26-7 is specifically named as one of the bourgeois and petit-bourgeois parties against whom this accusation is leveled. Though this is obviously unfair as, after all, it was the MR-26-7 who called the strike in Havana for August 5, what is certainly true is that the July 26th organization in Havana did not involve the PSP in the planning of the strike call. There had been some contact between the MR-26-7 and the communists through the Juventud Socialista (JS, Socialist Youth), but Luis Fajado, the PSP contact person, was not present at the meeting in the church of San Francisco where the decision to launch the strike on the 5th was taken, and it probably took the communists by surprise.[29] Therefore, in those areas of the capital's labor force, such as the docks, where the MR-26-7 appears to have had little influence in the summer of 1957, by the time word had spread of the strike call, its failure would already have been apparent. The fact that some areas of communist influence, mainly bus crews and tobacco workers, took part in the action testifies to the PSP's willingness to participate, whereas the disciplinary action taken against two hundred bus drivers for taking part in the strike can only have increased the communists' sense of bitterness.[30] The question of disciplinary reprisals brings us back to the strong support for the strike in Pinar del Rio. In the Minas de Matahambre, attempts were made to arrest some workers after the strike, but the rest of the miners refused to start work until their colleagues were released. The cry of "*¡O trabaja todos, o no trabajaremos ninguno!*" (Either all of us work or none of us will!) was successful and the detainees were released.[31]

Finally, we must consider the lack of response from Matanzas, despite its militant tradition and strong workers' section of the 26th July Movement among the textile workers. Neither of the detailed surveys of the revolutionary period conducted by Gladys García Pérez and Clara Chávez Alvarez give any indication of strike action in Matanzas in August 1957, but they do not offer any reason for the failure of the region to support the strike. Any explanation must be conjecture, but the previously mentioned lack of contact between the Matanzas militants and their comrades in the east may have meant that, by the time word had spread of the actions in Oriente, the strike had already passed its peak.

The search for explanations for the lack of success in Havana or Matanzas should not result in an underestimation of the speed with which the strike spread in Oriente, Camagüey, and Pinar del Rio, an impressive achievement in the circumstances. A general strike may start more or less spontaneously in a single town, but to spread it across three provinces in a matter of days demonstrates a significant level of organization. Thus the foregoing description of the spread of the strike paints a useful snapshot of the state of oppositional working-class organization in August 1957.

## *April 9, 1958*

The success in Oriente of the strikes in protest of Frank País's murder eclipsed the subsequent failure to spread the action further west. This would encourage the leadership of the MR-26-7 to call a general strike starting on April 9, 1958, which they envisaged as the final blow required to overthrow the dictatorship. However, it was a complete disaster, begging the questions: How can we explain the success of the strike in some areas and the lack of response in others? What is its significance and what lessons were drawn from it by the opposition?

The leaderships of both the PSP and the MR-26-7 were extremely impressed by the impact of the August 1957 strike, but drew different conclusions, both using the experience to reinforce an entrenched position. The MR-26-7 leadership concluded that one more push was all that was required for victory, without fully realizing the amount of work that still remained to be done in terms of building the networks, particularly in Havana, which was necessary to call a successful nationwide general strike. The PSP, on the other hand, having seen the widespread support of their proposals for a 20 percent wage claim, as well as the strikes against repression, felt that they had cause to believe that their approach, *la lucha de masas*, was bearing fruit. They concluded that the strike had weakened the government and had proved that strike action alone was the sufficient and only way to bring down the government.[32] Moreover, the MR-26-7 had not learned the lesson of the sugar strike, which had shown the importance of the economic struggles in radicalizing workers, and thus ignored the PSP's insistence on the importance of raising "immediate demands."[33] But with both organizations committed to a general strike, albeit with a completely different understanding of the term, there was some basis for the discussions between Fidel Castro and the veteran communist sugar workers' leader, Ursinio Rojas, which took place in the Sierra Maestra in October 1957.[34]

Following this meeting, an attempt was made to form a united workers' front. There were several meetings in Havana, with the CNDDO represented by Carlos Rodriguez Cariaga, Miguel Quintero, and occasionally Ursinio Rojas, while the MR-26-7 was represented by Ñico Torres, Octavio Louit, and Conrado Bécquer. However, these meetings failed to reach agreement because, according to Torres, the PSP was opposed to the armed struggle.[35] Nevertheless, these discussions produced a softening of the party's attitude to the guerrillas, which, though it still extolled *la lucha de masas* and condemned urban terrorism, pledged its support to the rebels in the Sierra Maestra in March 1958, with the reservation that armed action must support mass action rather than the other way round.[36] *Carta Semanal* also started to take a much less hostile line when speaking of Conrado Bécquer, having become aware that he was a member of the MR-26-7.[37] Furthermore, the PSP national committee decided, in February, to send one of its members, Carlos Rafael Rodriguez, to the Sierra for face-to-face discussions, but before this could be arranged, the 26th July Movement unilaterally called a general strike.[38]

By the spring of 1958, the guerrillas in the Sierra Maestra had survived for over a year and had grown into an efficient disciplined fighting force. With the help of the urban underground, they had established control over their area, carried out many successful attacks on government forces, and built up a considerable measure of support among the local *campesinos*.[39] Their continued existence helped maintain the atmosphere of crisis and gave hope and inspiration to the regime's opponents, while the army's obvious inability to destroy them militarily undermined Batista's waning credibility. Add to this the fact that, by the beginning of March 1958, a student strike had managed to close much of the country's educational system, and a general strike call appeared to be the logical next step.[40] Faustino Pérez, who was in overall charge of the operation, said in a later interview that the success of the August 1957 strike convinced him that conditions existed for the final uprising that would overthrow the regime and that this led to an unrealistic view of the balance of forces.[41] In a letter to Fidel Castro dated April 2, 1958, Pérez states that "all sectors look favorably on the strike and are ready to support," and a circular to all provincial heads of the *sección obrera* in early March says nothing about organizing for the strike, but is almost totally concerned with the steps necessary to take over the CTC after the strike had been won.[42] Having previously seen that it was possible to organize a general strike in the east, all sides saw the success or failure of the strike in Havana as key to the situation. However, though the organization of the FON had continued to grow and establish itself outside the capital, it had made only limited inroads in Havana itself. This was in part because anti-communist elements in the Havana MR-26-7 underground were unhappy with Castro's discussions with the PSP and, as a result, refused to organize joint strike committees in the capital with communists for sectarian reasons. It should be stressed that at this point the FON was far from being a unified organization and its practice varied enormously from region to region, depending on the politics and previous experience of its leaders in each locality. In particular, there was an east-west split with the concept of *movimiento obrero beligerante* being more dominant in the east, whereas in the west the role of the workers was seen as supporting the militias and raising money. This would affect the course of the April strike, because the importance of winning the capital meant that it was to be run from Havana.

Faustino Pérez wrote to Fidel Castro at the beginning of April expressing unhappiness at the manifesto that Castro had issued on March 26. This manifesto said that "the leadership of the FON will coordinate their efforts with the workers' sections of all political and revolutionary organizations," a policy that was not popular with the Havana MR-26-7 leadership.[43] Nevertheless, in some of the industrial suburbs of Havana, San Miguel del Padrón, Guanabacoa, Regla, Bejucal, San Jose de las Lajas, and Luyanó, joint committees had been established, but this was without the consent, perhaps without even the knowledge, of the Havana leadership of the 26th July Movement.

The MR-26-7, prior to April 1958, had an essentially military view of the general strike, and workers were expected to place the "national interest" above their perceived class interests.[44] This caused the MR-26-7 to give responsibility for the strike organization to the Movimiento de Resistencia Cívica in Havana, an organization that had neither the experience nor the networks capable of fulfilling their role. The national strike committee, which consisted of Faustino Pérez, Marcelo Salado, Manolo Rey, David Salvador, and Marcelo Fernández, had little experience or understanding of labor militancy.[45] Their conception of a general strike relied much more heavily on sabotage and the armed action of militia fighters than on the conscious self-activity of rank-and-file workers, more of an armed popular insurrection than a traditional workers' strike. This was not the opinion of everyone in the MR-26-7 *sección obrera*, as the bank worker José María de la Aguilera made clear in an interview with an Argentine journalist later in 1958.[46]

However, in the spring of that year, such voices as Aguilera's were in a minority in Havana. From the end of 1957, with Ñico Torres incapacitated by illness, the FON itself had been under the leadership of David Salvador, a sugar worker from Ciego de Avila. He was an ex-communist and a founding member of the 26th July Movement. Despite his occupational background, his involvement had been mainly in the general political arena and his experience of the working-class movement was limited. This inexperience prevented his appreciating the inadequacy of the organization in Havana, while the hangover from his previous relationship with the PSP meant that he had little inclination to work with them.[47]

Reading the Communist Party's literature of the time, it is obvious that they thought the strike would start on May Day.[48] Communists in the industrial suburbs of Havana started agitating for a general strike from the beginning of March. For example, on March 14 the Juventud Socialista in San Miguel del Padrón organized a march through the area, shouting "*¡Huelga General!*" (General Strike!) and "*¡Abajo Batista!*" (Down with Batista!), in which they managed to involve some of the youth section of the July 26th Movement.[49] This agitation in support of a general strike was combined with a series of open letters and appeals calling for the unity of the FON with the CNDDO.[50] Nevertheless, the secrecy about the start of the strike obviously irritated the PSP, which accused the MR-26-7 of sectarianism on several occasions, even while calling for unity.

Despite the insistence of many local FON organizers that they needed seventy-two-hours' notice to activate their networks, the strike organizers decided to keep the date of the proposed action secret, only telling MR-26-7 militants in Havana on the morning of April 9 itself.[51] If the date was secret, the fact that a strike was planned was not, Fidel Castro having announced a forthcoming revolutionary general strike when he made his declaration of "total war" on March 12. So forewarned, the government had suspended the constitution and placed the army and police on a war footing. The CTC bureaucracy had stepped up its anti-Castro propaganda, accusing the MR-26-7 of stabbing the working class in the back, while issuing threats that any workers supporting the strike would be dismissed and that the unions would not support them. To this end, the CTC bureaucracy drew up lists of suspected militants for the police and the employers.[52]

Thus, while the authorities were prepared, most workers were taken completely by surprise when the strike call came at 11 a.m. on April 9 and were thereby denied that feeling of ownership that is so essential to the success of a strike. The police and army, supported by a pro-government militia, the Tigers, rampaged through the streets of Havana, discharging their weapons at random. The poorly armed MR-26-7 militia was unable to wrest control—indeed, most members were not even in a position to defend themselves. In these circumstances, most workers found it impossible to leave their workplaces, and the strike failed.

In the Archivo Nacional in Havana, there is a typewritten account of the April 9 strike, written by Roger Venegas Calabuch, coordinator of the MR-26-7 grouping in the port of Havana. He paints a graphic image of chaotic organization; the first he hears of the strike is at half past ten on the morning of April 9, when he is ordered by the clandestine MR-26-7 leadership in Havana to "strike the port of Havana." He was astonished and replied that it was impossible to pull out 10,000 workers in thirty minutes. He says they had no weapons, while armed police were everywhere.[53] Meanwhile, the leaflets arguing for the strike did not arrive until two o'clock in the afternoon.[54] In the circumstances, it is hardly surprising that the strike failed. The government television station was able to dismiss the affair as "isolated groups of criminal elements under the leadership of the communist party," despite the fact that, on the morning of April 9, PSP members had been as much at a loss as everyone else.[55]

The CNDDO kept a tactful silence on the disaster, but *Carta Semanal* was vitriolic, attacking the MR-26-7 for sectarianism and for sterile commando raids producing the unnecessary deaths of brave young people.[56] Nevertheless, the paper admitted that the limited but courageous response showed that the workers saw the necessity of a general strike. *Carta Semanal* also noted the relative greater success in the eastern provinces and condemned divisions in the opposition; the subtext here is that in the east there was a greater tradition of united working-class action involving communist workers.[57] Outside the capital, the response to the strike call was mixed but far from insignificant, as Table 6.1 indicates.

Many workers in Havana had been able to protect their living standards and staffing levels because of the nature of the predominant industries. I discussed previously the port and tobacco industries, where the workers had avoided defeat. Another important sector in Havana was the tourist industry, to which the construction industry was closely linked, as the major building work in the capital was for new hotels. The tourist industry was still booming despite the growing crisis, and the U.S. Mafia made use of its participation in tourism to launder money from its illegal activities at

government forces, such as in El Cobre, this was as yet the only area in which rebel forces were sufficiently strong to neutralize the army locally, aided by the isolation of the region from the centers of power. The comparative success of the strike in the Guantánamo region would give those who advocated *movimiento obrero beligerante* the credibility they needed to spread their approach to the rest of the island.

## Picking Up the Pieces

The failure of the strike in Havana provoked an intense debate within the anti-Batista movement, and two documents reflect this debate. The first is a letter to Fidel Castro, copied to the MR-26-7 national directorate and to the leadership of the FON, signed by various Havana workers' organizers and militia captains. It is written in a critical tone and complains that the strike has played into the enemy's hands. It goes on to say that the July 26th Movement had insufficient penetration in the working class to call a general strike and had relied on armed action rather than the conscious will of the workers. However, this strategy was doomed because there were insufficient arms. Other problems outlined are that there was insufficient preparation, that important sectors such as the retail workers did not receive the strike call until too late, that there was a lack of communication between the leadership and local coordinators who had to organize the strike at base level, and that there was a failure to coordinate with other organizations. The letter concludes that the organization had lost touch with reality and had started to believe its own propaganda about the balance of forces.[59] Another letter, this one signed by the provincial leadership in Las Villas, made similar points, but in a much more measured tone, accepting that the failure was the fault of the whole organization, not any particular leader. This difference may be explained by the fact that the strike in Las Villas had been considerably more successful than the previous attempt in August 1957 and the authors had something to be proud of in a local context. It is worthy of note that the Las Villas letter starts by saying that the analysis it contains is the result of extensive consultation within the regional organization.[60] It is safe to assume that there would have been considerable debate within the MR-26-7, and that when the national leadership met at the beginning of May they would have been aware of the tenor of that debate.

The process of picking up the pieces therefore began with a meeting on May 3, 1958, at Los Altos de Mompié in the Sierra Maestra. From the point of view of working-class involvement in the insurrection, two important decisions were taken. One was to give future priority to the guerrilla struggle, and the other was to reorganize the FON. As part of this latter process, Ñico Torres, now recovered from his illness, was restored to the leadership of the FON, and David Salvador was given other responsibilities. Torres had been out of action for the early part of 1958, following an operation for a stomach ulcer and had only returned to activity when the plans for the April strike were well advanced.[61] The relatively greater success of the strike in areas that he had influenced and the particular success in his hometown of Guantánamo must have given him the necessary credibility to reorganize the FON, and he set about extending his network and methodology from Oriente toward the capital.

The FON showed an immediate change of style with the issue of a manifesto in May 1958 that took responsibility for the fiasco. Nevertheless, it maintained that a general strike was the most efficient way to defend and extend workers' rights, as well as "curbing the sinister despotism that is strangling our republic."[62] The manifesto attacked Mujal and the government in a detailed manner, highlighting the widely unpopular, corrupt practice of compulsory check off of union dues. It finished with a list of demands that mixed the economic and political in a way clearly designed to link the need for revolutionary change with workers' immediate concerns. An example of the new approach can be seen in a surviving FON leaflet calling for a railway strike in Las Villas in protest at the late payment of wages, which relates directly to a matter of immediate concern and contrasts to the general exhortations contained in the FON leaflet calling the April 9 strike.[63] This shows an increasing acceptance of the PSP's view of the importance of immediate demands and would have lent credibility to the other theme of the reorganized FON, the call to unity. This reflected the realignment toward the communists that was emerging with the discussions between Fidel Castro and the PSP delegate, Carlos Rafael Rodríguez.

In a much quoted article written in 1964, Che Guevara speaks of Ñico Torres being given instructions to work with the PSP in the labor movement and of his reluctant but disciplined agreement to do so.[64] It is likely, however, that his reluctant attitude was shared by others in the leadership, who might have been convinced of the need to work with the PSP but who were not happy with the prospect. The strained relationship between the PSP and the rest of the anti-government opposition demonstrates, in part, the divisive effect of Cold War anti-communist propaganda. The liberal opposition, often rather contemptuously referred to as *"los partidos burgueses"* (bourgeois parties) in PSP literature, did not wish to antagonize the United States by being seen to associate with the communists. Thus, for example, in November 1955 the fact that the PSP had organized a large turnout to support an opposition demonstration was condemned as "Communist sabotage" in the opposition press.[65] The PSP wrote endless open letters to the "bourgeois opposition" proposing a united front, although nearly always in terms that invited rejection, but they rarely if ever received a reply.[66] Of course, the PSP's uncritical support of the USSR, in particular its support of the crushing of the Hungarian uprising in 1956, played into the hands of its enemies.[67] These attitudes affected the relationship between the PSP and the July 26th Movement. Thus the bad start to relations as a result of the condemnation of the Moncada attack continued, and by the middle of 1958 a significant anti-communist faction had grown in the MR-26-7, particularly in Havana.

But it is important to differentiate between right-wing anti-communism that is opposed to the potential threat that communists pose to property relations, which is more common among the petit-bourgeoisie and the professions with property to lose and the left-wing anti-communism that saw the PSP as too moderate and overly prepared to make compromises, which is more common among working-class militants. Torres, as a sometime Trotskyist, fell into the latter camp.

The decision to work with the PSP had to be implemented in the aftermath of the failure of the April strike, about which, as outlined above, the PSP had been given no details and had not been involved in the planning process. The PSP leadership clearly felt considerable irritation at their exclusion from the strike, but this potential animosity seems to have been overcome by the decision of the July 26th Movement to begin serious negotiations. The PSP had been calling for unity for a long time and the approach from the rebels gave them reason to believe that their criticisms had been at least partially accepted. Moreover, the negotiations were given urgency by the ever-increasing wave of state-sponsored terror, which was widely reported in the party's press. The disappearance and subsequent murder of two of the most prominent and well-known communist leaders, Paquito Rosales, ex-mayor of Manzanillo, and José María Peréz, a bus workers' leader who had also been a congressional representative, appears to have shocked the rest of the PSP leadership.[68] Blas Roca, PSP general secretary, tells us that this terror started to convince the party leadership that there was no possibility of a legal solution to the crisis and that there was a need for armed protection before workers would take further action.[69]

### Convergence

The August 1957 strike occurred because of a convergence of the deeply felt anger of a mass of the population in eastern Cuba and a clandestine organization capable of capitalizing on the situation and spreading the action. The failure of the April 9 strike demonstrates that the "directing will of the center" is insufficient without mass involvement.

If chaotic organization and divisions within the opposition are a contributing factor in the failure of the April 1958 strike, they are not a sufficient explanation in themselves. The inability of the rebels to win a military confrontation with the government's armed forces in Havana must be seen as being decisive. Of course, any government's power is always concentrated in the capital, and this advantage was enhanced in this case by the fact that the influence of the trade union bureaucracy, upon which Batista depended so heavily, was also strongest in Havana.

Despite the failure of the August and April strikes to reach Havana, they were nevertheless impressive displays of opposition. Their ability to generate such widespread action, combined with the survival and growth of the rebel army in the mountains, made it clear that the MR-26-7 was now, irrespective of the defeated strike, the center of opposition to Batista and that other political organizations would have to orientate toward them. The PSP therefore had an interest in coming to an understanding with the MR-26-7 despite their annoyance at being excluded before the strike. With hindsight, it was probably politically fortunate for the PSP to have been so excluded, as it is unlikely that their involvement in the planning of the strike could have affected the outcome greatly, and their exclusion left them with the moral high ground.

The failure of the strike also convinced a significant group within the July 26th Movement that there would be advantages in working with the PSP, which still had sufficient roots in the labor movement to be of assistance. An analysis of the detail of both strikes certainly indicates that they were most successful in areas where militants of the two organizations worked together. The new leadership of the FON, though having no liking for the leadership of the PSP, was prepared to take a pragmatic approach and would begin serious negotiations over the summer of 1958. As can be seen from examining agitational material, there was much common ground between the egalitarian nationalist politics of the MR-26-7 and the communist notion of an *"amplia coalición democrática"* (broad democratic alliance), with both requiring a cross-class alliance fighting for democracy and national independence. The differences between the two organizations were at the tactical rather than the strategic level and circumstances were pushing both organizations to adopting a more accommodating attitude. Thus the failure of the strike on April 9 caused both the MR-26-7 and the PSP to change their approach and we see the start of a process of tactical convergence between the PSP and the MR-26-7, although the organizational convergence would be slower.

In this context, the other main decision taken by the MR-26-7 at Altos de Mompié, to give priority to the guerrilla struggle, though at first appearing like a turn away from the tactic of a general strike, in fact produced the conditions that would make such a strike possible.

## 7. LAST DAYS OF BATISTA

In an interview published shortly after the rebel victory in 1959, Faustino Pérez asserted that one of the reasons for the failure of the April 9 strike was that workers would not strike without adequate armed support.[1] The turn to a more militaristic approach by the MR-26-7 was not taken with a view to rectifying this inadequacy, but it did have that effect in the long term. Going on strike in Batista's Cuba could be a life-or-death decision, and workers had to feel some confidence in their chances of survival and in the possibilities of successfully gaining a result that would be in their political and economic interests. In the summer of 1958, however, the guerrillas still had to beat the encircling forces of Batista's army, which outnumbered them enormously. The events of the victory of the rebel army are well known, hence the need to examine the less well-known contribution of the working-class underground.

The rebel victory would give the MR-26-7 the most prominent position in the opposition forces and pave the way for a general strike that would sweep the July 26th Movement to power at the beginning of January 1959. The significance of this strike has been widely underestimated, and little work has been done to investigate how Fidel Castro was in a position to successfully call a strike when, only nine months before, his previous call had fallen so flat. Of course, the military victory was of great importance but was not sufficient by itself for the MR-26-7 to win power. Rather, the defeat of the government forces gave the workers the confidence to believe that they could go on strike without being brutalized by the security forces, who had been thoroughly demoralized by their treatment at the hands of a numerically inferior force. Moreover, nationwide general strikes require considerable organization. As the August 1957 strike shows, such spontaneity needs a base.

That organization developed through the unity discussions between the July 26th Movement and the communists, the organization of two workers congresses in rebel held territory, and the marginalization of the *mujalista* trade union bureaucracy. This shows the way in which the revolutionary general strike that overthrew Batista was organized and proved so powerful that it pulled the rest of the population in behind it. This leads to the conclusion that there was a convergence between the PSP and the MR-26-7 well before the rebel victory, that communists played a significant role in the success of the revolution, and that the general strike of January 1959 was the result of a high level of working-class organization and was crucial to the triumph of the revolution.

## Summer Offensive

In April 1958, the British vice consul in Santiago was clear that, in the provinces, the government's situation was increasingly precarious and that "everyone, rich as well as poor, appears to be in favor of Castro."[2] Despite thinking that "the present government has done more for Cuba than all previous administrations put together," he was also clear that "one of the reasons that the rebels have enjoyed so much immunity is in the very poor type of man in the Cuban Army. Being armed, they are living on the fat of the land, for every one of them is a grafter and has little inclination to get shot."[3] The British ambassador rather dourly added that "the Army is disinclined to undertake heroics."[4] This negative assessment of the fighting ability and morale of Batista's armed forces was to be borne out by the victory of the rebel forces over a government offensive launched in the wake of the failed strike of April 9, 1958. There was parallel growth in financial support coming from workers through late summer and autumn, as well as the increase in membership of the MR-26-7 *sección obrera*, which David Salvador estimated at 15,000 by the end of the year.[5] The logistical support for the guerrillas that was provided by the workers' underground was vital to their ability to continue the fight, whereas the rebel victory and the demoralizing effect it had on government armed forces gave ever-increasing numbers of ordinary working-class people the confidence to actively support the revolution. The priority of the *sección obrera* during the fighting was to ensure the logistical support of the guerrilla fighters, but once a rebel victory seemed assured, they turned their attention to the question of uniting all oppositional workers' organizations, which produced a united workers' organization, the Frente Obrero Nacional Unido (FONU, United National Workers' Front), that strengthened the hand of the rebel movement immensely.[6]

Following the defeat of the April 9 strike, Batista attempted to seize the advantage by means of a "summer offensive" that he dubbed Operación F-F *(Fase-Final* or *Fin-Fidel).* This offensive planned to use the army's greater firepower and numerical superiority to crush the rebels in the Sierra Maestra. Given that the dictatorship had somewhere in the region of 10,000 men at its disposal, supported by aircraft and artillery, whereas the rebels in the Sierra numbered only about 300 armed guerrillas, the outcome did not seem to pose any great problem for Batista. Fidel Castro's recently published account of the fighting from May to August 1958 fleshes out earlier accounts, showing both how the superior morale of the rebel fighters and intelligent tactical use of the mountainous terrain, enabled this small force to score victory after victory.[7]

The fighting in the Sierra Maestra quickly became the center of attention for all those opposed to the regime, overshadowing other matters. There is little record of any strikes or demonstrations over the summer of 1958, as it became clear that everything depended on the outcome of the battles in the mountains. In these circumstances, the priority for the MR-26-7 *sección obrera* was in organizing logistical support for the rebel army, engaging in sabotage, and preparing for a general strike in the event of a rebel military success. In terms of logistical support, the guerrillas in the hills were almost totally dependent for food and clothing on supporters in the towns.[8] Money could be raised from middle-class supporters and by "taxing" employers in the areas under rebel control, but this still had to be converted into material support. For this, workers in shops, warehouses, and distribution depots proved invaluable by large-scale organized pilfering of essentials, for which the *sección obrera* provided "shopping lists."[9] Railway workers were able to move these supplies under the noses of the police, while bus drivers formed propaganda distribution networks. Telephone operators in Santiago and Guantánamo eavesdropped on police conversations, reporting the information gleaned to the rebels. One particularly useful source of supplies was the U.S. base in Guantánamo Bay. In addition to the day-to-day items that could be pilfered, a quantity of arms and ammunition was purchased from U.S. Navy personnel. There was a considerable level of sympathy among the U.S. sailors on the base, and many contributed financially to the cause, and some security guards turned a blind eye to contraband material smuggled out of the base.[10] Without such support, the chances of the rebels resisting the regular army would have been slim indeed.

The government attempted to hide its failure to defeat the rebels by the imposition of strict media censorship. This was largely unsuccessful because the rebels had a radio station, Radio Rebelde, operating from the Sierra Maestra. This clandestine radio clearly had a powerful transmitter; its broadcasts were monitored by both the BBC World Service and at least one Mexican radio station.[11] The script of one broadcast, in the name of *Radio FON*, survives. As well as appealing for support for the continuing struggle of the *campesinos* on land owned by the King Ranch in Camagüey, it appeals to the common soldiers not to shoot their brother workers and either change sides or go home, saying that they were fighting for nothing in order to enrich their corrupt officers.[12] This appeal to the ordinary soldiers to change sides is a common theme at this time. In a similar vein, the Comité Obrero Revolucionario de San Miguel del Padrón issued a leaflet saying that not all the police were torturers and murderers, but those who did dishonor their uniform would be severely punished by future people's courts.[13] The army and police, though they had demonstrated ruthless efficiency when shooting down poorly armed students or unarmed striking workers, were not nearly so determined when faced with well-trained and politically motivated guerrillas. Army officers were frequently appointed and promoted more for their loyalty to Batista than for their martial competence. The rebel tactic of giving honorable and decent treatment to all military prisoners encouraged many to surrender or change sides. On the other hand, the well-known brutality of the military caused many guerrillas to fight to the death rather than surrender and face possible torture.

The rebel forces defeated the regime's summer offensive by August 1958, boosting the morale of the entire opposition and confirming the July 26th Movement as the real leader of the anti-Batista struggle. This position is highlighted by the terms of the Pact of Caracas, signed by all the opposition tendencies except the PSP on July 20, 1958. This gave the MR-26-7 complete freedom of movement while agreeing to a united front of the opposition, a position recognizing the de facto submission of the rest of the opposition to rebel army leadership. The agreement spoke clearly of the tactic to be employed: "an armed insurrection culminating in a great general strike on the civilian front."[14] The PSP was not included in the Pact of Caracas and the party leadership protested loudly in *Carta Semanal* for three weeks, then said no more as moves started toward separate discussions between the CNDDO and the FON.[15]Although the national meeting of the MR-26-7 leadership, held at Altos de Mompié, had decided to work together with the PSP, little progress was made over the summer. However, there was one campaign on which both groups expended some energy, taking a similar line: the long-running dispute at Coca-Cola. Twenty-six workers in the soft-drink company, some members of the PSP and others supporters of the MR-26-7, as well as independent militants, were dismissed. Their offense, according to both *Vanguardia Obrera* and *Carta Semanal*, was to "be against the dictatorship and the corrupt and traitorous leadership of the CTC."[16] This started a campaign to boycott Coca-Cola, and the company's workers dispatched committees to seek support from other workers. The CTC leadership tried to defuse the issue by negotiating the reinstatement of the twenty-six, provided they signed papers renouncing all political activity, a compromise denounced as shameful by the workers concerned.[17] The campaign was a live issue for the rest of the year, and they were only reinstated following the fall of Batista. Such collaboration at rank-and-file level helped the arguments of those in both organizations who wanted joint activity. So, once the government's summer offensive was repulsed, the leadership of the MR-26-7 turned its attention to the question of the workers' movement.

A circular issued by the national party leadersip on August 26, 1958, emphasized the changed situation with the military successes of the rebel army. It spoke of the need for "mobilization," using the term "*acción de masas*," previously associated with the PSP. This mass action was to be aimed at securing wage increases and price reductions, as well as opposing interventions in the unions and persecution. The final aim was, as always, a revolutionary general strike. While the circular spoke of the importance of building the FON committees through "unity from below," it equally stressed the need to maintain the independent existence of the *sección obrera* by distributing *Vanguardia Obrera* and other MR-26-7 propaganda.[18] Raúl Castro called a meeting of the provincial leaderships of the FON, which took place in the Sierra Cristal on September 12, 1958.[19] By this stage, Octavio Louit had been arrested and Julián Alemán had been killed, and Ñico Torres was now permanently stationed in the Segundo Frente Oriental "Frank País," as the area under the control of Raúl Castro's column in the Sierra Cristal was called.[20]

Following this meeting, Jesús Soto, a textile worker from the Havana suburbs and a strong advocate of collaboration, and David Salvador returned to Havana and contacted the PSP to arrange a meeting. David Salvador was arrested before the meeting could take place so Jesús Soto and José María de la Aguilera led for the MR-26-7, and Ursinio Rojas and Carlos Rodríguez Careaga spoke on behalf of the PSP.[21] This shows the seriousness with which the PSP national leadership treated this development as these two were the party's most senior trade union figures; Ursinio Rojas had replaced the murdered Jesús Menéndez as general secretary of the sugar workers' union and Carlos Rodríguez Careaga was leader of the CNDDO. Sometime in late October or early November 1958, it was agreed to form a joint organization to be known as the Frente Obrero Nacional Unido (FONU). A *circular de organización* from the MR-26-7 dated November 8 was still instructing its activists to form *comités del frente obrero nacional*, because they had been unable to arrive at a definite agreement with the union leaders of other organizations and urged their militants to proceed without waiting for the results of these meetings because workers' unity came from below.[22] The first manifesto of the FONU was issued on November 10, and there are at least three different printed versions of this, all with the same date, probably indicating a nationwide launch on this day.[23] This is a remarkable change from exactly a year before when an MR-26-7 leaflet was clear in saying that "the only proletarian force from which worker militants of the 26th July will accept instructions is the workers' section of the Movement."[24]

Once the FONU was formed, two committees were set up, one of which, with Miguel Quintero for the MR-26-7 and Carlos Rodríguez Careaga for the PSP, was to tour the provinces, charged with bringing the trade union militants of both organizations together in the localities and to form regional, district, and municipal sections of the FONU.[25] However, Carlos Rodríguez Careaga became the first high-profile martyr of the FONU, when he was caught up in a police raid at the house near Camagüey of a local communist sugar workers' leader, Saturnino Aneiro.[26] Both were beaten to death. The other committee went to Las Villas to help with the organization of a sugar workers' conference.

The political changes that happened within and between the MR-26-7 and the PSP are of immense importance for the revolutionary process, and it is significant that this coming together started at the working-class base of both organizations. Indeed, the MR-26-7 leadership in the Sierra Maestra still kept full knowledge of the rapprochement from their middle-class supporters. There was a solid base for unity, with the pressure coming from the already existing "committees of workers unity." This newfound collaboration would have its most complete expression in the "workers' congresses in liberated territory."

## Two Workers' Congresses

Once formed, FONU occupied itself with preparations for a general strike to overthrow the regime. Of particular significance in this respect were the two workers' congresses organized in the Sierra Cristal and in northern Las Villas. Having learned one of the lessons of the failures of April 1958, FONU planned this next strike to start in January 1959, coinciding with the start of the sugar harvest and thereby maximizing its economic effect. In the event, these preparations had to be brought forward to take advantage of the opportunity afforded by the flight of Batista on New Year's Day, 1959.

Two workers' congresses in liberated territory took place at the end of 1958, one in the Sierra Cristal in the area controlled by the Segundo Frente Oriental "Frank País," led by Raúl Castro, and the other in northern Las Villas Province in the area controlled by rebel forces under the command of Camilo Cienfuegos.[27] Despite the fact that these two meetings give us a valuable insight into the state of working-class politics at this crucial time, they have been largely overshadowed by the more dramatic events taking place on the guerrilla fronts as the rebel army turned the tide in its battles with Batista's forces. These two meetings were important events in themselves, the difficulties involved in assembling several hundred delegates in conditions of dictatorship and civil war showing an impressive level of organization. Furthermore, these congresses gave the rebel movement considerably increased legitimacy in working-class circles, showing that the opposition forces among organized labor were publicly united and capable of creating an alternative organizational structure.[28] As such, they played an important role in undermining the last remaining credibility of the *mujalista* CTC bureaucracy.

Soon after establishing the Segundo Frente Oriental "Frank País" in March 1958, Raúl Castro set up a *buró obrero* (labor bureau) to regulate industrial relations in the area under his command. In the early days of October of that year, Ñico Torres, in his role as national coordinator of the *sección obrera*, transferred to the Sierra Cristal to run the MR-26-7's intervention in the labor movement from there, as well as heading the Segundo Frente Oriental Buró Obrero.[29] Conrado Bécquer, now a wanted man, joined him, although, perhaps relieved to be able to discard the double life he had been living, expended most of his energy on a newly assigned combat role.[30] A successful *congreso campesino* (peasant congress) had been organized on September 21, a few days before Torres's arrival, to discuss the problems of the farmers of the region.[31] It was decided to organize a similar event for the sugar workers, and a preparatory plenary meeting took place in El Sigual on October 23.[32] This was initially called to consider how to deal with those sugar plantations in the area under rebel control, particularly the refusal of the employers to start repairs on their refineries in advance of the coming *zafra*. This situation was causing immense concern among the region's 36,000 sugar workers, who suspected that the employers were deliberately attempting to undermine support for the rebel army.[33] The discussions at the plenary soon expanded and, given the imminent launch of the FONU, it was decided to call a delegate conference representing all workers opposed to the regime.[34] This meeting was significant in that it was one of the first such meetings open to all political tendencies, including the communists. However, when the practicalities of assembling the delegates in the far east of the island for a national meeting were considered by the national leadership of the MR-26-7 *sección obrera*, now composed of Ñico Torres, Conrado Bécquer, and José Pellón, a distillery worker from Havana, it was decided to call two congresses, one near

Guantánamo for delegates from Oriente and the other for sugar workers in the recently liberated area of northern Las Villas Province.[35] Meanwhile, on the question of starting the preparation for the sugar harvest, an "intervention committee," jointly staffed by rebel soldiers and sugar workers, forced the issue. They toured the area under the control of the Segundo Frente Oriental "Frank País," ensuring that repairs were started, at gunpoint where necessary.[36]

The Congreso Obrero en Armas, as the conference in the Sierra Cristal was called, started on December 8. Delegates from areas under rebel control were elected in open assemblies, but, where this was not possible, they were designated by local cells of the MR-26-7 and/or the PSP. The industries represented included railway, sugar, ports, mining, pharmaceuticals, commerce, medicine, telephones, construction, printing, electricity, carpentry, baking, and the U.S. base. There were 110 delegates in all.[37] Many had a great deal of trouble getting there; for instance, the delegates from the U.S. base in Guantánamo had to walk and did not arrive until the 10th.[38] Twelve delegates from Santiago attempted to have the communist delegates barred from the meeting and, when they lost the vote, withdrew.[39] Following a report from Ñico Torres, the congress approved the formation of the FONU, pledged total support for the rebel army, and set out a familiar list of economic demands.[40] This congress appears to have adopted very similar policies to the conference in Las Villas, an event for which we have more details.

When the rebel detachment led by Camilo Cienfuegos arrived in Las Villas on October 7, 1958, he found a small PSP guerrilla group under the leadership of Félix Torres, who had become active in *campesino* politics after evictions by a particularly reactionary landlord in 1939–40. As a result of this and other activities, the PSP was especially strong in the northern part of Las Villas, which led to government repression being particularly severe in the region; many communist militants had been forced underground, where they took up arms in self-defense against the regime.[41] They had met with a certain hostility from the local MR-26-7 leadership, who had their own small guerrilla detachment.[42] However, Camilo Cienfuegos was fully informed about the new policy of cooperation with the communists, as his first proclamation indicates;[43] indeed, Osvaldo Sánchez of the PSP was acting as one of the liaison couriers linking Camilo Cienfuegos with Fidel Castro.[44] The most public demonstration of the new approach was that Gerado Nogueras, an experienced PSP workers' leader who had originally been a bus driver in Pinar del Rio Province, was appointed to run the *comisión obrera* (workers' committee), which the invading column set up upon its arrival.[45] The agreement seems to have been that the PSP was given the chair of the workers' committee in return for Félix Torres and his group submitting to MR-26-7 direction. Tito Igualada of the 26th July Movement was appointed as Gerado Nogueras's deputy, and Ramón "Mongo" Simonaca of the PSP was given responsibility for organizing the *campesinos*.[46] The principal task of the workers' committee was to organize assemblies on the sugar plantations and in the *centrales* in the province in order to elect new union representatives and to prepare for a sugar workers' conference, as well as providing logistical support for the guerrillas from the local rural population.[47]

When the column first arrived in northern Las Villas, delegations of sugar workers came looking for support for their demands, complaining of poor treatment by their employers and the army.[48] William Gálvez, an officer in the invading column, recalls that the rebel soldiers, most of whom were from urban backgrounds, were shocked by the levels of rural poverty.[49] With hindsight we know the regime would only survive for another two months, but the rebels were planning for a much longer campaign. It has already been mentioned that the founding meeting of the FONU had formed a committee to convene a conference of sugar workers.[50] At the beginning of December, they sent a letter to Che Guevara, who was commanding another column in Las Villas Province, requesting his support, which received a favorable response.[51] Following discussions with Camilo Cienfuegos, it was decided to send Ursinio Rojas to Las Villas to help the local *comisión obrera* with the preparations.[52] The others followed on the 14th.

As soon as local workplaces in the area under the influence of the rebels in northern Las Villas had started to reorganize, the *comisión obrera* called a series of district meetings to prepare for the congress. Camilo Cienfuegos personally chaired a meeting of workers from San Augustín and Adela *centrales* in the Alicante district in mid-November and planned to chair a larger meeting on the 28th.[53] In the event, he was caught in fighting in the Escambray mountains and delegated the responsibility to William Galvéz.[54] There were many similar meetings held during the second half of November and the early part of December, and Tito Igualada recalls a particularly militant assembly held in Güeba where 800 sugar workers elected new officials and planned the organization of workers in areas not yet under rebel control.[55] A similar assembly on December 7 in Jobo Rosado was attacked by aircraft of Batista's air force, but it continued after the all-clear.[56]

The final resolution of the plenary held on November 28 survives and provides some indication of the political feelings among the sugar workers of north Las Villas.[57] The resolution speaks of 728 delegates meeting under the protection of the invading column "Antonio Maceo," commanded by Camilo Cienfuegos, with the intention of discussing the demands for the forthcoming *zafra* as well as the wider political and social objectives of the Cuban people. It was resolved to:

1. Recognize the FONU as the leadership of the Cuban workers until such time as they might freely and democratically elect their leaders.
2. Declare the following December 7 a day of struggle against the dictatorship.
3. Call upon all sugar workers in Las Villas to prepare to fight for their demands for the forthcoming *zafra*. Call upon all other workers to fight for their own demands and in solidarity with the sugar workers.
4. Call upon all businessmen and industrialists to support the rebels' political demands, as this is the only way to develop their businesses with prosperity, respect, and peace.
5. Call upon the *campesinos*, small cane farmers, and professionals to join the fight of the Cuban people.
6. Call upon all members of the armed forces who are not complicit in murder and other bestial activities to cross over to the ranks of the rebel forces.
7. Condemn all countries that sell arms to the dictatorship, particularly the United States and England. These weapons are used to bomb and kill peaceful citizens.
8. For all Cubans, irrespective of social or political divisions to unite against the bloodstained government.

9.  To raise the following economic demands:
    - For a wage rise not less than 10%;
    - For a *diferencial* of 4.2%;
    - For the reemployment of all those dismissed or forced to leave their jobs by repression;
    - For land to be given to those agricultural workers who wish to cultivate it during the *tiempo muerto;*
    - Against the compulsory payment of union dues, but for voluntary payment;
    - For the payment of advances in wages free of interest;
    - For price reductions for basic household necessities;
    - For recognition of directly elected workers' representatives; until elections are possible, recognition of the clandestine *comités de lucha;*
    - Clean up living quarters and rebuild our houses;
    - For a general amnesty for all political and social prisoners, including those members of the armed forces who have been condemned for opposing the present regime;
    - For an end to censorship;
    - Reestablish constitutional guarantees;
    - For a provisional democratic government that will organize democratic elections as soon as possible in which all groups and parties opposed to the dictatorship may participate;
    - Return of all exiles so that they may resume their political activities;
    - Dissolve the BRAC, SIM and all other repressive bodies;
    - For the detention and condemnation of the assassin Pilar García and all others in the uniform of the armed forces who committed crimes and atrocities against the Cuban people;
    - For the most energetic condemnation of any nation that sold arms to the Batista dictatorship that were used to instill terror in the civilian population.[58]

The first thing that should be noted is that this is a significant number of delegates, particularly given the circumstances in which the assembly was called. It represents a qualitative increase in the strength and influence of the rebels within the labor movement, when compared to April

1958. What is most striking about the list of demands is their essential moderation. There is nothing here that is incompatible with a capitalist economy.[59] Given the earlier campaign for a 20 percent wage increase and a much larger *diferencial* than 4.2 percent, the comparatively low figures are surprising. The demands are posed in the context of a patriotic cross-class alliance, and it may have been that the sugar workers did not wish to alienate potential middle-class support for the rebels. However, given that the FONU was calling nationally for a 20 percent increase and a 40 percent price cut on basic items, it is unlikely that the FONU leadership was trying to restrict workers' demands.[60] It is more likely, in the face of the brutality of a dying regime, that the workers' main concern was to overthrow the government. There is also nothing in the list of demands that is incompatible with the previously held positions of either the MR-26-7 or the PSP. There clearly was some debate over the exact phrasing of the list, and the hand of the PSP can be seen in the detailed nature of many of the economic demands. Nevertheless, there are no substantive differences between this document and the previously issued statements of both parties, indicating that, at least among the militants active in the labor movement, political convergence had already occurred. The fact that there is little difference between the statements issued before and after the congress would seem to indicate that the rank-and-file delegates were also happy with the new situation.

This interpretation is borne out by a manifesto issued the same day in the name of *la Plenaria regional de trabajadores azucareros de la zona norte de Las Villas* addressed to *Los trabajadores azucareros de Las Villas*. This manifesto closely linked the economic demands with the fight for the political demands of the whole Cuban people, saying how this link made the fight over that year's *zafra* the most crucial ever. It urged sugar workers to turn their struggle into a wave of unstoppable resistance, which would lead the rest of the working class and all other classes of patriotic Cubans into a battle to overthrow the regime. Only by this method, it continued, could workers regain their rights and their self-respect. The manifesto concluded by claiming the position of honor for sugar workers, the most oppressed by the regime, who could become the vanguard of the struggle against tyranny. Such stirring rhetoric is evidence of a confidence that was lacking before the arrival of the rebel column.[61]

Guerrilla fighters from the rebel column in Las Villas started visiting the employers in the region, assigning to each one a tribute, or revolutionary tax, that they would be required to pay before being allowed to start harvesting sugar.[62] Employers were also required to recognize the newly elected workers' representatives and meet them to discuss their demands.[63] The position of the workers was further boosted by the rebels giving them arms recovered from supporters of the regime and forming them into militia companies, a move that must have further enhanced their position in negotiations with their employers.[64] Under the protection of the rebel soldiers and their own militias, local union assemblies prepared for the congress with traditional formality. For example, the workers of *central* Natividad in Guasimal, Las Villas, sent written motions to the congress calling for a 40 percent reduction in prices for basic items, for interest-free loans during the dead season (*tiempo-muerto*), and for equality of pay for office workers in private companies with state employees.[65]

It was in this atmosphere of excitement and tension that the "Congress of Sugar Workers in Liberated Territory" was summoned. Initially planned to take place in the Escambray Mountains, the military situation forced a change of plan and its eventual location was the small town of General Carrillo where Camilo Cienfuegos had his headquarters. Around 700 delegates took part, coming from all over Las Villas, Camagüey, Havana Province, Matanzas, and Pinar del Rio.[66] There were no delegates from Oriente because of the travel difficulties in time of war, but they had already held their congress in the Sierra Cristal. Ursinio Rojas delivered the keynote address, followed by both MR-26-7 and PSP speakers.[67]

The report of the organizing committee, which is paraphrased below, started by condemning Mujal's assertion that Cuba was prosperous due to increases in the price of sugar, arguing that the workers themselves had not benefited. The recent small salary increases that had been forced on the government had been eaten by inflation. Meanwhile, mechanization and *intensivismo* had increased productivity at the expense of thousands of jobs and accidents at work. While the workers' incomes between 1953 and 1957 had fallen by a total of 753 million pesos, the employers' profits had gone up enormously. Comparison was made between the years 1957 and 1951, when the same harvest of about 5 million tons was the same, and the sugar price for 1957 had risen back to 5.2 cents per pound, similar to the price of 5.29 cents per pound in 1951. The profits declared for 1951 had been 106 million pesos, but this figure had risen to 135 million pesos in 1957 while the total wage bill, at 321 million pesos, was 90 million pesos less. The report argued that this was partly because of wage cuts and partly because increased mechanization had enabled the same volume to be harvested in thirteen days less. In the days before Mujal and Batista, there had been an agreement to compensate workers for such "*superproducción*," but they had only received compensation for five days' loss of work rather than the thirteen they were owed. The minimum wage had been reduced from 3.14 pesos per day to 2.80 pesos. On top of this "official" reduction, union inactivity and state terror had permitted many employers to pay even less. The report concluded from this that the *zafra* could not continue under these conditions, and the list of demands adopted by the *Plenaria regional de trabajadores azucareros de la zona norte de Las Villas* (outlined above) was proposed.

The main question under discussion, the report continued, was to determine how to organize the struggle for these demands. Previous struggles had failed for lack of unity, which is why the FONU had been formed. It was seen as being of vital importance to build unity, and a large number of *comités de unidad* (unity committees) had already been set up. The other matter considered important was the development and strengthening of the rebel army. Important victories had been won over the army of the dictatorship, and the rebels were dominant in Oriente, north and south Las Villas, parts of Camagüey, Matanzas, and Pinar del Río. The document therefore claimed that the conditions existed for a successful general strike that, combined with revolutionary military activity, could bring down the dictatorship.

In areas where the rebels were in control, the report argued that the struggle would be easy. As soon as the employers agreed to the workers' demands, and the presence of rebel soldiers could assist in this, there was no reason not to immediately start the harvest. Where the dictatorship was still in control, the fight would be more difficult, but sugar workers had great experience learned from previous struggles. The report continued by saying that an essential part of this struggle would be to build the FONU, first in the workplaces and then at municipal and district level, with a view to calling a strike of all the sugar workers who labor in areas still under the

control of the dictatorship. The sugar workers were described as the vanguard of workers' movement and solidarity would be sought from all other
workers, as well as from small businesses, professionals, and small farmers,
leading to a revolutionary general strike. It concluded by saying that this
strike would have the full support and protection of the rebel army, and
sugar workers would do all they could to assist the rebel victory.[68]

The hand of the PSP is clearly visible in the phrasing of this document.
The close interlinking of immediate economic demands with anti-dicta-
torial political demands is typical of their approach to propaganda. The
frequent references to "unity" and the formula of "a democratic patriotic
government to implement agrarian reform, develop national industry,
freely trade with all countries, end racial discrimination, for peace and
national progress" with which the report ends, also reflects communist
political concerns.[69] MR-26-7 propaganda at this time tended to be
much less specific in its demands and generally contained much more
revolutionary rhetoric. Equally, the exact nature of the calculations of
the amount of money lost as a result of mechanization and wage cuts is
also much more in the communist style. Alfredo Menéndez, a clandestine
member of the PSP working as an economist in the Ministry of Sugar, had
access to the data necessary to prepare such a detailed account.[70] On the
other hand, the call for a revolutionary general strike was the main priority of the MR-26-7, which based all of its propaganda around this slogan.
The idea that the general strike should be started by the sugar workers
around both their economic demands and as a clear attempt to overthrow
the regime shows how much the rebels had learned since the fiasco of the
previous April.

The congress obviously had a very real effect on the morale and politics
of the participants. It gave a great boost to unity moves in the whole province, and assemblies were held in many places to elect *comités de unidad
obrera* (committees of workers unity).[71] These were decided on the basis
of parity between the revolutionary organizations, and places were also
given to two other minor opposition groups, the Organización Auténtica
(OA) and the Directorio Revolucionario (DR), which had little implanta-
tion in the working class, but which had made some contribution to the
fighting. In Santa Clara, the *comité de unidad obrera* allocated seats to the
OA and DR even though there was no one to fill them.[72] In the period that

followed, the idea of a united front between the PSP and the MR-26-7 came under attack from some elements within the latter organization, but was never seriously challenged in Las Villas Province.

## United Front

The nature of the alliance between the workers' organizations of the PSP and the MR-26-7 took the form of a united front. The implementation of this was viewed differently by the two component parts, and it may be useful to explore the nature of the relationships within the FONU as we find here the origins of the early disagreements between the parties during the first year of the revolutionary government.

The FONU did not become a real organization at the national level, but it was an important ideological symbol of unity. The agreement formulated in October called for the setting up of a formal structure, but, given the difficulties of clandestine organization, this was not possible and the organization was run on an ad hoc basis. Both *Vanguardia Obrera* and *Carta Semanal* continued publication. The CNDDO also continued to issue leaflets in its own name, but one of the first to follow the founding of the FONU was a leaflet calling for action to save the life of David Salvador, who was at that time still under arrest in Havana, saying that he was a workers' leader from the FONU. There were, however, no more statements issued in the name of the FON. It is interesting to compare two leaflets written about the murder of Carlos Rodríguez Careaga and Saturnino Aneiro. The first, dated November 27 and published in the name of the national committee of the CNDDO, refers to Rodríguez as secretary general of that organization and makes no mention of the FONU. The second, issued in the name of the national executive committee of the FONU, but clearly written by the same hand, stresses his contribution to workers' unity.[73] *Carta Semanal* displayed its enthusiasm for the new strategy combining *la lucha armada* with *la lucha de masas* in a series of high-profile articles and cartoons. Thus we see that, though they were sincere in their support for united action with the MR-26-7, the PSP leadersip was intent on making sure that its contribution to the united effort was fully recognized.

It was, however, not just the communists who were keeping their options open. The MR-26-7, when announcing the formation of the FONU in the

Santiago edition of *Vanguardia Obrera*, spoke glowingly of the benefits of unity without once mentioning that the unity of which they spoke involved the communists.[74] The archives of the Institute of Cuban History contain the first page of a draft of a manifesto announcing the formation of the FONU, which has been hand-annotated with suggestions for change. The final published version also survives. The draft starts with the fact that the FONU is a result of an agreement between the CNDDO and the FON, whereas the published version merely refers to agreement between *"distintas agrupaciones obreras"* (different workers' groups).[75] Yet, given the effort involved and the considerable danger to which both organizations were exposing themselves, there can be no doubt about the commitment at the national level to working together in the labor movement despite the apparent public reticence. One explanation for this seeming contradiction is that the other signatories of the Pact of Caracas were fiercely anti-communist, as were many of the MR-26-7 members involved in the Movimiento de Resistencia Cívica (civic resistance movement).[76] There would have been little to gain from drawing their attention too forcefully to the arrangement with the communists that would operate within the labor movement. On the other hand, we have already seen that in many areas there already existed a working relationship between communists and July 26th members in the workplace and neighborhood. These people would know exactly what was meant by "unity," and it would not have been necessary to spell it out. We can see this as an example of the balancing act needed to keep a cross-class movement together in the face of different sectional interests.

It is hardly surprising that the FONU did not have the opportunity to establish itself as a functioning national organization, because, within two months of its formal launch, Batista fled and the regime fell. It was established as a regional entity only in Las Villas and in the area under the influence of the Segundo Frente Oriental "Frank País," where the two conferences and the success of the rebel forces gave the necessary impetus. In Las Villas, Vicente Pérez, a PSP tobacco workers' leader, was appointed regional organizer, and there appears to have been a serious attempt to put the principles of uniting the workers' sections of the opposition movements into practice. The FONU became heir to previous initiatives of its component organizations; for example, a short railway strike had been called by the FON a short time earlier to protest the late payment of wages by the management of Ferrocariles Consolidados. The next leaflet in the dispute was then issued in the name of the Frente Obrero Nacional Unido, Comité Ferroviario (FONU railway committee), which speaks of the success of the strike, condemning the weakness of the *mujalistas* and calling on workers to build the FONU in preparation for the revolutionary general strike.[77]

Given the difficulties of communication in clandestine conditions, which were greatly exacerbated by the success of the rebel armies in cutting communications, the spread of a new organization would necessarily have taken time. *Carta Semanal* did not publish the FONU manifesto until December 3, 1958, and the local edition of *Vanguardia Obrera* in Santiago did not announce the formation of the FONU until December 29, 1958.[78] There is nothing sinister in this delay, which merely reflected the difficulties of communication and publication under a dictatorial regime. In areas where there were already working relationships between communist and July 26th Movement workers, particularly where there was some existing form of *comité de unidad*, the process would have been quick and easy. On the other hand, there was still considerable hostility toward the Communist Party in some sections of the MR-26-7, particularly in Havana, and this would not have disappeared because of a change in line from above. The new approach would have caused debate, disagreement, and, where there was a majority skeptical of the benefits of unity, no great urgency to start the process. Equally, some areas of the PSP were set in their ways and clung to the old *lucha de masas* approach, which had condemned armed action as terrorist. These would have viewed the new organization with suspicion and been slow to embrace the new line. As a result, the establishment of local or workplace FONU groups or unity committees was a varied patchwork, strongest in areas closest to the sites of the two workers' congresses and weakest in Havana.

The fact that the two organizations had agreed to work together did not mean that there was no longer any rivalry between them. The MR-26-7 still had a view of unity that was based on their hegemony rather than consensus or compromise, while the PSP considered itself to be the only real "party of the working class."[79] Such political rivalry is not unusual inside any united front; after all, if the constituent parts of an alliance agree completely, they might as well merge. In addition, the formation of a united front does not imply that the organizations involved will treat the new relationship as their highest priority. In this case, both organizations had ongoing projects within the milieu of the labor movement, and, for the people involved, these would retain their priority. The initial reaction to the formation of the FONU at rank-and-file level inside the MR-26-7 and the PSP would be to see the new formation in terms of its contribution to those existing projects. Thus, for example, the December 10 edition of *Carta Semanal* does not mention the FONU until page 2 and then ignores it until the end of the statement on page 4, which places the slogan "Strengthen the FONU" among many others in a long list although, at the top, we find "Build Unity Committees in every workplace."[80]

Santiago provides us with an example of the reality of collaboration in an area where there was a considerable history of united action, as we have seen earlier in the joint activity of the dockers and the Bacardi workers. However, there were also those in the MR-26-7 who were opposed to working with the communists, exemplified by the twelve delegates from Santiago who walked out of the Congreso Obrero en Armas. A *comité municipal de unidad obrera* was operating in Santiago in October 1958 that issued a leaflet containing detailed accounts of the grievances of the workers in many local workplaces. It confined itself entirely to economic issues without any mention of the rebel army or a revolutionary general strike. From this it is safe to assume that at this point in time the Santiago unity committee was dominated by the PSP with little MR-26-7 input. The next leaflet that survives, dated December 1, is titled "Against bombardments of the civilian population and against American intervention." It starts with a reference to Fidel Castro Ruz as "Commander in Chief of the Glorious Rebel Army" and roundly condemns the use of aircraft against civilians. It then immediately attacks the possibility of U.S. intervention, as in Korea and Lebanon, and reminds the reader of the level of racial discrimination in the United States, citing the incidents in Little Rock, Arkansas, as proof. The demands at the end are for trade union democracy, united action to overthrow the dictatorship, for a general strike, for donating a day's wages to the rebel army, reinstating all dismissed workers—and long live the second anniversary of the revolution. This is a leaflet written by a committee, with each organization comprising it wanting to get particular policies included. Thus the anti-imperialist part undoubtedly comes from the PSP, and references to the rebel army are from the MR-26-7.[81] The "second anniversary of the revolution" refers to the November 30 fighting in Santiago, which was launched by the MR-26-7, but supported by the Santiago PSP against the wishes of its national party leadership, now a point of regional pride.[82]

The existence of the Santiago *comité municipal de unidad obrera* did not prevent either organization continuing with its own propaganda; indeed, it seems to have inspired the local MR-26-7 to greater efforts. *Vanguardia Obrera* had published a special edition for Oriente Province since February 1958. The first two issues were reproductions of the national paper. Thereafter it contained increasing numbers of local references, both to industrial matters and the doings of the rebel army.[83] By December 1958, it had moved from a mimeographed format to a much more professional publication. Late 1958 seemed to produce a flurry of sectional publications: *La Voz* for press and radio workers, *Liberación Obrera* for medical workers, *El Portuario* for the dockworkers, and *Pantalla* for the cinematograph workers.[84] The July 26th *sección obrera* also issued a considerable number of manifestos in December 1958 in the name of its various sectoral committees: *Empleados Bancarios, Plantas Eléctricas, Refrescos Cerveza y Licores, del Puerto, del Comercio, Telefonico, del Transporte, Cinematógrafos, Prensa y Radio, de la Medecina, Gastronomico, Textilero, Tabaqueros,* and *Cemento Titan.*[85] This surge of activity would partly have its origins in an attempt to gain advantage in the changed situation and partly in the enthusiasm generated by the new sense of unity. Such a mixture of cooperation and competition is typical of any united front. Moreover, no united front operates in isolation from the political circumstances in which it is formed. Thus the feeling that things could not continue as they were, that change was imminent, which had in part been created by the forces of the opposition, in particular the guerrilla forces of the MR-26-7, both provided that opposition with an opportunity to force the pace of change still further and the encouragement to attempt to do so. Now, the hope for a general strike, which for so long had been an empty slogan, had become a distinct possibility thanks to the successes of the rebel army.

## The Last Days

The leaflets and manifestos from Santiago at the end of 1958, issued by the July 26 *sección obrera* and the Comité Municipal de Unidad Obrera, illustrate the crisis that was facing Cuban society in general and the working class in particular. They describe a situation in Santiago, confirmed by a report from the local office of Cable and Wireless, in which the Bacardi rum and Hatuey beer factories were virtually closed because the management claimed a shortage of bottles, most port workers were laid off because of a lack of ships coming into the harbor, and job losses in public transport as a result of cuts in service, as well as similar closures or layoffs in many other industries.[86] While the propaganda material from the time relates to the anger of the workers because of this situation, the lack of concrete proposals, other than a revolutionary general strike, reflects the difficulty faced in organizing industrial action when the economy is barely functioning. In such circumstances, workers could react by either blaming the rebels or the government. In this case, the overwhelming majority seem to have held the government responsible, and support for the rebels grew as they became seen as the only solution in desperate circumstances. Earlier in the year, following a rise in the official rate of inflation, the government had decreed a rise in the minimum wage and a 4 percent general wage increase. The Economist Intelligence Unit report saw this as "part of a campaign to keep them on the job and less open to the influence of the rebels." However, this approach by the government was so transparent that it increased MR-26-7 influence rather than reducing it, as the rebels were generally given credit for forcing Batista to award the increase. In any case, the official rate of inflation may have been only 2 to 3 percent, but the rise in the cost of basic necessities was closer to 20 to 30 percent, particularly in the east where the fighting made transport difficult. The demand for a reduction in the price of basic items and an end to speculation figures highly on all lists of workers' demands at this time. Moreover, any advantage the government might have gained from the increase was nullified by the fact that the increase was not enforced and many employers did not pay it, although they resented being placed in an awkward position.[87]

Support for Batista by employers was based on his ability to drive down wages, decrease staffing levels, and generally increase productivity, thereby helping profit margins. In return for this, there was a general acceptance by businessmen of the high levels of brutality and corruption associated with the dictatorship. By the end of 1958, a significant proportion of the employing class felt that the government had so mishandled the situation that any change, even a rebel victory, would be an improvement. The sugar magnate Julius Lobo is reported as saying, "It did not matter to us who got rid of Batista, as long as somebody did."[88] By December 1958, Batista's inability to ensure normal commercial activity, even to the extent of having lost control of the roads in the east of the island, meant that he had lost any usefulness to the business community.

The pressure from employers to maintain communications in the face of rebel forces cutting off roads and blowing up bridges gave rise to an attempt to protect the railways by using an armored train. This was being prepared in the Ciénaga railway workshops near Havana with the intention of transporting 700 soldiers to protect and repair the railway, initially between Havana and Santa Clara. Behind this incident is a good example of the manner of involvement of revolutionary workers in the final stages of the insurrection, when they concentrated on propaganda, sabotage, and aid to the guerrillas, rather than localized industrial action. The workers in the railway yard had considered refusing to work on the train, but following a meeting with the regional organizer of the July 26th underground, they decided to continue working, albeit slowly, while keeping the rebels informed of the progress and nature of their work, sending detailed sketches of their work directly to Che Guevara, who was in command of the rebel forces planning the attack on the city of Santa Clara in central Cuba. This gave them an opportunity to engage in propaganda work among the already demoralized soldiers who were to man the train and who were billeted in the works. This bore fruit, and, before the train left on December 23, thirty-nine soldiers deserted, aided by the railway workers who provided them with civilian clothing. Many more left the expedition en route, which arrived in Santa Clara with barely half its original complement. The train was finally derailed outside Santa Clara on the 30th during the final stages of the battle for that city. At this point, most of the soldiers deserted to the rebels, leaving the officers and remaining soldiers little choice but to surrender. The rebel army gained a considerable amount of supplies, arms, and ammunition from the ruined train.[89]

There was a functioning joint committee in Santa Clara composed of the local CDDO and MR-26-7 *sección obrera*, the former based mainly among the *gastronómicos* (hotel, restaurant, and catering workers), the latter among the bank workers. By the time the city fell, the *mujalistas* had already been purged, the local union offices seized, and the *gastronómicos* had taken charge of the provision of supplies for the civilian population and the rebel troops.[90] By the middle of 1958, the *mujalista* trade union bureaucrats had become irrelevant to both sides. Corruption and open support for Batista had so undermined their influence that they were of little further use to the regime. As Cuban politics became completely polarized between supporters of Batista and the rebels, an organization that relied for its existence on its ability to balance between capital and labor was swept aside. On New Year's Day 1959, Cuba awoke to the news that Batista had fled, but Mujal had become so marginalized that Batista did not bother to inform the CTC general secretary, who had to hurriedly seek refuge in the Argentine embassy.

The rebel army had driven the dictator from office, but it had not yet succeeded in seizing power or changing the political or economic system. The U.S. embassy was holding emergency talks with those generals who had not fled in an attempt to find an officer untainted by connection with the previous regime and who could lead a military coup to forestall a complete rebel victory. The columns led by Che Guevara and Camilo Cienfuegos were swiftly deployed to Havana, but were not sufficiently strong by themselves to overcome the enemy forces in the capital. There was a real possibility that an army coup, particularly if it was led by an honorable patriotic officer without previous close association with Batista, could have split some of the middle-class support away from the MR-26-7 and prolonged the civil war.[91] Such an intervention was greatly feared at the time, as can be seen by Lazaro Peña, communist ex-secretary of the CTC, writing of his concerns the previous November.[92] As the rebels moved in to seize Santiago on New Year's morning, Fidel Castro spoke over the radio from Santiago to condemn the coup attempts and to call for a revolutionary general strike. This call was directed at all workers in territory not yet liberated and told them to follow the lead of the Sección Obrera del Movimiento Revolucionario 26 de Julio, to seize all union offices and to organize in all workplaces to totally paralyze the country.[93]

From the moment the call went out, the strike was complete. Such a strike does not take long to describe; suffice to say that everything stopped and the scale of the action is evident from contemporary photographs, such as those of Burt Glinn.[94] Fidel Castro himself affirms that the general strike was decisive in delivering the fortresses of the capital of the republic, in defeating the final maneuvers of the enemies of the people, and in giving all power to the revolution.[95]

The strike provided such powerful evidence of the overwhelming popularity of the rebel victory that the army chiefs quickly abandoned their plans for a military coup. Furthermore, the strike gave an authority to and freed personnel for the MR-26-7 militias that were keeping order in the streets of Havana for that first week in January, thereby preventing the scenes of violent disorder and lynch mob rule that had followed the downfall of Machado.[96] Another important aspect of the general strike was the way in which it placed the MR-26-7 in complete control. The popular reaction to Fidel Castro's triumphant passage from Santiago to Havana demonstrated clearly who was the new power in the land. Equally significant was the way in which Castro was able to call for a return to work when he arrived in Havana, thereby demonstrating his authority once and for all.

## Convergence

Following the failure of the attempted general strike on April 9, 1958, the prospects of the revolutionary opposition must have seemed very bleak indeed, yet within a year, the regime had been overthrown and the rebels were in complete control of the country. The decisions taken at Altos de Mompié, to give priority to the guerrilla struggle and to work with the Communist Party in the labor movement, had borne fruit.

The success of the rebel army in repulsing the government's "summer offensive" heartened everyone who was opposed to Batista and established the July 26th Movement as the most important component of the opposition. Within the labor movement, this new prestige was reflected in increasing support for the MR-26-7 *sección obrera*. The center of gravity within the labor movement had now decisively shifted to the rebel side, and Mujal had become irrelevant. In the early days of the dictatorship, his control of the CTC had provided important cover for Batista. As late as April 1958 he had provided valuable service to the regime in undermining the rebels' attempted general strike, but by the end of 1958, he was so discredited that he was a positive liability. The ability of the rebels to organize large-scale workers' congresses in territory under their control marked the final transfer of working-class legitimacy from Mujal to the rebels. Everywhere they had the opportunity, aided by the rebel army, ordinary workers quickly removed Mujal's appointees. Where they could not, they simply ignored them. The failed strike of April 9 had proved that workers were reluctant to take action when faced with security forces that were prepared to use deadly violence to maintain order. The situation changed so dramatically over the summer that, by the autumn, there seemed little point in taking industrial action for narrow economic ends when the prize of a new political order suddenly appeared within reach. This enhanced standing of the MR-26-7 within the working class made an alliance with them more attractive to the Communist Party, which adopted a position of uncritical support for the rebel army and its tactical approach based on the armed struggle.

What, therefore, is the balance sheet of communist involvement in the Cuban insurrection? The main accusation of their enemies is that the PSP only jumped on the rebel bandwagon when victory was assured.[97] This ignores the fact that, when the PSP leadership first publicly announced its support for the guerrilla war in March 1958, rebel victory was far from a foregone conclusion. It also ignores the work of ordinary rank-and-file communists, who risked their lives distributing a constant stream of leaflets and underground newspapers, which contributed to maintaining and building a level of working-class discontent that responded so overwhelmingly to Fidel Castro's call for a general strike in January 1959. The sheer number and diverse origins of locally produced PSP agitational material serves to demonstrate the considerable numbers and widespread influence of communist militants in the labor movement; if this were not so, the MR-26-7 would not have bothered to negotiate with the PSP at the national level. It is true that the communists did not make a great contribution to the guerrilla struggle, but that was never their area of strength or expertise. The Communist Party's main influence was in the working-class movement, and it was this that they offered when negotiating with Fidel Castro. The course of those negotiations are shrouded in mystery as both parties played their cards close to the chest. Castro had the added difficulty of trying to get the PSP into the alliance without alienating his more anti-communist supporters. It is also true that after they decided to support the guerrilla campaign the PSP leaders were much keener on reaching an agreement than was the MR-26-7, which correctly recognized the relatively small contribution the communists could make to the advance of the rebel army, which was its main area of interest.

Nevertheless, the PSP did contribute a considerable amount to the growth of the revolutionary working-class movement, in particular helping to organize the two labor congresses in Las Villas and in the Sierra Cristal. The difficulties encountered in organizing such meetings have been widely underestimated. A workers' conference with 600 in attendance, which is organized in opposition to the official trade union bureaucracy, would be significant at any time, but to do it in the middle of a civil war, with many of the delegates coming from areas still under government control, is really impressive. One of the principal themes of these congresses was the Huelga General Revolucionaria, the revolutionary general strike. This final general strike was instrumental in preventing the projected coup and elevated the MR-26-7 to a position of hegemony. Without this strike, it is unlikely that the rebel victory would have been either so swift or so complete. Such general strikes do not materialize out of thin air; they have to be organized. As in the case of the strike that started in Santiago at the funeral of Frank País, apparent spontaneity requires considerable prior organization combined with a readiness to profit from a rapidly changing situation.

The convergence of the politics and tactics of the PSP and the MR-26-7 had been accompanied by the start of the organizational convergence of their work in the labor movement in the form of the FONU. This newfound unity was to prove very fragile.

## 8. THE FIRST YEAR OF THE NEW CUBA

With the overthrow of the Batista regime a new chapter in Cuban history began. The early period of the revolutionary government was deeply affected by the means by which it came to power, but many changes occurred in the world of organized labor over the first year of the new regime. In particular, the recently established alliance between the July 26 Movement and the Communist Party did not survive the arrival of the rebels in Havana. Given that the two organizations eventually merged, the realignment of forces within the MR-26-7 takes on considerable importance, in particular the contradictions between a new bureaucracy of the Confederación de Trabajadores de Cuba (CTC, Cuban Workers Confederation) and elements who wished to move the revolution in a more radical direction. The future Cuban Communist Party would emerge from the victory of the radicals in this faction fight.

### Division

As soon as it was known that Batista had fled, David Salvador was appointed the new general secretary of the CTC, an action that marked the end of the united front with the Communist Party. During the January 1959 strike, the FONU called for a mass meeting in the Parque Central in Havana on January 2, 1959, and another on January 8 to support the revolutionary government. This last appeal, signed by José Maria de la Aguilera for the MR-26-7 and Carlos Fernandez Rodriguez for the Comité Nacional de Defensa de las Demandas Obreras (CNDDO, National Committee for the Defense of Workers' Demands), is the last statement issued in the name of the FONU as a joint body, although Octavio Louit was still using the title Secretario de Organización del FONU in an interview on January 17.[1] Meanwhile, Ñico Torres and Conrado Bécquer, the latter still in his olive green uniform as a *comandante* of the rebel army, took the first flight from Santiago to Havana, where they immediately supervised the seizure of the CTC headquarters. This they did in the name of the *sección obrera* of the MR-26-7, whose leaders took all the seats on the CTC provisional executive committee, with David Salvador as secretary general.[2] The PSP was completely shut out, and, on January 13, the CNDDO wrote a furious letter to Salvador complaining that Torres and Bécquer had told them that the FONU was now dissolved and that they were excluded from decision making and even from entering the building.[3] Receiving no reply, the CNDDO, this time invoking the name of Lazaro Peña, called for a demonstration on January 21, only to be outflanked by David Salvador, who called a demonstration on the same day demanding justice for the 600 workers previously victimized by the Compañía Cubana de Electricidad and to celebrate the end of the compulsory check off of union dues that the government had decreed on January 20.[4]

With the establishment of the revolutionary government in Havana, the center of attention moved to the capital, and it was here that sentiment in the July 26 Movement was most hostile to working with the PSP. The journals *Bohemia* and *Revolución* became the mouthpieces for this approach, with frequent articles attacking communism in general and the Cuban communists in particular.[5] In a long interview published in *Bohemia* in February 1959, David Salvador argues that the FONU was a good idea, but the efforts spent trying to build it were a waste of time, that the communists were not a significant factor in the labor movement, and that only the MR-26-7 had any real presence in the working class.[6] The new leadership of the CTC set up the Frente Humanista (Humanist Front) and using this name succeeded in winning the overwhelming majority of the union elections.[7] Whatever Fidel Castro's personal views on relations with the communists may have been, and he was careful not to be too specific, his first priority was to keep his own organization together. Thus, when a group of angry communist railway workers knocked on the door of his apartment to denounce what they saw as undemocratic behavior by David

Salvador, he listened politely, expressed his interest, but did not pursue the matter further.[8]

As part of the attempt to reassure the more right-wing elements of the MR-26-7 and to confuse the U.S. government, the early "revolutionary government" was headed by a former judge, known for his honesty and his opposition to corruption rather than his radicalism, and many of the new ministers were equally moderate. The appointment of David Salvador to run the CTC, when his personal hostility to the PSP was well known, was the implementation of this strategy within the labor movement.

## Bureaucracy

A galloping bureaucratization of the CTC took place in the first months of 1959; many of the new officials quickly made themselves comfortable and began to resent the constant mobilizations and calls for action. They gravitated toward David Salvador and his associates in the anti-communist wing of the MR-26-7, who started to use crude anti-communism to attack those who wanted to push the revolution to take more radical steps. The more radical elements became known as the *"unitario"* group within the MR-26-7 *sección obrera*, among whose most prominent members were those who had been involved in the Las Villas congress: Jesús Soto, Lila León, and José Maria de la Aguilera. These *unitarios* soon attracted others in the CTC leadership, mainly those with long-term clandestine revolutionary experience such as Ñico Torres and Octavio Louit, who were disturbed by the growing bureaucratization. Seeking allies, they found them in the PSP, who agreed with the need to push the revolution further and who resented being excluded from the leadership of the labor movement.

The basis of the orthodox communist political approach was the theoretical position that history moved in stages and that it was first necessary to complete the "bourgeois democratic" phase of the revolution before moving to socialism. The Cuban Revolution was therefore defined as being "popular, patriotic, democratic, agrarian and for national liberation."[9] In line with this analysis, the leadership group of the PSP around Blas Roca were content to engage in the revolutionary process as it unfolded and, in particular, to support the wing of the MR-26-7 that seemed most progressive. This was also the section of the leadership that was most sympathetic to their inclusion, primarily those around Raúl Castro and Che Guevara, who condemned sectarianism and spoke publicly for the unity of all revolutionary forces including the PSP.[10] They continued working with those MR-26-7 trade unionists who had wished to carry on the united approach implied by the FONU.

What was the reaction of the rank-and-file workers to this? The first demands to be raised were for the reinstatement of those workers victimized for their militancy or made redundant as part of the old regime's productivity drive. There was particular joy at the reinstatement of the bank workers sacked for their strike in 1955 and the hundred bus workers dismissed after the coup in 1952.[11] Then there were wage claims, 10 or 20 percent, sometimes enforced by short strikes, more often just won by the threat of action. Some Shell refinery workers managed to double their wages.[12] Throughout 1959, the CTC was the main mobilizing force of the revolution and all of the major demonstrations were called in its name. May Day 1959 saw a million workers on the march, and hundreds of thousands went on strike and demonstrated on the streets to protest at the October airborne attack launched by right wing exiles from Miami.[13] During the government crisis of July 1959, workers' protests and a strike on July 26 were important factors in enabling Fidel Castro to remove Manuel Urrutia from the presidency and to secure the post of prime minister for himself. Thus we see a growing rift between the increasing radicalism among ordinary workers contrasting with a tendency to bureaucratization among a section of the CTC officialdom.

Within the CTC, matters came to a head at the 10th Congress of the CTC held in Havana in November 1959. The delegates were 90 percent July 26th Movement supporters, but were deeply split between the anticommunist faction lead by David Salvador and the *unitarios* fronted by Soto and Aguilera. Conrado Bécquer, who chaired proceedings. had some difficulty in maintaining order. Fidel Castro opened the proceedings, and spoke of the need for unity. Both sides interpreted this to suit their own entrenched position, and matters were no nearer a resolution as the closing session approached. Castro returned, upbraided the delegates for their uncomradely behavior, and it was agreed that a committee composed of Fidel Castro, David Salvador, Conrado Bécquer, José Pellon, and Jesús Soto should compose a compromise list for the executive. The posts were divided between the two factions with an anti-communist deputy to a *unitario* executive officer, or vice-versa in most positions. Two notable absences were Bécquer and Torres, now leaders of the FNTA and the railway federation respectively. This list was carried by acclaim, with the communist delegates abstaining, and the congress ended in relative harmony.[14]

Che Guevara called the 10th Congress "an arduous war against the representatives of *mujalismo*, representative of the old CTC gang."[15] Modern Cuban writing tends to adopt this line, although this was not the case at the time, even in the heated atmosphere of the congress hall, with neither of the newspapers of the PSP and MR-26-7, *Hoy* and *Revolución*, using the term *mujalista*.[16] On the other hand, anti-Castro writers such as Robert Alexander and Efrén Córdova discuss the 10th Congress of the CTC entirely at the level of the bureaucracy itself and see the fight as being between honest officials who respect private property and those who Robert Alexander refers to as "Melons," green on the outside, red on the inside.[17] The eventual triumph of the *unitarios* is seen as an imposition by Castro as part of his plot with the communists. Neither of these explanations are satisfactory. In January 1959, the CTC bureaucracy was effectively purged both *de jure* and *de facto*. Mujal himself,had sought refuge in the Argentine embassy, from where he was allowed to leave for Miami. The rest of his bureaucratic associates were removed from office and were well enough known by the ordinary membership to have no chance of regaining their positions. However, many of those who took their place quickly adopted bureaucratic attitudes and started using some of the old *mujalista* techniques such as voting irregularities and anti-communist demagogy. In a manner commonly found among opportunist trade union bureaucrats, they resented the work implied by constant mass mobilization. Aguilera and Louit were particularly vocal in criticizing this trend. The right wing of the bureaucracy, in return, used the accusation of communist influence to attack those who wanted a more radical approach to running the economy. One can say that they adopted similar bureaucratic methods to the *mujalistas*, but we have to be clear that they did not represent the return to office of the old *mujalista* bureaucrats themselves.

David Salvador did not last long as general secretary. Events outside the union forced the pace of change, and 1960 was a year in which, following the obvious popularity of the agrarian reform program of the previous year, large-scale nationalizations of foreign-owned enterprises took place. These, if the size of the demonstrations in their support are anything to go by, were very popular, and this radical economic approach, combined with the hostile reaction from the United States, seemed to launch a new wave of popular nationalism among the working class. The more radical political circumstances, combined with the threat of U.S. intervention, pushed the balance inside the CTC in the direction of the *unitarios*. David Salvador disappeared from view almost immediately after the 10th Congress, and for the rest of 1960 the most prominent CTC spokesman was Conrado Bécquer, with Jesús Soto and Octavio Louit also much in evidence. Salvador resigned in February 1960 and in June joined the "November 30 Movement," which was linked to the right-wing guerrillas operating in the Escambray mountains. He was arrested in November of that year, expelled from the CTC, and charged with treason. The victory over the U.S.-supported invasion at Playa Girón in April 1961 sealed the dominance of the *unitarios* within the CTC, and in July 1961 Lazaro Peña, the communist tobacco worker who had been ousted in 1947, assumed leadership of the federation.

The PSP leadership continued its almost unquestioning support for Fidel Castro while maintaining its organizational independence. However, they did not see the revolution as being socialist or communist, rather defining it as "national, emancipatory, agrarian, patriotic and democratic," and Blas Roca told the 1960 PSP Congress that "Cuba should not go down the road of rapid radicalization."[18] However, they were soon swept along by the course of events and, with increasing polarization, both internally and internationally, firmly supported the more radical line adopted by those around the Castros and Che Guevara. Carlos Rafael Rodriguez, the most pro-rebel leading member of the party, now became its principal public spokesman.[19] The turn toward the Soviet Union, following the break with the United States, had of course received the PSP leadership's full support. The logic of this situation would lead to the merging of the Directorio Revolucionario, the PSP, and the MR-26-7, first as the Organizaciones Revolucionarias Integradas (ORI, Integrated Revolutionary Organizations) in 1961, then the Partido Unido de la Revolución Socialista de Cuba (PURSC, United Party of the Cuban

Socialist Revolution) in 1962, and finally as the Partido Comunista de Cuba (PCC, Communist Party of Cuba) in 1965. As the leadership of the PSP was carried along by the tide of revolution, what of the ordinary workers?

The first wave of localized strikes in 1959 was for immediate demands: wage increases, union recognition, reinstatement of those who had lost their jobs under the dictatorship and the dismissal of scabs and other supporters of the regime.[20] As the rebel leadership consolidated its grip on power, this initial strike wave receded and the MR-26-7 newspaper *Revolución* asked, "Strikes? Against whom? For what?"[21] While set-piece mass mobilizations accompanied agrarian reform and the nationalizations, first of foreign oil companies, then foreign banks, and, very quickly, the whole of the economy, there was also considerable local activity driving forward the nationalization process, as the following two examples demonstrate.

At the beginning of July 1959, the workers in *central* Covadonga in Cienfuegos Province demanded payment of *superproducción*. In reply, the owners said they had no money, so the workers obtained a promise from the Ministry of Finance to make a loan to pay the wage demand, but the owners refused to sign the papers. The workers then went into permanent assembly, effectively occupying the premises and demanded that the state intervene to expropriate the whole property, while at the same time denouncing the links between the owners and the Batista dictatorship. In a move that showed that the old militant networks were still intact, local railway workers pledged their support and three other *centrales* in the area also went into permanent session raising the same demands. Once the nationalizations had taken place the workers renamed the *central* for Antonio Sánchez, a MR-26-7 underground activist who had been murdered by the police following the failure of the April 9 strike. It is clear from the reports in *Revolución* and *Hoy* that both MR-26-7 and PSP activists were involved in these actions.[22]

If this gives an example of the proactive nature of rural workers in the nationalizations, the takeover of the newspaper *Diario de la Marina*, nearly a year later, serves to show the process in an urban industrial setting. *Diario de la Marina*, the oldest and most right-wing newspaper in Cuba, continued publishing after the rebel victory and became a center around which reactionary forces could coalesce. In June 1960, the print workers presented a series of demands to management, including the dismissal of the managing editor, José Ignacio Rivero, whom they denounced as a counterrevolutionary. When they received the inevitable rejection, the workers occupied the premises, wrote and printed a last issue, and 15,000 people marched through the streets of Havana in their support, holding a mock funeral for the newspaper. The company was then expropriated and the presses converted to publishing other material.[23] There are many similar examples of the direct involvement in the nationalization process. Once the nationalization had taken place, many of the managers and technicians fled and the workers had to organize the continuation of production themselves. This was particularly true in the case of the nationalization of the U.S.-owned oil companies when the multinational owners withdrew their staff. In many ways, defense of the revolution became a battle for production in the face of destabilization from domestic and foreign capitalists and their supporters. The government, the unions, the MR-26-7, and the PSP all pushed the same line on this issue and it appears to have received popular support.[24] However, despite this active involvement, one does not see the development of independent workers' democratic institutions capable of holding the government to account. It was a period when there was great popular support for, and trust in, the revolutionary government and the majority of workers and the national leaders seemed to be pushing in the same direction, so there may not have appeared the need to create such institutions—after all, unofficial networks of activists allied with the guerrillas had brought down the dictatorship, so such a configuration would probably have seemed sufficient to build a socialist future. The most trusted revolutionary workers' leaders were now either running the union federations or working as officials in the ministries. Ñico Torres, who played such an important part in this story, remained as leader of the railway workers federation, played a part in the early contacts with the USSR, visiting Moscow in 1960, and, on his retirement, became an active member of the National History Commission. He died in Havana in 1991 at the age of seventy-nine.[25]

How can we account for this sudden about-face from the apparently genuine attempt to build a united front in the labor movement? First, it is in the nature of united fronts with a limited goal that they fall apart in the face of political differences of participants when that goal has been achieved. The goal of the FONU had been the overthrow of the dictatorship; when that had been achieved, many in the MR-26-7 saw no further use for the alliance with the PSP. The July 26th Movement had a hegemonic view of revolution; they sought unity under their unchallenged leadership. On the other hand, in colonies or countries considered to be "semi-colonial," like Cuba, orthodox communist policy called for an alliance between the working class and the progressive, patriotic bourgeoisie and petit-bourgeoisie with the aim of achieving full national independence. It is easy to see how an alliance with the MR-26-7 could be seen to fit this model. The PSP therefore consistently called "for a broad coalition government of all democratic forces," which was not at all what the MR-26-7 leadership had in mind. Both Conrado Bécquer and David Salvador pointed out that the old Communist Party newspaper *Hoy* had been permitted to resume publication without censorship and that democratic elections would be held in the not too distant future. The implication was that the PSP should be thankful for this and stop complaining. Furthermore, it was not only the PSP that was excluded. The Directorio Revolucionario fared no better; its leader, Faure Chaumón, was denied a platform at the first May Day celebrations on the grounds that there was not enough time.[26]

Second, the July 26th Movement was a coalition of different class interests and political opinions, united by a hatred of the dictatorship, but with very different ideas about the future direction of the revolution. There was a clear division within the movement between a right and a left wing, with many of the better-off supporters of the movement being opposed to the communists for fear that they might represent a challenge to their economic and property interests. Among this faction, the use of the expression "growing communist influence" became a stick with which to beat the more radical sections of the July 26th Movement.

Third, there was a real fear of U.S. intervention and the feeling that, if the U.S. government felt that the revolution was under communist influence, it would be more likely to intervene. It was considered prudent therefore to distance the leadership from an association with the PSP. The MR-26-7 trade union cadres' use of crude anti-communism during the trade union elections that took place throughout the early part of 1959 helped to buy time for the revolutionary regime. The British and U.S. governments were unsure, but on balance thought that Castro was not influenced by communists; he was considered to be an "extremist," but they were not sure of what type.[27]

So, why did the MR-26-7 subsequently split and its left wing realign with the Communist Party? Revolutions never stand still. The increasing radicalization of the revolution alienated many of the middle and upper classes who wished that change could have stopped with the removal of Batista and who stood to lose money from the reductions in rent and utility charges. They also feared the effects on business profits from workers' wage increases. This was reflected inside the MR-26-7 and the revolutionary government, but also had repercussions in the labor movement.

Fidel Castro worked with the more radical elements of the MR-26-7 to move the CTC to the left. In part, this was done by using both his undoubted popularity and considerable political maneuvering skills to secure leadership positions for his supporters among the new trade union leaders. The outcome of the elections at the 10th Congress of the CTC is a good example of this.[28] The purges of the rightist elements from the bureaucracy in 1960 aroused no particular outcry from the rank-and-file membership, but to merely describe these officials as "the old CTC gang" is inaccurate, as the old *mujalistas* had already been comprehensively removed in early 1959. A more convincing explanation can be found in the nature of trade union bureaucracy.

Trade union bureaucracy is an inherently conservative force that balances between capital and labor, gaining privileges and a certain independence in the process. Moreover, the CTC under Eusebio Mujal was thoroughly corrupt and completely undemocratic. However, removing the abuse and corruption did not deal with the essential nature of trade union bureaucracy—that required a political understanding. In the second half of 1959, the national leadership of the revolution grappled with the problems they faced in attempting to take hold of a state structure that had developed to serve the interests of capitalism, a situation further complicated by the domination of the economy by foreign, mainly U.S., capital. It was becoming obvious that merely correcting the abuses of the Batista regime was not enough. If Cuban society was to change, the core nature of the state had to change as well. This battle was reflected in the CTC and fought out at the 10th Congress.

There was considerable popular support for the revolutionary government as the state took increasing command of the economy. Nationalization of foreign-owned enterprises had long been a popular demand in the Cuban labor movement, and the large turnouts for the demonstrations in support of the nationalizations in 1960 seem to indicate the widespread popularity of these moves.[29] The CTC was one of the prime movers in these demonstrations, and the ascendancy of the left following the 10th Congress was a significant factor in providing an institutional vehicle for the expression of this support.

Just as the revolutionaries found that they could not achieve their ends by merely taking over the old state machine, so revolutionary workers' leaders found that they could not just take over the old CTC structure. Revolutionary change of both the state and the unions was necessary if they wanted to revolutionize society as a whole.

## CONCLUSION: WHAT WAS THE ROLE OF ORGANIZED LABOR IN THE CUBAN INSURRECTION?

The untold history of working-class involvement in the Cuban insurrection of the 1950s emerges from the archives as a fascinating story of courage and organization. Recovering from the defeat of an important series of industrial battles in 1955, a small but determined group of workers managed to build a clandestine labor movement in the face of an entrenched trade union bureaucracy and a brutal military dictatorship. This movement refused to accept the logic of capitalist industrial relations, which relates workers' demands to the employers' ability to pay. They organized unofficial strikes, produced a lively underground press, and combined industrial action with sabotage and armed conflict, thereby providing valuable support for the rebel guerrillas. By the end of 1958, they were able to organize two revolutionary workers' congresses composed of hundreds of delegates and, finally, the most complete general strike in Cuban history.

Given such an impressive record, one wonders why this story is untold, particularly as the evidence is available in the archives for any researcher who cares to look. Perhaps it is because so much historical writing prefers to concentrate on the actions of "great men" and is blind to the ability of ordinary workers to take an independent and often decisive collective role in the development of events. In attempting to bring this hidden history to light and to provide an answer to the question "What was the role of organized labor in the Cuban insurrection?," several subsidiary questions arose. In answering these, a fuller picture of the actual role played by the workers emerges.

*What were the problems facing Cuban workers during the 1950s?*

A profound contradiction existed at the heart of the Cuban economy: the national income, principally derived from the export of sugar, which provided 80 percent of the country's exports, was insufficient to maintain the wage rates and staffing levels historically expected by the workers and at the same time provide the employers the profit margins they expected. In order to maintain their profits, business interests needed to increase productivity, which they sought to do by cutting wages, decreasing staffing levels, and introducing new machinery. Such a redivision of the national income in favor of capital at the expense of labor did not prove possible under a democratic regime. This caused significant sectors of Cuban and U.S. business to support the authoritarian solution offered by Fulgencio Batista, in the expectation that an authoritarian regime would break workers' resistance to the implementation of cost-cutting measures.

The Batista government supported and coordinated an offensive by the main groups of employers aimed at reducing wage costs, having first secured the support of the trade union leadership by corruptly advancing the personal interests of the bureaucracy. This productivity drive was conducted sector by sector, ensuring that no two significant groups of workers came under attack at the same time, thereby undermining the possibility of generalized resistance. This process was aided by the trade union bureaucracy, which played a moderating and conservative role. Whenever there was a danger of groups of workers bypassing the limits set by the bureaucracy, the government used repressive force to defeat them. This dual strategy of repression and corruption, which was employed throughout 1955, succeeded in defeating workers in the railway, banking, textiles, and brewing industries, as well as, most importantly, the sugar workers. The tobacco workers and the dockers, however, managed to resist the increased mechanization of their industries. As a result of the defeats of 1955, important sections of the Cuban working class adopted other methods of organization and struggle to defend their interests.

*How was the Cuban working class organized?*

The trade union bureaucracy under capitalism is predominantly a conservative social group, with interests independent of the workers they purport to represent. This results in a tendency to accommodate to the status quo. This conservative self-interest made the trade union officials around Mujal susceptible to the offers of corruption coming from the regime. Up to 1955, the CTC bureaucracy had appeared to defend wages and conditions and had largely maintained its hegemonic position. However, in the face of the concerted employers' offensive, which started in earnest that year, it revealed itself as unable or unwilling to safeguard working-class living standards and was increasingly seen as part of the problem rather than contributing to a solution.

The term "organized labor" can be used to describe working-class organization at a number of levels. There are the formal structures of the trade unions and then there are a multiplicity of unofficial, informal structures through which ordinary workers defend their interests, often in the face of obstruction from the official bureaucracy. The role played by the *mujalistas* in undermining working-class resistance has led to an underestimation of the role played by workers in the insurrection. However, when the division of interest between the bureaucracy and the rank and file is taken into account, the way is opened to search for evidence of involvement by workers that is distinct from the conventional view obtained by merely considering official union activity.

Thus the categorization of the general strikes of August 1957 and January 1959 as "spontaneous" is an example of the tendency for historians to see an event as spontaneous when in reality they just do not know, or do not wish to admit, who actually organized it. This use of the idea of "spontaneity" to dismiss events for which a researcher has no explanation ignores and dismisses grassroots organization. These two strikes, as well as a large amount of other militant working-class activity, were the work of the network of activists linked to the rebel movement. This organization, which was started by revolutionary militants from Guantánamo, drew on preexisting unofficial relationships within the labor movement and spread westward to cover much of the island. As well as organizing strikes and demonstrations, these activists engaged in sabotage and provided logistical support for the guerrillas. This network was organized in some areas on the basis of a formal cell structure, in others less formally. These activists sometimes collaborated with Communist Party members and supporters, according to local circumstances, traditions, and personal relationships. Sometimes this network operated under the name of the Frente Obrero Nacional, sometimes under the name of a local committee of workers' unity or some such, and sometimes was completely anonymous. Whatever form this network took in the localities, it proved highly effective in organizing material and political support for the rebels in the hills, as well as localized industrial action. The most significant achievement, however, was that these activists provided the basis for Fidel Castro to call the most complete general strike in Cuban history in January 1959.

### *What political forces were active in working-class politics?*

It can be confusing to refer to the "labor movement" as if it were a single entity, as there were clearly a variety of different movements operating within the working class in Cuba during the period under consideration. It may be more helpful to refer to "poles of political attraction" within the wider context of organized labor. There were three such poles of attraction within the broad labor movement: the communist Partido Socialista Popular, the Movimiento Revolucionario 26 de Julio led by Fidel Castro, and the trade union bureaucracy led by Eusebio Mujal. From 1955 onward, the main question in working-class political life was the competition for support between the PSP, the MR-26-7, and the official union machine.

The *mujalista* trade union bureaucracy started to lose credibility after the defeats of 1955 and became increasingly dependent on state intervention to maintain its position. There were some splits in the union leadership that took two forms: on the one hand, internal jealousies and arguments over the division of the spoils of corruption and, on the other, honest officials who opposed what they saw as a sellout of workers' interests. The latter group, small in number but significant in their effectiveness, moved toward the MR-26-7. By the end of 1958, Mujal and his associates were effectively marginalized.

The PSP found its main support in those industries that were able, for various reasons, to resist the employers' offensive of 1955–56 and defend their conditions of employment, principally the docks, tobacco, and hotel and catering. In these industries, the communist line of "mass struggle" still appeared to provide a way forward. However, in those industrial sectors that suffered defeat in the class battles of 1954–55, particularly railways, banking, textiles, and sugar, small but growing groups of local workers' leaders turned to a more radical policy. They became convinced that the only way workers could reclaim their rights and regain democratic control over their trade unions was by the revolutionary overthrow of the regime. These militant workers were attracted to the armed struggle approach advocated by the July 26th Movement. Of particular importance were a group of railway workers from Guantánamo, in the extreme east of the island, who developed a tactical approach that they called *movimiento obrero beligerante*, combining traditional industrial action, such as strikes, slowdowns, and demonstrations with sabotage, bombing, and other armed actions. This dovetailed with the MR-26-7's revolutionary approach, which relied on a general strike supported by guerrilla action to overthrow the dictatorship. The fact that these workers adopted revolutionary tactics did not affect their basic demands, which were reformist in the sense that they sought improvements within capitalism rather than its overthrow.

### What was the relationship between the PSP and the MR-26-7?

The growth of the MR-26-7 *sección obrera* inevitably brought them into contact with PSP militants at the workplace level. The dynamics of workplace organization forced these two groups of militants to interact, and though there was continued political debate and disagreement a process of convergence started to occur, which was considerably in advance of the developing relationship at the leadership level. The two organizations had much in common politically, both advocating an egalitarian nationalist solution to the social and economic crisis, assuming the necessity of a cross-class alliance, and seeing the revolutionary process as one that progressed by stages. Neither grouping openly advocated socialism. Their differences were largely tactical, with the PSP promoting unarmed mass struggle and the MR-26-7 seeing the need for armed action to defeat the forces of state repression. Both organizations placed the general strike at the center of their approach, but they had a very different conception of tactic. To the PSP it represented a traditional stoppage of work by the overwhelming majority of workers, who would thereby achieve their objective by sheer weight of numbers and by paralyzing the economy. To the MR-26-7, the general strike was more akin to a mass armed popular insurrection. As opposition to the Batista regime grew, the difference between these tactical approaches was tested in practice. The PSP leadership learned the need for armed support and the MR-26-7 leadership realized that popular support could not just be summoned but had to be built by relating to workers' economic and social interests.

The process of tactical convergence first began at the workplace level, as local solidarity pushed militants from both organizations to work together. This convergence was boosted by the increasing brutality of the regime, particularly in the east. As the army and police became frustrated by their inability to defeat the guerrillas, they vented their feelings on the civilian population. In addition to this random unofficial violence, there was increased activity by government death squads, which targeted all sections of the opposition, but made a particular target of known working-class activists, including communists, despite the opposition of the communists to the armed struggle. The sheer horror of the state violence meted out by the Batista dictatorship has dropped from sight in recent studies, but it needs to be remembered as an important factor contributing to the increasing popular hatred of the regime. The common danger was another factor in pushing rank-and-file communists and *fidelistas* together as well as producing a feeling among many ordinary PSP supporters that they needed to arm themselves, if only in self-defense.

Although there was a political convergence between the two organizations, the process of organizational convergence was slower, in part due to anti-communist attitudes within sections of the MR-26-7, particularly in Havana. However, anti-communism takes different forms and there are both right-wing and left-wing varieties, with the former being opposed to the communists because of opposition to the collectivization of property, and the latter frequently feeling the communists are insufficiently militant and overly bureaucratic, with a poor commitment to democracy. It is important to differentiate between these two phenomena, as left-wing critics of the Communist Party were frequently prepared to collaborate with communist militants once these adopted a more radical approach, and the right wing was generally opposed in all circumstances. The leading members of the MR-26-7 *sección obrera*, with the notable exception of David Salvador, fell into the left-wing category and, following the PSP acceptance of armed action, did work with the communists.

A view of the Cuban Revolution that sees the rebel victory as entirely the work of the guerrilla army will necessarily see little contribution from the communists. If the role of organized labor is taken into account, the communist contribution becomes considerably more significant, as this is the area in which they operated most effectively. Thus their systematic agitation and propaganda was a key factor in helping maintain independent working-class organization, and their organizational experience and preexisting militant networks complemented the work of the MR-26-7 *sección obrera*.

## To what extent were regional differences important?

In all of this, opposition to the regime was generally stronger in the east of the island and least pronounced in Havana. The arrival of the nucleus of the rebel army in the *Granma* gave the advocates of *movimiento obrero beligerante* their first test. There were strikes and sabotage in Guantánamo in solidarity with the armed actions in Santiago in November 1956. This drew the attention of leadership of the MR-26-7 to the contribution that could be made by organized labor, and the Guantánamo workers were encouraged to spread their organization and activities. Relationships between the MR-26-7 and the PSP were also better in the east of the island and, in a parallel move, the local communist leadership in Santiago supported the MR-26-7 armed uprising of November 1956 by organizing a dock strike in solidarity. This aided the process of convergence between the two organizations, which was slow and uneven, but was most pronounced among workers in the east and center of the island.

Moreover, the importance and influence of working-class members of the MR-26-7 was greater in Oriente, Matanzas, and Las Villas provinces, whereas the leadership of the urban underground in Havana tended to be drawn more from professional and petit-bourgeois backgrounds. Partly as a result of this, there was a better relationship between the MR-26-7 and the PSP in the provinces than in the capital, for, as previously stated, workplace solidarity and the pressure of unaligned workmates tends to lessen sectarian party differences. Another factor in considering regional differences was that the influence of the trade union bureaucracy diminished away from the capital, where the head offices of the federations were situated. On the other hand, government capital expenditure was concentrated in Havana, with such projects as the Havana Bay Tunnel providing employment; the tourist industry and its associated hotel-building program were also concentrated here and in nearby Varadero. As a result, there was less economic pressure on workers in the capital and therefore less reason to seek a revolutionary solution. Recognition of these regional differences is crucial to understanding the course of the insurrection.

*How significant was the involvement of organized labor in determining the outcome of the conflict?*

As the crisis deepened, the army and police engaged in a campaign of terror, including the use of death squads and torture, which was particularly fierce in Oriente Province. Militant workers, even when unconnected to the rebels, were a particular target of this state repression. The initial working-class response to state terror comprised a series of strikes in Manzanillo, Bayamo, and Santiago. These, while helping to raise levels of opposition to the regime, proved ineffective in preventing government violence, with the result that many workers, including sectors of the Communist Party, were drawn to support the rebel forces. Even the August 1957 strike, despite being the biggest demonstration against Batista before he fled, did not seriously threaten the regime. In circumstances where a regime is prepared to use high levels of brutality to suppress workers' attempts to defend their wages and conditions, then conventional methods of mass action, such as the strike, the demonstration, the boycott, etc., are insufficient. Equally, armed guerrilla action without mass support normally leads to isolation and defeat. The victory of the revolutionary forces in Cuba in 1959 was due to a successful combination of these tactics.

The failure of the regime's summer offensive of 1958 gave the rebel forces immense prestige and resulted in the loss of support for Batista from within the business class. The subsequent rebel advances led Batista to flee the country, but, while this removed the dictator, it did not ensure the victory of the revolutionary forces. Rather, the general strike called by Fidel Castro at the beginning of January 1959 was crucial in preventing an army coup that would have prolonged the war. This general strike was in no way spontaneous, but was the result of careful preparation. The FONU was responsible for convening two well-attended workers' congresses in rebel-held territory in December 1958. These congresses agreed to organize a general strike at the start of the next sugar harvest, due to begin in the following January. However, Batista fled before this, and the general strike had to be brought forward to prevent a military coup designed to prevent a rebel victory. This strike was the most complete in Cuban history and ensured the overthrow of the old regime. The importance of this in determining the future course of events cannot be overestimated.

### How can the Cuban Revolution be characterized?

In common with many conflict situations, a number of parallel struggles took place in the revolution, and most combatants participated in some elements but not others according to their political beliefs and class interests. The insurrection was a civil war, a class struggle, an anti-imperialist movement, a democratic revolution, a fight for national independence against neo-colonialism, a campaign against corruption, and an episode in the Cold War. However, in the period between 1952 and the end of 1958, there was no faction or interest group publicly arguing for socialism. Many supporters of the revolution from petit-bourgeois, professional, and managerial social strata were concerned with democracy and anti-corruption, as well as being sickened by the regime's brutality, but had an economic interest in the productivity measures enforced by the government. Those big-business elements who came to support the revolution, switching their allegiance from their previous support for Batista and his productivity drive, did so because they felt that matters could not continue as they had  been and that any solution promising a return to stability on any terms was an improvement over the prevailing chaos. To this may be added that there would have been personal reasons for many, reacting against the repressive violence that left few families untouched. These pro-capitalist sectors would have had little interest in the anti-imperialist and Cold War aspects of the conflict, although many outside the sugar oligarchy may have been attracted to economic nationalist arguments, though they were mainly hostile to increased workers' rights.

The workers who supported the rebel cause did so on a number of levels. As citizens they were party to the general revulsion with corruption and a desire for the return of democracy. In working-class politics, this was reflected in the demand for the cleansing of the trade unions and the right to elect their chosen leaders. This was not an abstract demand, but linked to reestablishing the trade union movement as a vehicle to defend wages, jobs, and workplace rights and it was thus inextricably linked with the class struggle. The publicly expressed demands of the rebel workers' movement were, in themselves, reformist and related to a return to earlier higher wage and staffing levels. However, though there was nothing intrinsically incompatible with capitalism in the workers' demands, these demands were not affordable for Cuban capitalism in the light of its position in the world capitalist economic order. International competition meant that they were effectively pricing themselves out of a market that was able to tour the world seeking the lowest wage costs. This contradiction would lead to working-class support for anti-capitalist measures following the rebel victory.

In the period from 1952 to 1959, working-class involvement in the insurrectionary process took place as part of a cross-class alliance, within which specifically working-class forms of struggle made a vital contribution to the success of the rebellion. Without this contribution from organized labor, the Cuban Revolution would not have succeeded.

# BIBLIOGRAPHY

## ARCHIVAL RESOURCES

Archives consulted in Havana, Cuba:
   ***Instituto de Historia de Cuba*** (IHC), Institute of Cuban History
      Papers of the *Comité Nacional de Defensa de las Demandas Obreras y por la
      Democratización de la CTC* (1956–58)
      Papers of the *Comités de Unidad Obrera* (1958)
      Papers of the *Frente Obrero Nacional* (1957–58)
      Papers of the *Frente Obrero Nacional Unido* (1958)
      Papers of the *Partido Socialista Popular* (1955–58)
   ***Archivo Nacional***
      Papers of *Movimiento Revolucionario 26 de Julio*
   ***Biblioteca Nacional "José Martí"***

Provincial Archives in Cuba:
      Archivo Provincial de Manzanillo
      Archivo Provincial de Guantánamo
      Archivo Provincial de Las Villas, Santa Clara
   ***Biblioteca Provincial de Guantánamo*** (newspaper archive)
   ***Museo Provincial de Ciega de Avila***
   ***Archivo Provincial de Oriente, Santiago de Cuba***
   ***Biblioteca Elvia Carpe, Santiago de Cuba***
   ***Universidad de Oriente, Santiago de Cuba***

Personal Collections in Cuba:
   **Alcibíades Poveda Díaz, of the Oficina del Historiador de Santiago de Cuba**
   **Angelina Rojas, of the Insituto de Historia de Cuba**
   **Reinaldo Suárez Suárez, of the Universidad de Oriente**
   **Vicente Pérez, PSP trade union organizer from Caibarién**

Archives in UK:
**British National Archives, Kew**
References to archival material in the National Archive at Kew start with the folder reference FO 371, which refers to records created and inherited by the Foreign Office, General Correspondence from Political and Other Departments from 1906 to 1966. This is followed by the document reference AK, which refers to Cuba-related material originating in the American Department of the Foreign Office/
**British Library Newspapers, Colindale**
**TUC Archives, London Metropolitan University**
**British Library**

## ONLINE MATERIAL

**Confidential U.S. State Department Central Files**:
Available at http://www.latinamericanstudies.org/us-cuba.htm

## INTERVIEWS

**Interviews by the Author:**
Julio García Oliveres, Directorio Revolucionario student leader, Havana, May 2014.
Francis Velázquez Fuentes, rebel army veteran, Santiago, April 2009.
Alfredo Menéndez, Ministry of Sugar, PSP member, Havana, March 2009.
Francisco Monserrat Iser, PSP factory worker, Manzanillo, March 2009.
María Victoria Antúnez Salto, Juventud Socialista activist, Manzanillo, March 2009.
Alcibíades Poveda Díaz, MR-26-7 activist, Santiago de Cuba, March 2009.
Vicente Pérez, PSP trade union organizer, Havana, June 2008.

**Interviews by Other Researchers:**
Antúnez Salto, María Victoria, testimony of Wilfredo de la O Estrada, PSP leader in Manzanillo, Manzanillo, n.d..
Luis Figueras, Semblanza de Antonio Torres Chedebaux, Guantánamo, n.d..
Jana Lipman, interview with coordinator of the MR-26-7 group at the U.S. base at Guantánamo, Havana, December 2004.
Delio Orozco, interview with Ñico Torres, MR-26-7 head of the Frente Obrero Nacional, Havana, April 1990.
Gary Tennant, interview with Octavio Louit, MR-26-7 revolutionary railwayman from Guantánamo, Havana, 1997.

CONTEMPORARY PERIODICALS

*Bohemia* (Havana) 1952–77
*Carta Semanal* (Havana) 1954–58
*Daily Worker* (New York) 1953
*Diario de Cuba* (Santiago) 1952–53
*Diario de la Marina* (Havana) 1952–58
*El Mundo* (Havana) 1954–60
*Havana Post* (Havana) 1952
*La Calle* (Havana) 1955
*Le Villereño* (Santa Clara) 1955–58
*Noticias de Hoy* (Havana) 1953
*Oriente (Santiago)* 1952–53
*Prensa Universal* (Santiago) 1952–53
*Revolución* (Havana) 1959
*Voz del Pueblo* (Guantánamo) 1955–56

ARTICLES, BOOKS, AND OTHER PRINTED MATERIAL

Agee, Phillip. *Inside the Company: CIA Diary* (Harmondsworth: Penguin, 1975).
Alexander, Robert. *Organized Labor in Latin America* (New York: Free Press, 1965).
Alexander, Robert Jackson. *A History of Organized Labor in Cuba* (Westport, CT: Praeger, 2002).
Alvarez, José. *Principio y fin del mito fidelista* (Bloomington: Trafford, 2008).
Alzugaray, Carlos. *Crónica de un fracaso imperial* (Havana: Editorial de Ciencias Sociales, 2008).
Ameringer, Charles. *The Cuban Democratic Experience: The Auténtico Years, 1944–1952* (Gainesville: University Press of Florida, 2000).
Anderson, Jon Lee. *Che Guevara: A Revolutionary Life* (London: Bantam, 1997).
Andrews Thomas, Jorge. "La huelga de 9 de abril en Guantánamo," Research paper, Universidad de Oriente, Santiago de Cuba, 1982.
Baklanoff, Eric N. "Cuba on the Eve of the Socialist Transition: A Reassessment of the Backwardness-Stagnation Thesis," Papers and Proceedings of the 8th Annual Meeting of the Association for the Study of the Cuban Economy (ASCE) (Miami, August 6–8, 1998).
Balfour, Sebastian. *Castro* (Harlow, UK: Pearson, 2008).
Barquín López, Ramón. *Las luchas guerrilleras en Cuba: De la colonia a la Sierra Maestra* (España: Editorial Playor, 1975).
Bécquer, Conrado. *El porqué de la congelación de los salarios, la productividad y los sindicatos en el proceso revolucionario* (Havana: CMQ, 1960).
Bell Lara, José, Delia Luisa López García and Tania Caram León. *Documentos de la Revolución cubana, 1959* (Havana: Editorial de Ciencias Sociales, 2006).
Berdayes Garcia, Hilda Natalia. *Papeles del Presidente: Documentos y discursos de José Antonio Echeverría Bianchi* (Havana: Casa Editorial Abril, 2006).

Blackburn, Robin, "Class Forces in the Cuban Revolution," *International Socialism*, vol.2, no.9, Summer, 1980

Blackburn, Robin. "Prologue to the Cuban Revolution," *New Left Review* 1/21 (October 1963).

Bonachea, Ramón, and Marta San Martín. *The Cuban Insurrection, 1952-1959* (New Brunswick, NJ: Transaction Books, 1974).

Bonachea, Rolando, and Nelson Valdés. *Cuba in Revolution* (Garden City, NY: Anchor Books, 1972).

Bornot, Thelma. "Esa tarde me pusieron a la frontera," *Santiago*18-19 (June and September 1975).

Cannon, Terence. *Revolutionary Cuba* (New York: Crowell, 1981).

Cardona Bory, Pedro. *Memorias del Congreso Obrero en Armas, Segundo Frente "Frank País"* (Cuba: Pilar Casada Gonzalez, ca. 1995).

Carr, Barry. "Mill Occupations and Soviets: The Mobilisation of Sugar Workers in Cuba 1917-1933," *Journal of Latin American Studies* 28/1 (1996).

Castro, Fidel. *La victoria estratégica* (Havana: Consejo de Estado, 2010).

———. "Manifesto No. 1 del 26 de Julio al pueblo de Cuba, 8 August 1955," *Pensamiento Critico*, vol. 21, 1968.

———. *Discursos de comandante Fidel Castro en el X Congreso Nacional Obrero* (Havana: COD de publicidad de la CTC, 1959).

Cepero Bonilla, Raúl. "Política azucarera," *Obras históricas* (Havana: Instituto de Historia, 1963).

Chávez Alvarez, Clara Emma. *Matanzas de rojo y negro 1952-1958* (Matanzas: Ediciones Matanzas, 2007).

Chevandier, Christian. *Cheminots en grève: la construction d'une identité (1848-2001)* (Paris: Maisonneuve & Larose, 2002).

Chomsky, Aviva. *A History of the Cuban Revolution* (Chichester: Wiley-Blackwell, 2011).

Cirules, Enrique. *El imperio de La Habana* (Havana: Casa de las Américas, 1993).

Coma, Ismael Alonzo. "El Movimiento 26 de Julio en Guantánamo," Research paper, University of Oriente, Santiago de Cuba, 1981.

Córdova, Efrén. *Clase Trabajadora y Movimiento Sindical en Cuba (1959-1996)*, vol. 2 (Miami: Ediciones Universal, 1996).

———. *Castro and the Cuban Labor Movement: Statecraft and Society in a Revolutionary Period (1959-1961)* (Lanham, MD: University Press of America, 1987).

Coya, María Modesta "El movimiento obrero en Santiago de Cuba 1952-1958," Research paper, Universidad de Oriente, Santiago de Cuba, 1982.

Curry-Machado, Jonathan. 'Sin azúcar no hay país': The Transnational Counterpoint of Sugar and Nation in Nineteenth-Century Cuba," *Bulletin of Hispanic Studies* 84/1 (January 2009).

Cushion, Steve. "Cuban Popular Resistance to the 1953 London Sugar Agreement," in *Global Histories, Imperial Commodities, Local Interactions*, ed. Jonathan Curry Machado (Basingstoke: Palgrave Macmillan, 2013).

Darushenkov, Oleg. *Cuba, el camino de la revolución* (Moscow: Editorial Progreso, 1979).

Dávila Rodríguez, Rolando. *Lucharemos hasta el final* (Havana: Oficina de Pulicaciones del Consejo de Estado, 2011).

Departamento Obrero II Frente Oriental "Frank Pais," Comisión Nacional de Historia, *Provincia Guantánamo* (Havana: manuscript in IHC Archives, 1980).

Díaz Pendás, Horacio. *Textos sobre Historia de Cuba* (Havana: Editorial Pueblo y Educación, 2009).

Draper, Theodore. *Castroism: Theory and Practice* (London: Pall Mall, 1965).

———. *Castro's Revolution: Myths and Realities* (New York: Praeger, 1962).

Duarte Hurtado, Martin. *La maquina torcedora de tabaco y las luchas en torno a su implementación en Cuba* (Havana: Ciencias Sociales, 1973).

Durán Cremet, Dagmary. "Movimiento obrero en el sector ferroviario en Santiago de Cuba 1925-1945," Research paper, Universidad de Oriente, Santiago de Cuba, 1988.

Dye, Alan, and Richard Sicotte. "The U.S. Sugar Program and the Cuban Revolution," *Journal of Economic History* 64/3 (2004).

Economist Intelligence Unit (EIU), "Cuba, Dominican Republic and Puerto Rico," *Quarterly Economic Review* 13 (1956).

———. "Cuba, Dominican Republic and Puerto Rico," *Quarterly Economic Review* 9 (1955).

Espín, Vilma. "Déborah," *Santiago* 18-19 (June and September 1975).

Farber, Samuel. *The Origins of the Cuban Revolution Reconsidered* (Chapel Hill: University of North Carolina Press, 2006).

Farber, Samuel. "The Cuban Communists in the Early Stages of the Cuban Revolution: Revolutionaries or Reformists?," *Latin American Research Review* 18/1 (1983).

Figueras Pérez, Luis, and Marisel Salles Fonseca. *La lucha clandestina en Guantánamo, 1952-1958* (Guantánamo: Editorial El Mar y La Montña, 2011).

Fuente, Alejandro de la. *A Nation for All: Race, Inequality, and Politics in Twentieth-Century Cuba* (Chapel Hill/ London: University of North Carolina Press, 2001).

García Faure, Martha Albys, and Margarita Canseco Aparicio. *Algunas Manifestaciones Políticas en Guantánamo* (Guantánamo: El Mar y la Montana, 2009).

García Galló, Gaspar Jorge. *General de las cañas* (Havana: Editora política, 1998).

García Montes, Jorge, and Antonio Alonso Avila. *Historia del Partido Comunista de Cuba* (Miami: Ediciones Universal, 1970).

García Oliveras, Julio. "El movimiento estudiantil antibatistiano y la ideología de la Revolución," *Ruth Cuadernos 3* (2009).

———. *Contra Batista* (Havana: Editoral Ciencias Sociales, 2008).

———. *José Antonio Echeverría: La lucha estudiantil contra Batista* (Havana. Editora Política, 1979).

García Pérez, Gladys Marcl. *Insurrección y Revolución, 1952-1959* (Havana: Ediciones Unión, 2006).

———. *Insurrection and Revolution: Armed Struggle in Cuba, 1952-1959* (Boulder: Lynne Rienner Publishers, 1998).

Gávlez, William. *Camilo, Señor de la vanguardia* (Havana: Cincias Sociales, 1979).

Glinn, Burt. *Havana: The Revolutionary Moment* (Stockport, UK: Dewi Lewis Publishing, 2001).

Gonzalez Pedrero, Enrique. *La Revolución cubana* (Mexico City: Escuela Nacional de Ciencias Politicas y Sociales, 1959).

Gonzalez, Mike. *Che Guevara and the Cuban Revolution* (London: Bookmarks, 2004).

Guérin, Daniel. *Rosa Luxemburg et la Spontanéité Révolutionnaire* (Paris: Flammarion, 1971).

Guevara, Ernesto. *Pasajes de la guerra revolucionaria* (Havana: Editora Política, 2001).

Halperin, Ernst. *Fidel Castro's Road to Power* (Cambridge, MA: MIT Center for International Studies, 1970).

Harman, Chris. "The Return of the National Question," *International Socialism* 2/56 (1992). ———. "1984 and the Shape of Things to Come," *International Socialism* 2/ (Summer 1985).

Hart Phillips, Ruby. *Cuba: Island of Paradoxes* (New York: McDowell, 1959).

Hart, Armando. *Aldabonazo, en la clandestinidad revolucionaria cubana, 1952-58* (New York: Pathfinder, 2004).

Hatzky, Christine. *Julio Antonio Mella* (Santiago de Cuba: Editorial Oriente, 2008).

Instituto de Historia del Movimiento Comunista y de la Revolución Socialista de Cuba, Partido Comunista De Cuba (PCC), *Historia del movimiento obrero cubano*, vol. 2 (Havana: Editora Política, 1985).

Huberman, Leo, and Paul Sweezy. *Cuba: Anatomy of a Revolution* (New York: Monthly Review Press, 1968).

Ibarra Cuesta, Jorge. *Prologue to Revolution: Cuba, 1898-1958* (London: L. Rienner Publishers, 1998).

Ibarra Guitart, Jorge. *Sociedad de Amigos de la República* (Havana: Editora Ciencias Sociales, 2003).

———. *El fracaso de los moderados* (Havana: Editora Política, 2000).

Kapcia, Antoni. *Leadership in the Cuban Revolution: The Unseen Story* (London: Zed Books, 2014).

———. *Cuba in Revolution: A History Since the Fifties* (London: Reaktion, 2008).

Karol, K. S. *Guerrillas in Power: The Course of the Cuban Revolution* (New York: Hill & Wang, 1970).

Le Riverend, Julio. *La República* (Havana: Instituto Cubano del Libro, 1973).

Lipman, Jana K. *Guantánamo: A Working-Class History between Empire and Revolution* (Berkeley: University of California Press, 2009).

Machado, Pedro. *El movimiento obrero henequenero después del golpe de estado del 10 de marzo. Etapa conspirativa de Julián Alemán* (Havana: unpublished ms., 2011).

Marques Dolz, Maria Antonia, and Luis Alberto Fierro. "The Non-Sugar Industrial Bourgeoisie and Industrialization in Cuba, 1920-1959," *Latin American Perspectives* 22/4 (1995).

Masetti, Jorge Ricardo. *Los que luchan y los que lloran* (Buenos Aires: Editorial Jorge Alvarez, 1969).

Massón Sena, Caridad. "Proyectos y accionar del Partido Socialista Popular entre 1952 y 1958," in *1959: Una rebellón contra las oligarquías y los dogmas revolucionarios*, ed. Jorge Ibarra Guitart (Panamá: Ruth, 2009).

McGillivray, Gillian, *Blazing Cane: Sugar Communities, Class, and State Formation in Cuba, 1868-1959* (Durham, NC: Duke University Press, 2009).

Méndez Oliva, Esperanza. *La estirpe de Mariana en Las Villas* (Santa Clara: Editorial Capiro, 2006).

Mendoza Bú, Gabriela, "El movimiento 26 de julio en el sector ferroviario en Santiago de Cuba," Research paper, Universidad de Oriente, Santiago de Cuba, 1988.

Monserrat Iser, Francisco. "Luchas obreras en Manzanillo" (Manzanillo: unpublished ms., 2009).

Montoto, Newton Briones, and Rita Vilar. *Una hija reivindica a su padre* (Panama: Ruth, 2011).

Morley, Morris H. *Imperial State and Revolution: the United States and Cuba, 1952-1986* (Cambridge: Cambridge University Press, 1987).

O'Connor, James. *The Origins of Socialism in Cuba* (Ithaca, NY: Cornell University Press, 1970). O'Donnell, Guillermo. *Modernization and Bureaucratic-Authoritarianism: Studies in South American Politics* (Berkeley: Institute of International Studies, University of California, 1973).

Olutski Ozacki, Enrique, Héctor Rodríguez Llompart and Eduardo Torres Cueva. *Memorias de la Revolución* (Havana: Imagen Contemporanea, 2007).

Orozco, Delio. "Manzanillo en los 50, rebeldía y revolución" (Manzanillo: unpublished ms ., n.d.t).

———. *Manzanillo: "El Movimiento Revolucionario 26 de Julio y el apoyo a la Sierra"* (Manzanillo: unpublished ms., 1989).

Osa, Enrique de La *En Cuba: Tercer tiempo 1955-1958* (Havana: Ciencias Sociales, 2008).

———. *En Cuba: Tercer tiempo 1952-1954* (Havana: Ciencias Sociales, 2006).

Padrón, José Luis, and Luis Adrián Betancourt. *Batista: El Golpe* (Havana: Ediciones Unión, 2013).

———. *Batista: Últimas días en el poder* (Havana: Ediciones Unión, 2008).

Page, Charles. "Development of Organized Labor in Cuba," PhD diss. (University of California, Berkeley, 1952).

Pearce, Brian. "Some Past Rank-and-File Movements," *Labour Review* 4/1 (April–May 1959).

Pérez Garcia, Mayda, Angel E. Cabrera-Sánchez and Luis Vázquez-Muñoz. "Invierno Caliente" (Ciego de Avila: unpublished ms., 2008).

Pérez Linares, Ramón. "La agro-manufactura tabacalera de la antigua provincia de Las Villas y las principales luchas de sus trabajadores en el periodo de 1940 a 1058," PhD diss. (Universidad Central 'Marta Abreu' de Las Villas, Santa Clara, 2005).

———. "La lucha de los tabacaleros villareños contra la mecanización integral del torcido (1952-1958)," *Islas* 138 (October–December 2003).

Pérez Pérez, Angel. *La huelga de 55 en el Central Estrella* (Havana: Departament de
Orinetación Revolucionaria del Partido Comunista de Cuba, 1974).

Pérez Stable, Marifeli. *The Cuban Revolution* (Oxford: OUP, 1999).

Pérez, Faustino. "La sierra, el llano: eslabones de un mismo combate," *Pensamiento Crítico* 31 (1969).

Pérez, Louis. *Cuba: Between Reform and Revolution* (Oxford: Oxford University Press, 2006).

———. *Cuba and the United States: Ties of Singular Intimacy* (Athens: University of Georgia Press, 1990).

Pino Santos, Oscar. *Los años 50* (Havana: Editorial Arte y Literatura, 2008).

———. *El asalto a Cuba por la oligarquía financiera yanqui* (Havana: Casa de las Americas, 1973).

———. *Historia de Cuba: Aspectos fundamentales* (Havana: Editora del Consejo Nacional de Universidades, 1964).

Pollitt, Brian H. "The Rise and Fall of the Cuban Sugar Economy," *Journal of Latin American Studies* 36/2 (2004).

———. "The Cuban Sugar Economy and the Great Depression," *Bulletin of Latin American Research* 3/2 (1984).

Portuondo Lopez, Yolanda. *José Tey Saint-Blanchard, su última cita de honor* (Santiago: Editorial Oriente, 2006).

Poveda Diaz, Alcibíades. *Propaganda y revolución en Santiago de Cuba 1952–1958* (Santiago de Cuba. Oficina de la Historiador de la Cuidad, 2003).

Quesada González, Pilar. "El congreso obrero en armas," in *II Taller Científico Internacional, Movimiento Obrero y 1ero de Mayo: Memoria*, ed. Marcelo González Bustos, José Alfredo Castellanos Suárez, Luis Hipólito Serrano Pérez, Marco Antonio Anaya Pérez, and Alvaro González Pérez (Texcoco, México: Editorial Futura, 1999)

Ramero Granado, Marlene. "El movimiento 26 de julio en Bayamo," Research paper, Universidad de Oriente, Santiago de Cuba, 1988.

Regalado, Antero. *Las luchas campesinas en Cuba* (Havana: Editora Política, 1979).

Reyes Pérez, Miriam, and Ramón Batista López. "El movimiento 26 de julio en los municipios de Tunas y Puerto Padre," Research paper, Universidad de Oriente, Santiago de Cuba, n.d..

Rodrígiez López, Facundo Alexis, and Diosdado Martínez Rodríguez. "La huelga de 9 de abril de 1958 en la cuidad de Camagüey," Research paper, Universidad de Oriente, Santiago de Cuba, 1984.

Rodriguez Ramirez, Aleida, and Liduvina Ramos Cabrales. "El Movimiento Revolucionario en manzanillo de 1950 a 1959," Research paper, Instituto Superior Pedagogico, Manzanillo, 1988.

Rojas Blaquier, Angelina. "A propósito del asalto mujalista a al CTC en 1947," in *II Taller Científico Internacional, Movimiento Obrero y 1ero de Mayo: Memoria*, ed. Marcelo González Bustos et al. (Texcoco, México: Editorial Futura, 1999).

———. *El Primer Partido Comunista de Cuba 1952–1961*, vol. 3 (Santiago de Cuba: Editorial Oriente, 2011).

———. *1955: Crónica de una marcha ascendente* (Havana: Instituto de Historia de

Cuba, 1998).———. "El mujalismo en el movimiento obrero cubano," PhD. diss. (Instituto de Marxismo-Leninismo, Sofia, 1983).

Romualdi, Serafino *Presidents and Peons: Recollections of a Labor Ambassador in Latin America* (New York: Funk & Wagnalls, 1967).

———. "Labor and Democracy in Latin America," *Foreign Affairs* 25/1–4 (April 1947).

Sánchez Guerra, José, and Margarita Canseco Aparico. *El eco de las voces: La prensa en Guantánamo de 1902 a 1962* (Guantánamo: Historia, 2006).

Santamaría García, Antonio. *Sin azúcar no hay país: La industria azucarera y la economía cubana (1919–1939)* (Seville: Universidad de Sevilla, 2001).

Sección de historia del comité provincial del partido en Guantánamo. *Reseña histórica de Guantánamo* (Santiago de Cuba: Editorial Oriente, 1985).

Sección de historia del comité provincial del PCC en Guantánamo, *Guantánamo, apuntes para una cronología historíca* (Santiago de Cuba: Sección de historia del comité provincial del PCC en Guantánamo, n.d.).

Serra, Jorge Alberto. "El Movimiento de Resistencia Cívica en La Habana," in *Memorias de la Revolución,* ed. Enrique Olutski Ozacki, Héctor Rodríguez Llompart, and Eduardo Torres Cueva (Havana: Imagen Contemporanea, 2007).

Silva Leon, Arnaldo. *Cuba y el mercado internacional azucarero* (Havana: Editorial de Ciencias Sociales, 1975).

Sims, Harold. "Cuba's Organized Labour from Depression to Cold War," *MACLAS Latin American Essays* 11 (1997).

———. "Cuban Labor and the Communist Party, An Interpretation," *Cuban Studies* 15/1 (Winter 1985).

Smith, Kirby, and Hugo Llorens. "Renaissance and Decay: A Comparison of Socioeconomic Indicators in Pre-Castro and Current-Day Cuba," *Cuba in Transition,* Papers and Proceedings of the 8th Annual Meeting of the Association for the Study of the Cuban Economy (ASCE), vol. 8, Miami, August 6–8, 1998.

Soler Martínez, Rafael. "El partido bolchevique leninista," in *II Taller Científico Internacional, Movimiento Obrero y 1ero de Mayo: Memoria,* ed. Marcelo González Bustos et al. (Texcoco, México: Editorial Futura, 1999).

Spalding, Hobart. *Organized Labor in Latin America: Historical Case Studies of Workers in Dependent Societies* (New York: New York University Press, 1977).

Stubbs, Jean. *Tobacco on the Periphery: A Case Study in Cuban Labour History, 1860–1958* (Cambridge: Cambridge University Press, 1985).

———. "The Cuban Tobacco Industry and Its Workings: 1860–1958," PhD diss. (University of London, 1975).

Suchlicki, Jaime. *University Students and Revolution in Cuba, 1920–1968* (Coral Gables, FL: University of Miami Press, 1969).

Sweig, Julia. *Inside the Cuban Revolution: Fidel Castro and the Urban Underground* (London: Harvard University Press, 2002).

Swerling, Boris C. "The International Sugar Agreement of 1953," *American Economic Review* 44/4 (December 1954).

——. "A Sugar Policy for the United States," *American Economic Review* 42/3 (1952).

Taquechel, Rafael, and María Poumier. *Juan Taquechel López y el movimiento obrero en Santiago de Cuba* (Santiago de Cuba: Colleción El Cobre, 2009).

Tennant, Gary. *The Hidden Pearl of the Caribbean* (London: Porcupine Press, 2000).

——. "Dissident Cuban Communism: The Case of Trotskyism, 1932–1965," PhD diss. (University of Bradford, UK, 1999).

Thomas, Hugh. *Cuba, or, the Pursuit of Freedom* (New York: Da Capo Press, 1998).

Toirac Adames, Joaquín. "El Movimiento Obrero en la Base Naval Norteamericana," *El Managui* (1988).

Truslow, Francis Adams. *Report on Cuba* (Washington, D.C.: International Bank for Reconstruction and Development, 1951).

Velazquez Fuentes, Francis. *Josué* (Santiago: Edisciones Santiago, 2008).

Whitney, Robert. *State and Revolution in Cuba* (Chapel Hill: University of North Carolina Press, 2001).

Winocur, Marcos. "¿Dónde estaba la clase obrera cubana cuando la revolución?: 1952–1959," *Secuencia* 13 (1989).

——. *Las clases olvidadas en la revolución cubana* (Buenos Aires: Contrapunto, 1987).

Zanetti, Oscar. *La República: Notas sobre economía y sociedad* (Havana: Ciencias Sociales, 2006).

Zanetti, Oscar, and Alejandro García. *Sugar and Railroads: A Cuban History 1837–1959* (Chapel Hill. University of North Carolina Press, 1998).

——. *Caminos para azúcar* (Havana: Editorial de Ciencias Sociales, 1987).

——. *United Fruit Company, un caso del dominio imperialista en Cuba* (Havana: Editorial de Ciencias Sociales, 1976).

Zeitlin, Maurice. *Revolutionary Politics and the Cuban Working Class* (Princeton: Princeton University Press, 1967).

# NOTES

### Foreword

1. Fidel Castro, *Informe Central, Primer Congreso del Partido Comunista de Cuba* (Havana: Departamento de Orientación Revolucionaria del Comité Central del Partido Comunista de Cuba, 1975), 29.
2. Chapter 4.
3. Chapter 3.
4. Chapter 6.
5. Chapter 3.
6. Chapter 4.
7. Chapter 5.
8. Chapter 7.
9. Chapter 8.

### Introduction

1. Steven Soderbergh, dir., *Che*, 2008; Rebecca Chavez, dir., *Ciudad en Rojo*, 2009.
2. Liner notes on the DVD of Soderbergh's *Che*.
3. Antoni Kapcia, *Cuba in Revolution: A History since the Fifties* (London: Reaktion, 2008).

### 1. Organized Labor in the 1950s

1. Hobart Spalding, *Organized Labor in Latin America: Historical Case Studies of Workers in Dependent Societies* (New York: New York University Press, 1977), 227–38.
2. Brian H. Pollitt, "The Cuban Sugar Economy and the Great Depression," *Bulletin of Latin American Research* 3/2 (1984): 11.
3. Spalding, *Organized Labor in Latin America*, 227.
4. Robert Whitney, *State and Revolution in Cuba* (Chapel Hill: University of North Carolina Press, 2001), 169.
5. The *Partido Auténtico,* also known as the Cuban Revolutionary Party–Auténtico

or PRC–A, was a liberal nationalist party founded in 1933. Its two most prominent leaders had been presidents Grau San Martín and Prío. By 1952 it had become a byword for corruption.

6.  "El no. 1 de la cordialidad, " *Bohemia* (October 24, 1948), quoted in Enrique de La Osa, *En Cuba: Segundo tiempo 1948–1952* (Havana: Ciencias Sociales, 2005) , 1–5. Gillian McGillivray, *Blazing Cane: Sugar Communities, Class, and State Formation in Cuba, 1868–1959* (Durham, NC: Duke University Press, 2009), 254; Martin Duarte Hurtado, *La maquina torcedora de tabaco y las luchas en torno a su implementación en Cuba* (Havana: Ciencias Sociales, 1973), 242. The weekly magazine *Bohemia* was particularly useful as it covered developments in the labor movement in considerable detail. *Bohemia* also had many other articles on the general political situation and organized written debates between leading political figures that provide a deeper understanding of contemporary arguments. In order to verify these reports, I have cross-checked with other newspapers when they report the same incident, and, once allowance has been made for the political bias of the other journals, found sufficient correlation to make the *Bohemia* accounts believable. The Instituto de Historia de Cuba has a complete run of *Diario de la Marina* for the 1950s and the British Library Newspaper Archive has all the editions of *El Mundo* for the period.

7.  Harold Sims, "Cuba," in Leslie Bethell and Ian Roxborough, eds., *Latin America between the Second World War and the Cold War, 1944–1948* (Cambridge: Cambridge University Press, 1992), 230–36.

8.  U.S. Embassy Havana, Dispatch 2099, *Labor Developments in Cuba 1950,* 1951. References to U.S. Department of State confidential files follow the listing in the most readily available digital source, http://www.latinamericanstudies. org/us–cuba.htm.

9.  U.S. Embassy Havana, Dispatch 170, *Cuban Labor Developments*, 1950.

10.  Sims, *Cuba,* 1992, 217; U.S. Embassy Havana, Dispatch 1309, Membership of the CTC, June 29, 1955.

11.  FO371/103377-AK1016/1 *Communism in Cuba*, 1953; U.S. Embassy Havana, Dispatch 1271, Joint Weeka No. 7 for State, Army, Navy, and Air Departments from SANA, February 13, 1953.

12.  Robert Jackson Alexander, *A History of Organized Labor in Cuba* (Westport, CT: Praeger, 2002), 148; Ricardo Melgar Bao, *El movimiento obrero latinoamericano: Historia de una clase subalterna* (Madrid: Alianza Editoria, 1988), 348–52.

13.  Harry Kelber, "AFL–CIO's Dark Past," *Labor Educator*, November 29, 2004; Phillip Agee, *Inside the Company: CIA Diary* (Harmondsworth: Penguin, 1975), 620.

14.  Serafino Romualdi, "Labor and Democracy in Latin America," *Foreign Affairs* 25/1–4 (April 1947).

15.  Serafino Romualdi, *Presidents and Peons: Recollections of a Labor Ambassador in Latin America* (New York: Funk & Wagnalls, 1967), 5.

16.  FO371/97516–AK1015/11, *ORIT,* 1952.

17.  Instituto de Historia del Movimiento Comunista y de la Revolución Socialista

de Cuba Partido Comunista De Cuba (PCC), *Historia del movimiento obrero cubano, tomo II* (Havana: Editora Política, 1985), 256.

18.  U.S. Department of State Memorandum of Telephone Francisco Aguirre, Serafino Romualdi, John T. Fishburn, *Cuban Labor at the Time of the Coup,* March 17, 1952.

19.  U.S. Embassy Havana, Dispatch 1552, *Mujal Attack on Communists,* March 21, 1952.

20.  U.S. Embassy Havana, Dispatch 1073, *Check-Off of Union Dues Imposed in Sugar Industry,* March 4, 1954.

21.  *Carta Semanal,* March 2, 1955. From 1954, when the Partido Socialista Popular (PSP) newspaper *Hoy* was banned, the Communist Party replaced it with a weekly clandestine paper called *Carta Semanal,* a complete set of which is held in the IHC library. This paper had a regular column, *Lucha de Masas* (Mass Struggle), which gives details of a large number of industrial disputes. A communist militant would interview workers engaged in industrial action and write a story for the *Carta Semanal.* He or she would then return the following week to attempt to sell the paper on the basis of the story in the hope that some new regular readers would be found. Any inaccuracies would have undermined this tactic, so this can be considered a reliable source of information. When accounts of such disputes that appeared in the clandestine *Carta Semanal* are compared with the less frequent references in the mainstream press, such as *El Mundo* or *Diario de la Marina,* there is a high level of consistency when the different political orientations of the sources are taken into account.

22.  Efrén Córdova, *Castro and the Cuban Labor Movement : Statecraft and Society in a Revolutionary Period (1959-1961)* (Lanham, MD: University Press of America, 1987), 55.

23.  Angelina Rojas Blaquier, "El mujalismo en el movimiento obrero cubano," PhD diss., Instituto de Marxismo-Leninismo, Sofia, 1983, 92; U.S. Embassy Havana, Dispatch 1856, *May Day Observed without Major Incident,* May 5, 1952.

24.  U.S. Embassy Havana, Dispatch 1837, *Weeka No. 18 for State, Army, Navy, and Air Departments from SANA.,* May 2, 1952.

25.  Quoted in Rojas, *El Mujalismo,* 99–100 (my translation).

26.  Jana K. Lipman, *Guantánamo: A Working-Class History between Empire and Revolution* (Berkeley: University of California Press, 2009), 75–87; U.S. Embassy Havana, Dispatch 413, *Trouble with Union at Guantanamo Naval Base,* October 20, 1954.

27.  Jorge Ibarra Cuesta, *Prologue to Revolution: Cuba, 1898-1958* (London: L. Rienner Publishers, 1998) , 21–22.

28.  Ibid., 31–32.

29.  Charles Page, "Development of Organized Labor in Cuba," PhD diss., University of California, Berkeley, 1952 , 167.

30.  Jorge Mañach, "El canal y la soberanía", *Bohemia* 47/1 (January 2, 1955); *El Villareño,* January 4, January 6, 1955.

31.  Fulvio A. Fuentes, "La FEU contra el canal Vía-Cuba," *Bohemia* 47/2 (January 9, 1955): 64–65; *Voz del Pueblo,* January 3, 1955.

32. *Carta Semanal,* December 8, 1954.
33. *Carta Semanal,* December 22, 1954.
34. Instituto de Historia de Cuba (IHC) ref:1/8:13/38.1/66A1–A2, *Los portuarios y el canal rompe a Cuba,* December 8t, 1955. The archives of the *Instituto de Historia de Cuba* contain a large collection of leaflets and pamphlets issued by the principal clandestine workers' organizations and local workers' committees.
35. The Partido Ortodoxo (Orthodox Party), also known as the Partido del Pueblo Cubano (Party of the Cuban People), was founded in 1947 by Eduardo Chibás. Its main platform was opposition to corruption.
36. Jorge Ibarra Guitart, *El fracaso de los moderados* (Havana: Editora Política, 2000).
37. The *Hermandad Ferroviaria* (Railway Brotherhood) was divided into *delegaciones,* roughly corresponding to a local branch. Each one covered the workers in a particular area working for the same employer. Each one had a number.
38. Dagmary Durán Cremet, *Movimiento obrero en el sector ferroviario en Santiago de Cuba 1925-1945,* Universidad de Oriente, Santiago de Cuba, Trabajo de diploma, 1988, 51–53.
39. Gary Tennant, *The Hidden Pearl of the Caribbean* (London: Porcupine Press, vol.7, no.3, 2000), 141.
40. This had previously been known as the Partido Bolshevique Leninista (PBR).
41. Gary Tennant, "Dissident Cuban Communism: The Case of Trotskyism, 1932-1965," University of Bradford, UK, 1999, 194–257 and 302–19; Rafael Soler Martínez, "El partido bolchevique leninista," in *II Taller Científico Internacional, Movimiento Obrero y 1ero de Mayo: Memoria,* ed. Marcelo González Bustos, José Alfredo Castellanos Suárez, Luis Hipólito Serrano Pérez, Marco Antonio Anaya Pérez, and Alvaro González Pérez (Texcoco, México: Editorial Futura, 1999), n.p.
42. For more information on the struggles of Realengo 18 see Sección de historia del comité provincial del partido en Guantánamo, *Reseña histórica de Guantánamo* (Santiago de Cuba: Editorial Oriente, 1985), 98–102.
43. Luis Figueras, *Semblanza de Antonio Torres Chedebaux* (n.d.), n.p.
44. Oleg Darushenkov, *Cuba, el camino de la revolución* (Moscow: Editorial Progreso, 1979), 68–80; see also Aviva Chomsky, *A History of the Cuban Revolution* (Chichester, UK: Wiley-Blackwell, 2011), 35–47.
45. Sebastian Balfour, *Castro* (Harlow: Pearson, 2008), 36–38; see also Ernst Halperin, *Fidel Castro's Road to Power* (Cambridge, MA: MIT Center for International Studies, 1970), 69–76.
46. "Continuara su lucha por lograr la amnestia el lider Conrado Rodriguez," *El Villareño,* April 4, 1955.
47. "Quieren matar a Fidel," *La Calle,* May 13, 1955, cited in Rolando Dávila Rodríguez, *Lucharemos hasta el final* (Havana: Oficina de pulicaciones del Consejo de Estado, 2011), 99; *Carta Semanal,* June 8, 1955.
48. Castro, *Manifesto No. 1 del 26 de Julio al pueblo de Cuba* (1955), in Horacio Díaz Pendás, *Textos sobre la historia de Cuba* (Havana: Editorial Pueblo y Educación, 2009), 242–254.

49. Dávila Rodríguez, *Lucharemos hasta el final*, 133.

50. Alcibíades Poveda Diaz, *Propaganda y revolución en Santiago de Cuba 1952–1958* (Santiago de Cuba: Oficina de la Historiador de la Cuidad, 2003), 364; María Antonia Figueroa, "Un centavo del más humilde de los cubanos," *Santiago* (Santiago de Cuba: Universidad de Oriente, no. 99–112, June and September 1975), 102.

51. Gladys Marel García Pérez, *Insurrection and Revolution: Armed Struggle in Cuba, 1952–1959* (Boulder, CO: Lynne Rienner Publishers, 1998), 44–47.

52. Luis Aguilar, *Marxism in Latin America* (New York: Knopf, 1968), 28.

53. Whitney, *State and Revolution in Cuba*, 93–94.

54. Barry Carr, "Mill Occupations and Soviets: The Mobilization of Sugar Workers in Cuba 1917–1933," *Journal of Latin American Studies*, 28/1 (1996): 130.

55. Samuel Farber, *The Origins of the Cuban Revolution Reconsidered* (Chapel Hill: University of North Carolina Press, 2006), 141–42.

56. PCC, *Historia del movimiento obrero cubano II*, 102.

57. Melgar Bao, *El movimiento obrero latinoamericano*, 334.

58. O'Connor, *The Origins of Socialism in Cuba*, 179.

59. *Hoy*, March 11, 1952.

60. K. S. Karol, *Guerrillas in Power: The Course of the Cuban Revolution* (New York: Hill & Wang, 1970), 129.

61. *Oriente*, March 10, 1952.

62. U.S. Embassy Havana, Dispatch 162, *Closure of Communist Newspaper*, July 27, 1953; U.S. Embassy Havana, Dispatch 165, *Attacks against Armed Forces in Santiago de Cuba*. July 28, 1953; U.S. Embassy Havana, Dispatch 1501, *CTC Anti-Communist Resolution*, June 11, 1954; PCC, *Historia del movimiento obrero cubano*, 274–76.

63. Suárez Collection, *Carta Abierta a los Putchistas y Terroristas*, n.d..

64. Newton Briones Montoto and Rita Vilar, *Una hija reivindica a su padre* (Panama: Ruth, 2011), 66–74; Rojas Blaquier, *El Primer Partido Comunista de Cuba 1952–1961*, vol. 3, 59–74; *Carta Semanal*, August 4, 1954; U.S. Embassy Havana, Dispatch 243, *Communist Party*, September 8, 1954.

65. "The Recent Insurrection in Cuba," *Daily Worker*, August 4, 1953.

66. "Fascist Terror Grips Cuba," *Daily Worker*, August 10, 1953.

67. *Carta Semanal*, May 1, May 22, 1954.

68. U.S. Embassy Havana, Dispatch 167, *PSP Election Stand*, August 11, 1954.

69. *Carta Semanal*, November 3, 1954.

70. *Carta Semanal*, October 20, 1954.

71. *Carta Semanal*, November 17, 1954.

72. *Carta Semanal*, November 24, 1954.

73. *Carta Semanal*, November 17. 1954. Sims, in *Cuba*, gives a date of 1948 for the origin of the CDDOs (236), but he only cites Jorge García Montes and Antonio Alonso Avila, *Historia del Partido Comunista de Cuba* (Miami: Ediciones Universal, 1970), 403, which in turn provides no reference. Every other source that gives a date speaks of late 1954 or early 1955.

74. *Carta Semanal*, August 16, 1955.

75.  *Carta Semanal,* April 4, 1956.
76.  Aguilar, *Marxism in Latin America,* 28.
77.  García-Pérez, *Insurrection and Revolution,* 72.

## 2. A Crisis of Productivity

1.   Antonio Santamaría García, *Sin azúcar no hay país: la industria azucarera y la economía cubana (1919–1939)* (Seville: Universidad de Sevilla, 2001); Jonathan Curry-Machado, 'Sin azúcar no hay país': The Transnational Counterpoint of Sugar and Nation in Nineteenth-century Cuba," *Bulletin of Hispanic Studies* 84/1 (January, 2009).
2.   For example, Eric N. Baklanoff, "Cuba on the Eve of the Socialist Transition: A Reassessment of the Backwardness-Stagnation Thesis," 262; and Kirby Smith and Hugo Llorens, "Renaissance and Decay: A Comparison of Socioeconomic Indicators in Pre-Castro and Current-Day Cuba," Cuba in Transition Project, Papers and Proceedings of the 8th Annual Meeting of the Association for the Study of the Cuban Economy (ASCE), vol. 8, Miami, August 6–8, 1998, 247–5.
3.   Jorge Ibarra Cuesta, *Prologue to Revolution: Cuba, 1898–1958* (London: L. Rienner Publishers, 1998), 5–20.
4.   See, for example, Samuel Farber, *The Origins of the Cuban Revolution Reconsidered* (Chapel Hill: University of North Carolina Press, 2006), 71–72; Louis Pérez, *Cuba: Between Reform and Revolution* (Oxford: Oxford University Press, 2006), 189–228; Marifeli Perez Stable, *The Cuban Revolution* (Oxford. OUP, 1999), 15–17; Terence Cannon, *Revolutionary Cuba* (New York: Crowell, 1981), 37–43; Jorge Ibarra Guitart, *El Tratado anglo–cubano de 1905* (Havana: Editora Ciencias Sociales, 2006), 50–59.
5.   Brian H. Pollitt, "The Cuban Sugar Economy and the Great Depression," *Bulletin of Latin American Research* 3/2 (1984): 3.
6.   Ibid., 22.
7.   Brian H. Pollitt, "The Rise and Fall of the Cuban Sugar Economy," *Journal of Latin American Studies* 36/2 (2004): 320–21.
8.   Pérez, *Cuba,* 280.
9.   Oscar Pino Santos, *El asalto a Cuba por la oligarquía financiera yanqui* (Havana: Casa de las Americas, 1973), 198.
10.  Arnaldo Silva Leon, *Cuba y el mercado internacional azucarero* (Havana: Editorial de Ciencias Sociales, 1975), 139.
11.  Robin Blackburn, "Prologue to the Cuban Revolution," *New Left Review* 1/21 (October 1963): 60–61.
12.  Ibarra Cuesta, *Prologue to Revolution,* 21–26.
13.  Oscar Zanetti and Alejandro García, *Caminos para azúcar* (Havana: Editorial de Ciencias Sociales, 1987).
14.  Francis Adams Truslow, *Report on Cuba* (Washington, D.C.: International Bank for Reconstruction and Development, 1951), 856–64.
15.  See, for example, "El pueblo de Cuba debe estar vigilente," *Bohemia,* November 27, 1955, 3; U.S. Embassy Havana, Dispatch 1290, *Cuban Labor Leader*

*Suggests Nationalization of American-Owned Electric and Telephone Companies,* December 18, 1950.

16.  Pedro Machado, "El movimiento obrero henequenero después del golpe de estado del 10 de marzo: Etapa conspirativa de Julián Alemán," 2011, unpublished study of the textile industry in Matanzas Province combined with a biography of Julian Alemán, copy in author's possession; U.S. Embassy Havana, Dispatch 1586, *Labor Difficulties at Textile Plant,* June 30, 1954.

17.  Maria Antonia Marques Dolz and Luis Alberto Fierro, "The Non-Sugar Industrial Bourgeoisie and Industrialization in Cuba, 1920-1959," *Latin American Perspectives* 22/4 (1995): 65-74; Charles Ameringer, *The Cuban Democratic Experience: The Auténtico Years, 1944-1952* (Gainesville: University Press of Florida, 2000), 136.

18.  Marques Dolz and Fierro, "The Non-Sugar Industrial Bourgeoisie and Industrialization," 66.

19.  Enrique Cirules, *El imperio de La Habana* (Havana: Casa de las Américas, 1993).

20.  David J. Gerber, "The United States Sugar Quota Program: A Study in the Direct Congressional Control of Imports," *Journal of Law and Economics* 19/1 (1976): 103-11.

21.  Pérez Stable, *Cuban Revolution,* 14-16.

22.  Raúl Cepero Bonilla, "Política azucarera," *Obras históricas* (Habana: Instituto de Historia, 1963), 321; U.S. Embassy Havana, Dispatch 45, *Review of the 1951 Sugar Crop,* 1951.

23.  Cepero Bonilla, *Política azucarera,* 347.

24.  Ibid., 329-30.

25.  Ibid., 339.

26.  Clara Emma Chávez Alvarez, *Matanzas de rojo y negro 1952-1958* (Matanzas: Ediciones Matanzas, 2007), 16.

27.  "Azúcar," *Bohemia,* January 23, 1955.

28.  José Antonio Guerra, "La industria azucarera cubana: 1932-1957," *Diario de la Marina,* September 15, 1957.

29.  Cepero Bonilla, *Política azucarera,* 310-12.

30.  Chávez Alvarez, *Matanzas de rojo y negro,* 33-34.

31.  Oscar Pino Santos, *Los años 50* (Havana: Editorial Arte y Literatura, 2008), 141.

32.  *Convenio Internacional del Azucar* (Havana: Gaceta Oficial, No. 7645), January 11, 1954.

33.  Boris C. Swerling, "The International Sugar Agreement of 1953," *American Economic Review* 44/5 (December 1954): 845-49.

34.  Swerling, *The International Sugar Agreement of 1953,* 841.

35.  Silva Leon, *Cuba y el mercado internacional azucarero,* 123-43.

36.  *Carteles,* January 16, 1955, 46-49, 97, repr. in Pino Santos, *Los años 50,* 135-40.

37.  Stuart Marshall Jamieson, *Labor Unionism in American Agriculture* (New York: Arno Press, 1976), 243-44.

38. U.S. Embassy Havana, Dispatch 1452, *Campaign against Modification of U.S. Sugar Act*, June 2, 1954.

39. Oscar Pino Santos, "La cuota azucarera de Cuba en Estados Unidos," *Carteles*, Havana, February 13, 1955, 46–48; Alan Dye and Richard Sicotte, "The U.S. Sugar Program and the Cuban Revolution," *Journal of Economic History* 64/3 (2004): 673–704.

40. "Obreros," *Bohemia*, May 14, 1955; Mario del Cueto, "La delegación obrera cubana en Washington," *Bohemia*, May 14, 1955.

41. Carlos Casteñeda, "Azúcar: causa común de todo un pueblo," *Bohemia*, July 3, 1955.

42. Francisco Riveron Hernadez, "Tiempo Muerto," *Bohemia*, August 28, 1955.

43. Agrupación Católica Universitaria, "Encuentra de Trabajadores Rurales, 1956–57," *Economía y Desarrollo*, July–August 1972.

44. Truslow, *Report on Cuba*, 10.

45. Pérez, *Cuba*, 224–30.

46. Truslow, *Report on Cuba*, 60.

47. Ibid., 372.

48. Ibid., 388.

49. Ibid., 98.

50. U.S. Embassy Havana, Dispatch 193, *Labor Developments in Cuba—Second Quarter, 1950.*

51. Interview with Alfredo Menéndez, Ministry of Sugar, PSP member, Havana, March 2009.

52. Truslow, *Report on Cuba*, 309.

53. Interview with Vicente Pérez, PSP trade union organizer, Havana, June 2008.

54. Truslow, *Report on Cuba*, 136.

55. U.S. Embassy Havana, *Labor Developments in Cuba—Second Quarter, 1950.*

56. A survey published in *Bohemia* in January 1952 gave Agramonte a 12-point lead over Hevia and double the score of Batista. Cited in José Luis Padrón and Luis Adrián Betancourt, *Batista: El golpe* (Havana: Ediciones Unión, 2013) .

57. U.S. Embassy Havana, Dispatch 185, *Policies and Prospects of Senator Eduardo Chibas*, August 2, 1951.

58. Carlos Alzugaray, *Crónica de un fracaso imperial* (Havana: Editorial de Ciencias Sociales, 2008), 72–78; U.S. Embassy Havana, Dispatch 1994, *Weeka No. 13 for State, Army, Navy, and Air Departments from SANA; Eduardo Chibas lack of balance*, March 30, 1951.

59. Ameringer, *The Cuban Democratic Experience,* 107.

60. U.S. Embassy Havana, Dispatch 1575, *Weeka No. 4 for State, Army, Navy, and Air Departments from SANA; Eduardo Chibas*, January 26, 1951.

61. Alcibíades Poveda Diaz, *Propaganda y revolución en Santiago de Cuba 1952–1958* (Santiago de Cuba: Oficina de la Historiador de la Cuidad, 2003), 17–48.

62. Rafael García Bárcena, "Elecciones ¿para qué?," *Bohemia*, April 6, 1952.

63. Enrique de La Osa, *En Cuba: Tercer tiempo 1952-1954* (Havana: Ciencias Sociales, 2006), 33–37.

64. Pérez Stable, *The Cuban Revolution*, 52–53; Pérez, *Cuba*, 288–289; Salvador

Morales Pérez, "La dictadura de Batista," *Cuba Now*, February 17, 2009; Morris H. Morley, *Imperial State and Revolution : The United States and Cuba, 1952–1986* (Cambridge: Cambridge University Press, 1987), 143–45.

65. *Havana Post*, March 14, 15, 19, 1952; *El Mundo*, March 14, 15, 19, 1952.
66. *Diario de la Marina*, February 29, 1952, had a special 16-page supplement titled *"Batista es el hombre"* (Batista is the man).
67. Quoted in *Havana Post*, March 16, 1952.
68. FO 371/97516/7-AK1015/33, *Cuban Political Situation*, 1952.
69. FO 371/97516-AK1015/18, *Cuba under General Batista*, 1952.
70. U.S. Embassy Havana, Dispatch 1561, *Recognition*, March 24, 1952.
71. Truslow, *Report on Cuba*, 359.

### 3. The Employers' Offensive

1. FO 371/108990-AK1015/3, *Internal Situation in Cuba*, 1954.
2. Mario del Cueto, "Las condiciones de trabajo hacen insostenible a los Consolidados," *Bohemia*, November 21, 1954.
3. *The Economist*, May 27, 1978, 21–23.
4. U.S. Embassy Havana, Dispatch 15, *Army Occupied Autobuses Modernos and Arrested Marco A. Hirigoyen*, July 3, 1952.
5. U.S. Embassy Havana, Memorandum, *Opposition to Batista Administration*, May 15, 1952.
6. U.S. Embassy Havana, Dispatch 60, *Further Report on Autobuses Modernos Situation and Its Effects on the CTC*, July 11, 1952.
7. FO 371/97516 - AK1015/33, *Political Situation in Cuba*, July 11, 1952.
8. FO 371/97516/7-AK1015/9, *General Batista's Coup d'Etat*, 1952.
9. Oscar Zanetti and Alejandro García, *Sugar and Railroads: A Cuban History 1837–1959* (Chapel Hill: University of North Carolina Press, 1998).
10. Dagmary Durán Cremet, "Movimiento obrero en el sector ferroviario en Santiago de Cuba 1925-1945," Universidad de Oriente, Santiago de Cuba, Research Paper, 1988, 6.
11. London *Times*, November 30, 1950, 10.
12. Oscar Zanetti and Alejandro García, *Caminos para azúcar* (Havana: Editorial de Ciencias Sociales, 1987), 358–59.
13. *Noticias de Hoy*, September 18, 1949, 6.
14. U.S. Embassy Havana, Dispatch 264, *Labor Notes—Habana*, 1950; U.S. Embassy Havana, Dispatch 2494, *Annual Economic Review 1950*, 1951.
15. FO 371/103386, *Negotiations over United Railways of Havana*, 1953.
16. *Noticias de Hoy*, July 3 and 9, 1953.
17. *Noticias de Hoy*, July 17, 1953.
18. See chapter 1.
19. FO371/108990-AK1015/16, *Reports that the Election Campaign Is Passing Quietly*, 1954.
20. Zanetti and García, *Caminos para azúcar*, 370.
21. *El Mundo*, November 9, 1954.

22.   "Los Conflictos Sociales," *Bohemia*, November 12, 1954.
23.   *Voz del Pueblo*, November 13, 1954.
24.   The term literally means "to move at the pace of a turtle."
25.   Cueto, *Las condiciones de trabajo hacen insostenible a los Consolidados*.
26.   *Voz del Pueblo*, November 17–22, 1954; U.S. Embassy Havana, Dispatch 522, *Consolidated Railroad Lay-Offs Suspended*, November 24, 1954.
27.   *Carta Semanal*, January 12, 1955.
28.   *Bohemia*, December 26, 1954, 23; *Voz del Pueblo*, December 21–24 1954.
29.   Raul Martinez Nogales, "Ferrocarriles Consolidados! Una empresa que salvar!," *Bohemia*, December 12, 1954.
30.   *Carta Semanal*, January 3, 12 and 26, 1955.
31.   *Voz del Pueblo*, January 21, 1955.
32.   *Carta Semanal*, February 9, 1955.
33.   "Trabajo," *Bohemia*, February 6, 1955; *El Villareño*, February 4, 1955.
34.   *Carta Semanal*, February 23, 1955.
35.   *Voz del Pueblo*, February 3, 1955.
36.   *Carta Semanal*, February 23, 1955.
37.   *Carta Semanal*, February 16 and 23, 1955.
38.   "Trabajo," *Bohemia*, February 13, 1955; *El Villareño*, February 9, 1955.
39.   *Voz del Pueblo*, February 11, 1955; *Carta Semanal*, February 23, 1955.
40.   *El Villareño*, February 17, 1955.
41.   *Carta Semanal*, March 23, 1955.
42.   *Carta Semanal*, March 30, 1955; *El Villareño*, March 25, 1955.
43.   *Carta Semanal*, June 15, 1955; *Diario de la Marina*, June 8, 1955.
44.   Zanetti and García, *Caminos para Azucar*, 371.
45.   *Voz del Pueblo*, June 8, 1955; *El Villareño*, June 9, 1955.
46.   *Carta Semanal*, May 25 and June 8, 1955; *El Villareño*, June 18, 1955; Rolando Dávila Rodríguez, *Lucharemos hasta el final* (Havana: Oficina de pulicaciones del Consejo de Estado, 2011).
47.   *El Villareño*, June 16, 1955.
48.   *Voz del Pueblo*, June 16, 1955.
49.   "Obreros," *Bohemia*, August 28, 1955; *Diario de la Marina*, July 7, 1955.
50.   U.S. Embassy Havana, Dispatch 1272, *Consolidated Railroads Labor Dispute*, June 20, 1955.
51.   *Carta Semanal*, June 15, 22 and 29, July 13, 1955; *Diario de la Marina*, July 7, 1955; *La Calle*, June 14, 1955.
52.   Author's interview with Vicente Pérez, Communist trade union organizer from Caibarién, Havana, June 21, 2008.
53.   *Carta Semanal*, June 8, 1955.
54.   Angelina Rojas Blaquier, *1955: Crónica de una marcha ascendente* (Havana: Instituto de Historia de Cuba, 1998), 41.
55.   *Diario de la Marina*, July 1, 1955.
56.   *Diario de la Marina*, July 8, 1955; Mario del Cueto, "La opinión obrera," *Bohemia*, July 17, 1955, 64–65.

57. "Bancarios," *Bohemia*, July 24, 1955, 68.
58. Andres Valdespino, "El Problema Bancario: Capitalismo y Justicia Social," *Bohemia*, July 24, 1955, 50.
59. The term literally means "strike of fallen arms."
60. *Carta Semanal*, August 3, 1955; *Diario de la Marina*, July 22, 1955.
61. *Diario de la Marina*, September 2, 1955.
62. *Diario de la Marina*, September 3, 1955.
63. "Bancarios," *Bohemia*, September 11, 1955, 72; U.S. Embassy Havana, Dispatch 106, *Labor Developments*, August 3, 1955.
64. Mario del Cueto, "Una Polémica de Actualidad," *Bohemia*, September 18, 1955.
65. *Carta Semanal*, September 21, 1955.
66. *Diario de la Marina*, September 9, 10, 1955.
67. *Diario de la Marina*, September 7, 1955.
68. *Diario de la Marina*, September 13, 14, 1955.
69. *Diario de la Marina*, September 20, 1955.
70. *Revolución*, February 14, 1959.
71. *Diario de la Marina*, November 1, 1955; *Carta Semanal*, November 9, 1955; U.S. Embassy Havana, Dispatch 466, *Labor Developments: Cuba, August–December 1955*, December 30, 1955.
72. Andres Valdespino, "¿De quien ha sido el triunfo en el conflicto bancario?," *Bohemia*, September 25, 1955.
73. "Telegrafistas," *Bohemia*, August 28, 1955, 78; *Carta Semanal*, August, 24, 31, 1955; U.S. Embassy Havana, Dispatch 151, *Telegraph Strike*, August 23, 1955; *El Villareño*, July 8, August 16, 17, 20, 22. 1955.
74. Mario del Cueto, "En la Rayonera hace tiempo que los obreros están 'levantando parejo,'" *Bohemia*, December 4, 1955, 54–55 (my translation).
75. U.S. Embassy Havana, Dispatch 510, *Henequen Workers Strike*, October 3, 1952.
76. Clara Emma Chávez Alvarez, *Matanzas de rojo y negro 1952–1958* (Matanzas: Ediciones Matanzas, 2007), 94–97.
77. U.S. Embassy Havana, Dispatch 1586, *Labor Difficulties at Textile Plant*, June 30, 1954.
78. *Carta Semanal*, September 28, 1955.
79. Rojas, *1955*, 53–54; "Conflicto." *Bohemia*, October 30, 1955, 69–71.
80. Pedro Machado, "El movimiento obrero henequenero después del golpe de estado del 10 de marzo. Etapa conspirativa de Julián Alemán," unpublished ms., 2011.
81. Alcibíades Poveda Diaz, *Propaganda y revolución en Santiago de Cuba 1952–1958* (Santiago de Cuba: Oficina de la Historiador de la Cuidad, 2003), 59–61.
82. U.S. Embassy Havana, Dispatch 1100, *Student Riots Quelled by Police and Firemen*, January 16, 1953; U.S. Embassy Havana, Dispatch 1271, *Joint Weeka No. 7 for State, Army, Navy, and Air Departments*, February 13, 1953. Mella was a founding member of both the FEU and the Cuban Communist Party. He fled to Mexico to escape the Machado dictatorship but was murdered there,

probably by an assassin employed by the Machado regime. For more details see Christine Hatzky's biography, *Julio Antonio Mella* (Santiago de Cuba: Editorial Oriente, 2008).

83.  *Diario de Cuba,* December 9, 1952.

84.  *Diario de Cuba,* May 3, 1953.

85.  Julio García Oliveras, "El movimiento estudiantil antibatistiano y la ideología de la Revolución," *Ruth Cuadernos 3* (2009): 15.

86.  Poveda Diaz, *Propaganda y revolución,* 91.

87.  "Elecciones en la FEU," *Bohemia,* April 24, 1955, 72.

88.  "La FEU protesta," *Bohemia,* May 15, 1955; U.S. Embassy Havana, Dispatch 1105, *Student Disturbances,* May 10, 1955.

89.  "Registro en la universidad," *Bohemia,* July 17, 1955; U.S. Embassy Havana, Dispatch 127, *University Disturbances,* August 16, 1955.

90.  Julio García Oliveres, *Contra Batista* (Havana: Editoral Ciencias Sociales, 2008), 173; Author's interview with Julio García Oliveres, Havana, May 2014.

91.  Hilda Natalia Berdayes Garcia, *Papeles del Presidente: Documentos y discursos de José Antonio Echeverría Bianchi* (Havana: Casa Editorial Abril, 2006), 56–63.

92.  Frank Josué Solar Cabrales, "El Directorio, revolucionario de su tiempo," *Ruth Cuadernos 3* (2009): 24–50.

93.  García–Oliveres, *Contra Batista,* 231; Cushion interview with Julio García Olivores

94.  "Disturbios estudantiles," *Bohemia,* December 4, 1955.

95.  *Carta Semanal,* December 28, 1955.

96.  Rolando Bonachea and Nelson Valdés, *Cuba in Revolution* (Garden City, N.Y.: Anchor Books, 1972), 56.

97.  "Estudiantes," *Bohemia,* December 18, 1955, 64–65.

98.  "Mantendremos sin tregua nuestra lucha," *Carteles,* January 1, 1955.

99.  U.S. Embassy Havana, Dispatch 1203, *High Court Rules against Payment of Union Dues by Employers,* February 4, 1953.

100. "Azucar," *Bohemia,* January 2, 1955.

101. U.S. Embassy Havana, Dispatch 434, *Labor Developments,* October 25, 1954.

102. FO 371/108990-AK1015/1&3, *Internal Situation in Cuba,* 1954.

103. Mario del Cueto, "El problema social de la zafra," *Bohemia,* January 9, 1955, 52–53.

104. *El Mundo,* December 16, 1954.

105. "Azucar," *Bohemia,* January 23, 1955; *El Villareño,* January 11, 12, 1955.

106. Pardo Llada, "La pobre zafra de 55," *Bohemia,* February 6, 1955, 59; *El Mundo,* January 20, 1955; *El Villareño,* January 21, 1955.

107. U.S. Embassy Havana, Dispatch 955, *Labor Developments,* March 31, 1955.

108. "Obreros," *Bohemia,* January 30, 1955, 65; *El Villareño,* January 22, 1955.

109. The term *"central"* refers to the sugar processing factory at the center of a plantation. This would frequently be surrounded by workers' accommodation, the company offices, and the company store, effectively making a large village.

110. "Trabajo," *Bohemia,* February 6, 1955.

111.  *El Villareño*, March 15, 1955.

112.  *El Villareño*, January 24, 1955.

113.  FO 371/108990-AK1015/3, *Possible Labor Developments*, 1954.

114.  "Trabajo," *Bohemia*, February 24, 1955.

115.  Gillian McGillivray, *Blazing Cane: Sugar Communities, Class, and State Formation in Cuba, 1868–1959* (Durham, NC: Duke University Press, 2009), 261–63; Díaz, "La huelga que dicidieron las mujeres," in *Memorias de un Viejo Mundo Azucarero*, ed. Colectivo de Authores (Havana: Editorial de Cíencias Sociales, 1990), 60–167. McGillivray based her research on interviews with survivors, as did Díaz in his earlier account; their versions of events tally with contemporary details in *Carta Semanal*.

116.  Dates in first column are for issues of *Carta Semanal*, unless specified otherwise.

117.  U.S. Embassy Havana, Dispatch 916, *Congressman Detained by Military*, March 22, 1955.

118.  *Carta Semanal*, January 3, 1955.

119.  McGillivray, *Blazing Cane*, 261-63.

120.  Literally, "dead time," as the period outside the sugar harvest period was known, when sugar workers had no income from their trade and had to subsist as best they could on other employment, subsistence farming, etc.

121.  *Carta Semanal*, August 24 and September 14, 1955; *El Villareño*, September 3, 1955.

122.  "Azucareros," *Bohemia*, September 11, 1955, 69; *El Villareño*, October 28, 1955.

123.  Carlos Marquez Sterling, "Injusticia con el Trabajador del Azúcar," *Bohemia*, April 17, 1955; Mario del Cueto, "Otro Escándalo en el Retiro Azucarero," *Bohemia*, April 17, 1955; "Azúcar," *Bohemia*, June 26, 1955; "Obreros" *Bohemia*, July 10, 1955, 67; Carlos Casteñeda, "Azúcar: causa común de todo un pueblo," *Bohemia*, July 3, 1955.

124.  *Superproducción* is the term for the increase in production due to mechanization. In the face of such mechanization it was a common demand of Cuban workers to be paid the same as before the new machinery arrived. This was strongly contested by the employers for whom mechanization was aimed at reducing the wage bill.

125.  *Carta Semanal*, November 23, 1955.

126.  "Obreros," *Bohemia*, January 1, 1956, 68.

127.  Author's interview with Alfredo Menendez, economist at the Ministry of Sugar who had been a member of both the PSP and the *M-26-7*, March 8, 2009.

128.  Samuel Feijoo, "Desocupación endémica, el ciclo del tiempo muerto," *Bohemia*, October 7, 1956.

129.  Conrado Rodriguez, "La industrial azucarera ha obtenido fabulosas ganancias," *Bohemia*, December 18, 1955, 71.

130.  "Obreros," *Bohemia*, January 8, 1956; José Lorenzo Fuentes, "La huelga azucarera," *Bohemia*, January 8, 1956; Rojas-Blaquier, *1955*, 68–76.

131.  Julio García Oliveres, *José Antonio Echeverría: la lucha estudiantil contra Batista* (Havana: Editora Política, 1979), 258.

132. See for example Caridad Massón Sena, "Proyectos y accionar del Partido Socialista Popular entre 1952 y 1958," in *1959: Una rebellón contra las oligarquías y los dogmas revolucionarios,* ed. Jorge Ibarra Guitart (Panamá: Ruth, 2009), 233.

133. *Carta Semanal,* January 11, 1956.

134. Conrado Bequer Diaz, "Vendió Mujal las demandas azucaras," *Bohemia,* January 22, 1956, 61.

135. Mario del Cueto, "El pleito sindical de los trabajadores azucareros," *Bohemia,* January 15, 1956; "Obreros," *Bohemia,* January 15, 1956, 61.

136. "Obreros," *Bohemia,* January 22, 1956.

137. Andres Valdespino, "Mas allá del Diferencial," *Bohemia,* January 22, 1956, 55.

138. Economist Intelligence Unit (EIU), "Cuba, Dominican Republic and Puerto Rico," *Quarterly Economic Review* 9 (1955), and 13 (1956).

139. Francis Adams Truslow, *Report on Cuba* (Washington, D.C.: International Bank for Reconstruction and Development, 1951), 391–402.

140. Author's interview with Alfredo Menéndez.

141. Angelina Rojas Blaquier, "El mujalismo en el movimiento obrero cubano," PhD diss., Instituto de Marxismo-Leninismo, Sofia, 1983, 84.

142. *Carta Semanal,* May 22, 1954.

143. *Carta Semanal,* February 9, 1955.

144. *El Mundo,* January 30, 1955.

145. *Carta Semanal,* February 16, 1955; *El Mundo,* January 30, 1955; U.S. Embassy Havana, Dispatch 955, *Labor Developments,* March 31, 1955; *El Villareño,* February 9, 1955.

146. *Carta Semanal,* March 16, 1955.

147. *El Villareño,* February 9, 1955.

148. Alejandro de la Fuente, *A Nation for All : Race, Inequality, and Politics in Twentieth-Century Cuba* (Chapel Hill, NC, and London: University of North Carolina Press, 2001), 242; *Carta Semanal,* March 30, 1954.

149. *Carta Semanal,* April 6, 1955.

150. "Azucar," *Bohemia,* January 23, 1955; *El Mundo,* January 7, 1955.

151. *Carta Semanal,* April 13, 1955.

152. *Carta Semanal,* February 23, 1955.

153. U.S. Department of Agriculture Commodity Stabilization Service Sugar Division, *Sugar Reports,* no. 83, March 1959.

154. Jerry Hagelberg, *Bulk Loading of Sugar in Cuba,* email to author, November 16, 2009.

155. Fidel Castro, *Speech at the Dedication of a Bulk Sugar Terminal,* Puerto Carupano, Las Tunas Province, January 20, 1978.

156. Truslow, *Report on Cuba,* 856–64.

157. Jean Stubbs, *Tobacco on the Periphery : A Case Study in Cuban Labour History, 1860-1958* (Cambridge: Cambridge University Press, 1985), 153.

158. *Carta Semanal,* February 15 and 29, March 21, 1956.

159. U.S. Embassy Havana, Dispatch 551, *Labor Notes on Havana,* 1950.

160. Ramón Pérez Linares, "La agro-manufactura tabacalera de la antigua provincia

de Las Villas y las principales luchas de sus trabajadores en el periodo de 1940 a 1058," PhD diss., Universidad Central 'Marta Abreu' de Las Villas, Santa Clara, 2005, 95–96; U.S. Embassy Havana, Dispatch 885, *"Cuban Labor Developments,"* 1950.

161. U.S. Embassy Havana, Dispatch 1138, *Communist-Sponsored Labor Meeting Broken Up by Police,* 1950.

162. Francisco Romero Ríos, "Aspectos fundamentales de la situación objetiva de la clase obrera en Pinar del Río y algunas de sus luchas en 1947–52," PhD diss., Universidad Central 'Marta Abreu' de Las Villas, Santa Clara, 1986, 104–7.

163. Jean Stubbs, "The Cuban Tobacco Industry and Its Workings: 1860–1958," PhD diss., University of London, Birkbeck College, 1975, 280–81; Ramón Pérez Linares, "La lucha de los tabacaleros villareños contra la mecanización integral del torcido (1952-1958)," *Islas* 138 (October–December 2003): 96–101.

164. Pérez Linares, *La lucha de los tabacaleros villareños,* 145–46.

165. U.S. Embassy Havana, Dispatch 19, *Six Communists Selected to the Executive Committee of the Tobacco Workers Federation,* July 3, 1953; U.S. Embassy Havana, Dispatch 434, *Labor Developments,* October 25, 1954; "Obreros," *Bohemia,* October 4, 1954, 82.

166. In Spanish: *"un fondo para utilizar con carácter 'persuasivo.'"*

167. "Tabaco," *Bohemia,* October 16, 1955; *Carta Semanal,* November 23, 1955.

168. *Carta Semanal,* February 15, 29, March 7, 21, April 11, 1956.

169. Archivo Histórico Provincial de Sancti Spiritus, Fondo 70, Expediente 130–C, Legajo 3, *La lucha de los tabacaleros cabaiguanenses contra el Mujalismo durante los años 1956 y 1957,* 1994.

170. Pérez Linares, "La agro-manufactura tabacalera de Las Villas," 106.

171. Chávez Alvarez, *Matanzas de rojo y negro,* 34.

172. Herminio Portell-Vilá, "El puerto más caro del Mundo," *Bohemia,* January 22, 1950, 45, 112; U.S. Embassy Havana, Dispatch 75, *Labor Notes on Havana,* 1950.

173. *Prensa Universal,* December 29, 1955, cited in María Modesta Coya, "El movimiento obrero en Santiago de Cuba 1952-1958," Universidad de Oriente, Santiago de Cuba, Research Paper, 1982, 25.

174. Gladys Marel García Pérez, *Insurrección y Revolución (1952-1959)* (Havana: Ediciones Unión, 2006), 105–6.

175. Marifeli Pérez Stable, *The Cuban Revolution* (Oxford: OUP, 1999), 55.

176. *¡Las máquinas salen, aunque sean bañadas con sangre!*

177. Mayda Pérez Garcia, Angel E. Cabrera-Sánchez and Luis Vázquez-Muñoz, *Invierno Caliente* (Ciego de Avila: Archivo Histórico Provincial de Ciego de Ávila, 2008), 105.

### 4. Workers Take Stock

1. Epigraph: Chris Harman, "1984 and the Shape of Things to Come," *International Socialism* 2/29 (Summer 1985): 115–16.

2. Vilma Espín, "Déborah," *Santiago* 18–19 (June and September 1975): 67–68.

3.    Nydia Sarabia, "...y mi honda es la de David," *Bohemia*, July 28, 1967, 7–8.

4.    Gladys Marel García Pérez, *Insurrección y Revolución 1952–1959* (Havana: Ediciones Unión, 2006), 72.

5.    Espín, "Déborah," 73.

6.    "Detenidos por el SIM 3 Obreros Acusados de Actividades Comunistas," *Voz del Pueblo*, July 4, 1955.

7.    This isolation has helped to obscure the history of that movement from later researchers. Jana Lipman is the major exception, in *Guantánamo: A Working-Class History between Empire and Revolution* (Berkeley: University of California Press, 2009), 134–43. Cuban historians have not shown significantly greater interest, and other than occasional scattered references, we have to rely on the work of local historians for published details: See Sección de historia del comité provincial del partido en Guantánamo, *Reseña histórica de Guantánamo* (Santiago de Cuba: Editorial Oriente, 1985). The report on the Guantánamo workers' movement by the Comisión Nacional de Historia (National History Commission) has never been published and exists only in manuscript: Comisión Nacional de Historia Departamento Obrero II Frente Oriental "Frank Pais," *Provincia Guantánamo* (Havana: manuscript, 1980). We are thus fortunate that the University of Oriente in Santiago ran a project in the 1980s, which required some final-year history undergraduates to write their dissertations on the struggles of the 1950s using interviews with surviving militants.

8.    Antero Regalado, *Las luchas campesinas en Cuba* (Havana: Editora Política, 1979), 65 77; Martha Albys García Faure and Margarita Canseco Aparicio, *Algunas Manifestaciones Políticas en Guantánamo* (Guantánamo: El Mar y la Montana, 2009), 41.

9.    *Carta Semanal*, March 23, 1955.

10.    *Voz del Pueblo*, February 7, 1955.

11.    *Carta Semanal*, July 20, 1955.

12.    Author's interview with Luis Figures of the Casa de la Historia, Guantánamo, April 1, 2009.

13.    Ismael Alonzo Coma, "El Movimiento 26 de Julio en Guantánamo," Research Paper, University of Oriente, Santiago de Cuba, 1981, 31; Comisión Nacional de Historia, *Provincia Guantánamo*, 5–7; Luis Figueras Pérez and Marisel Salles Fonseca, *La lucha clandestina en Guantánamo, 1952–1958* (Guantánamo: Editorial El Mar y La Montña, 2011), 31–34.

14.    Sección de historia, *Reseña histórica de Guantánamo*, 123–25.

15.    Brian Pearce, "Some Past Rank-and-File Movements," *Labour Review* 4/1 (May 1959): 13–24.

16.    *Carta Semanal*, July 18, 1956.

17.    Comisión Nacional de Historia, *Provincia Guantánamo*, 4–7.

18.    Gillian McGillivray, *Blazing Cane: Sugar Communities, Class, and State Formation in Cuba, 1868–1959* (Durham, NC: Duke University Press, 2009), 140.

19.    Coma, "El Movimiento 26 de Julio en Guantánamo," based on interviews with Enrique Soto, Luis Lara, Antonio Torres, Octavio Louit, Caridad Rosa Rossell, Benito Bell, Bernado Betancourt, and workers in *central* Ermita.

20.   Author's interview with Luis Figueras Pérez of the Casa de Historia, Guantánamo, 2010, following his own interviews with surviving veterans.

21.   *Carta Semanal,* January 11, 1956.

22.   IHC 1/8:13A1/6.1/1.1/1 CDDO de Güines, December 12, 1954; IHC 1/8:13A1/3.1/1 CDDO de Trabajadores Azucareros de la Provincia de la Habana, January 1955; IHC 1/8:13A1/4.1/1 CDDO de la Habana *"Todos a la plenaria nacional azucarera,"* January 1955.

23.   IHC 1/8:13A1/2.1/1.1/1 Comité en Defensa de los Demandas de la Zafra de 1955, *";Alerta!,"* January 1955; *El Mundo,* January 20, 1955.

24.   *Carta Semanal,* April 4, August 29, 1956.

25.   IHC 1/8:13A1/1.1/31–33 CNDDO, *"Informe a la reunión nacional del CNDDO,"* October 1956.

26.   IHC 1/8:13A1/9.1/1 CDDO de Matanzas, December 29th 1955; IHC 1/8:13A1/9.1/2 CDDO de Matanzas, September 30, 1956; IHC 1/8:13A1/11.1/1 CDDO de Las Villas, February 1, 1956; IHC 1/8:13A1/13.1/1–2 CDDO de Pieles, Santa Clara, n/d; IHC 1/8:13A1/15.1/1–2 CDDO de Puerta Padre, November 1956.

27.   *Carta Semanal,* July 25, 1956; IHC 1/8:13A1/5.1/4–13 CNDDO, *"¿Qué es un comité de defensa de las demandas obreras?,"* 1956.

28.   IHC 1/8:13A1/5A1/1–4, CDDO, *"A todos los trabajadores de los Ómnibus Aliados,"* July 1956.

29.   IHC 1/8:13A1/12.1/1–2, CDDO, *"Reunión azucarera de Las Villas,"* October 14, 1956.

30.   See, for example, Harold Sims, "Cuban Labor and the Communist Party, an Interpretation," *Cuban Studies* 15/1 (Winter, 1985): 50–56; Samuel Farber, "The Cuban Communists in the Early Stages of the Cuban Revolution: Revolutionaries or Reformists?," *Latin American Research Review* 18/1 (1983): 59–61; Hugh Thomas, *Cuba, or, the Pursuit of Freedom* (New York: Da Capo Press, 1998), 923, 929, 981.

31.   *Bohemia,* January 22, 1956, 55.

32.   *Carta Semanal* special issue, February 1956.

33.   *Carta Semanal,* January 18, 25, 1956; special issue, February 1956.

34.   *Carta Semanal,* special issue, February 1956.

35.   IHC 1/8:13/A1/1.1/27 CNDDO, *"Carta Abierta,"* October 12, 1956.

36.   *El Mundo,* November 22, 1956; U.S. Embassy Havana, Dispatch 651, *Sugar; Conrado Becquer* [sic]; *CTC,* April 3, 1957; U.S. Embassy Havana, Dispatch 678, *Labor Briefs for March, 1957: Sugar Wage Increase 6 Percent,* April 12, 1957.

37.   Multiple examples in *Carta Semanal* during April 1955.

38.   Theodore Draper, *Castroism: Theory and Practice* (London: Pall Mall, 1965), 28–29; Angelina Rojas Blaquier, *El Primer Partido Comunista de Cuba 1952–1961,* vol. 3 (Santiago de Cuba: Editorial Oriente, 2011), 180–204.

39.   *Carta Semanal,* August 15, 1956.

40.   *Carta Semanal,* August 8, 1956.

41.   Archivo Provincial Histórico de Matanzas (APHM) Fondo Tribunal de

Urgencia, Legajo 161, Caja 128, *A los trabajadores*, 1956, cited in García Pérez, *Insurrection and Revolution*, 72, 122; Robert Whitney, *State and Revolution in Cuba* (Chapel Hill: University of North Carolina Press, 2001), 101–48.

42. FO 371/67972-AK1689/14, *Labor and Communism in Cuba*, 1948.
43. *Carta Semanal*, March 14, 1956,; Andres Valdespino, "Agresión totalitaria a la libertad sindical," *Bohemia*, March 18, 1956.
44. *Carta Semanal*, March 14, 1956; *El Villareño*, March 5, 1956; Andres Valdespino, "Agresión totalitaria a la libertad sindical," *Bohemia*, March 18, 1956.
45. *Carta Semanal*, October 26, 1956; Mario del Cueto, "El 26 de julio en la dirección sindical," *Bohemia*, January 11, 1959.
46. *El Villareño*, January 4, 1956.
47. "Obreros," *Bohemia*, January 15, 1956, 61–65; "Obreros," *Bohemia*, January 22, 1956; *Voz del Pueblo*, January 5, 1956; Mario del Cueto, "El pleito sindical de los trabajadores azucareros," *Bohemia*, January 15, 1956; "Huelga de Hambre," *Bohemia*, January 27, 1956, 65–70; U.S. Embassy Havana, Dispatch 536, *Conrado Rodriguez; Conrado Becquer* [sic], January 31, 1956.
48. "Obreros," *Bohemia*, January 15, 1956, 62.
49. *El Villareño*, January 7, 1956.
50. *Carta Semanal*, February 1, 1956; "CTC," *Bohemia*, January 27, 1956; *El Villareño*, January 12, 14, February 3, 1956.
51. Archivo Provincial de Camagüey, Fondo Movimiento Obrero, Expediente 59, Legajo 2.
52. *"Que quieren? Los sellos del buen cotizante no son para repartirlos entre los que nos hacen la oposición sindical. . . . Si los enemigos se deciden por la violencia el día de las elecciones, correrá la sangre, pero no la nuestra, sino la de ellos."* From "Obreros" *Bohemia*, September 2, 1956. My translation.
53. *Carta Semanal*, October 26, 1956.
54. Samuel Feijoo, "Obreros de la Zafra," *Bohemia*, February 12, 1956; "Obreros" *Bohemia*, September 2, 1956, 61–2; *Carta Semanal*, August 22, 29, 1956; Eusebio Mujal, "Verdad contra infamia," *Bohemia*, October 14, 1956; "Obreros" *Bohemia*, October 14, 1956, 72–73.
55. U.S. Embassy Havana, Dispatch 10, *Labor Developments–Cuba: January–June 1956*, July 6, 1956; U.S. Embassy Havana, Dispatch 509, *Labor Briefs for January 1957*, February 19, 1957.
56. *El Villareño*, January 7, 1956.
57. Antonio Bosque, "*1957*, Una etapa de Avance Progresivo del Movimiento Obrero Cubano," *Revista Azúcar*, December 1957, 31.
58. Andres Valdespino, "El decreto 538: ¿contra el comunismo o contra la libertad?," *Bohemia*, April 7, 1956, 51, 99.
59. U.S. Embassy Havana, Dispatch 630, *Two Labor Federations Oppose Decree 538*, March 28, 1957.
60. U.S. Embassy Havana, Dispatch 486, *Angel Cofiño Replaced by Oscar Salamea as President of Electrical Workers' Retirement Fund*, February 7, 1957.
61. "Obreros," "Conflictos sociales," *Bohemia*, April, 21 1957; "Obreros," *Bohemia*, April 28, 1957; *Carta Semanal* (April, May 5, May 22, 1957).

62. "Obreros," *Bohemia*, June 2, 1956, 91, 92; U.S. Embassy Havana, Dispatch 831, *Chronology re Intervention of the Federation of Electric, Gas and Water Plants*, June 5, 1957.

63. "Obreros," *Bohemia*, April 28, 1956, 85–86, 94–95.

64. Lisandro Otero Gonzalez, "¡La confraternidad humana no permite discriminación alguna!," *Bohemia*, April 28, 1957.

65. "Santiago de Cuba," "Desembarco," "Los Sucesos de Santiago," *Bohemia*, December 9, 1956.

66. Rafael Taquechel and María Poumier, *Juan Taquechel López y el movimiento obrero en Santiago de Cuba* (Santiago de Cuba: Colleción El Cobre, 2009), 120.

67. Coya, "El movimiento obrero en Santiago," 79.

68. Taquechel and Poumier, *Juan Taquechel*, 120–127.

69. IHC 1/8:13/38.1/1–66/A3–A4, CDDO de Santiago de Cuba, *Carta Abierta*, 1957; U.S. Embassy Havana, Dispatch 509, *Labor Briefs for January 1957*, February 19, 1957.

70. Comisión Nacional de Historia, *Provincia Guantánamo*, 7, 8; Coma, "El Movimiento 26 de Julio en Guantánamo" 34–37; Sección de historia, *Reseña histórica de Guantánamo*, 125–31.

71. Comisión Nacional de Historia, *Provincia Guantánamo*, 7, 8, 17,18; Coma, "El Movimiento 26 de Julio en Guantánamo," 37–39; Luis Figueras, *Semblanza de Antonio Torres*; Gary Tennant, interview with Octavio Louit, revolutionary railwayman from Guantánamo, August 13, 1997.

72. Christian Chevandier, *Cheminots en grève: la construction d'une identité (1848–2001)* (Paris: Maisonneuve & Larose, 2002), 204–18.

73. FO 371/126467 – AK1015/1, *Reports on the unrest in Cuba*, January 1957.

74. U.S. Embassy Havana, Dispatch 610, *Labor Briefs for February 1957; Dissension among Electrical Plant Workers*, March 21, 1957; U.S. Embassy Havana, Dispatch 678, *Labor Briefs for March, 1957; Electrical Workers Attempt to Withdraw from the CTC*, April 12, 1957; U.S. Embassy Havana, Dispatch 709, *Labor Problem of Electrical Workers Continues*, April 24, 1957; U.S. Embassy Havana, Telegram 548, *Cuban Electric Company Strike*, May 16, 1957; U.S. Embassy Havana, Telegram 560; *Government Military Interventor at Electric Generating Plants and Substations*, May 22, 1957; U.S. Embassy Havana, Telegram 565, *Cofiño May Attempt to Create Blackout over Weekend To Be Coordinated with Insurrectionary Activities of "26 of July" Movement*, May 24, 1957; U.S. Embassy Havana, Dispatch 807; *Labor Briefs for April 1957*, May 27, 1957; U.S. Embassy Havana, Telegram 577, *Cofiño in Hiding Called Off Strike; Cables Dynamited at Suarez Street*, May 29, 1957; U.S. Embassy Havana, Dispatch 831, *Labor Chronology re Intervention of the Labor Federation of Electric, Gas and Water Plants*, June 5, 1957.

#### 5. Responses to State Terror

1. FO 371/126467-AK1015/8, *Political Situation in Cuba*, February 22, 1957.

2. FO371/126467-AK1015/28, *Review of the Opposition Parties in Cuba*, June 28, 1957.

3.    See, for example, Oleg Darushenkov, *Cuba, el camino de la revolución* (Moscow: Editorial Progreso, 1979), 163–74; Partido Comunista De Cuba (PCC) Instituto de Historia del Movimiento Comunista y de la Revolución Socialista de Cuba, *Historia del movimiento obrero cubano*, vol. 2 (Havana: Editora Política, 1985), 320–33; Terence Cannon, *Revolutionary Cuba* (New York: Crowell, 1981), 76–91.

4.    Theodore Draper claims that there was even a division of opinion in the leadership but, as before, there is no real evidence as discipline was maintained: Theodore Draper, *Castroism: Theory and Practice* (London: Pall Mall, 1965), 31.

5.    *Carta Semanal*, July 11, August 22, 29, 1956.

6.    *Carta Semanal*, July 18, August 8, 1956.

7.    *Carta Semanal*, February 20, 1957.

8.    ANC 7-191-1391, *Trabajadores de La Concordia Textil SA*, March 26, 1957.

9.    *El Impacial*, March 9, 1957.

10.    Gladys Marel García Pérez, *Insurrección y Revolución (1959)* (Havana: Ediciones Unión, 2006), 104.

11.    *Carta Semanal*, November 28, December 12, 1956.

12.    *Carta Semanal*, January 9, 16, 1957.

13.    *Carta Semanal*, February 20, 1957.

14.    Marcelo Parrado Falco and José Lino Pérez González, "Breve relato histórico del surgimiento, fundación y desarrollo de los gremios, uniones y federaciones del sector marítimo-portuario de Caibarién," in *Los obreros hacen y escriben su historia* (Havana: Editorial de Ciencias Sociales, 1979), 162.

15.    IHC 1/8:13A1/1.1/31-33 CNDDO, *"Reunión nacional,"* October 1956.

16.    *Carta Semanal*, January 2, 16, 1957.

17.    *Carta Semanal*, March 29, 1957.

18.    *Carta Semanal*, April 17, May 29, November 20, 1957.

19.    FO 371/97516-AK1015/33, *Political Situation in Cuba*, 1952.

20.    IHC 1/8:13A1/5A1/1-4 CDDO, *"A todos los trabajadores de los Ómnibus Aliados,"* July 1956.

21.    IHC 1/8:13A1/1.1/31-33 CNDDO, *"Reunión nacional,"* October 1956.

22.    IHC 1/8:13A1/1.1/22 CNDDO, *"Llamamiento a los obreros azucareros,"* July 1956; IHC 1/8:13A1/1.1/23 CNDDO, *"Trabajador azucarero,"* October 4, 1956; IHC 1/8:13A1/1.1/49 CNDDO, *";Trabajadores azucareros!,"* March 20, 1957; IHC 1/8:13A1/12.1/1-2 CNDDO, *"Reunión azucareros de Las Villas,"* October 14, 1956; IHC 1/8:13A1/12.1/1-2 CDDO de Puerto Padre *"A los obreros azucareros,"* November 1956.

23.    *El Mundo*, December 2, 1956.

24.    U.S. Embassy Havana, Dispatch 610, *Labor Briefs for February 1957*, March 21, 1957.

25.    *Carta Semanal*, September 11, 1956.

26.    *Carta Semanal*, February 20, March 6, 1956.

27.    Eric N. Baklanoff, "Cuba on the Eve of the Socialist Transition: A Reassessment of the Backwardness-Stagnation Thesis," Papers and Proceedings of the 8th Annual Meeting of the Association for the Study of the Cuban Economy

(ASCE), Miami, August 6–8, 1998, 262; Kirby Smith and Hugo Llorens, "Renaissance and Decay: A Comparison of Socioeconomic Indicators in Pre-Castro and Current-Day Cuba," *Cuba in Transition,* Papers and Proceedings of the 8th Annual Meeting of the Association for the Study of the Cuban Economy (ASCE), vol. 8, August 6–8, 1998, 247–59.

28. Morris H. Morley, *Imperial State and Revolution: The United States and Cuba, 1952–1986* (Cambridge: Cambridge University Press, 1987), 39.

29. ANC 5-74-868, *PSP al Tribunal Supremo,* December 28, 1956.

30. *Carta Semanal,* January 2, 9, 1957; "Navidades de Sangre," *Bohemia,* January 6, 1957.

31. U.S. Embassy Havana, Dispatch 389, *26 Killed in Holguin; Sabotage at Chaparra and Delicias Sugar Mills; Shooting at Nicaro,* January 3, 1957.

32. FO371/126466-AK1012/2, *Report on Leading Personalities in Cuba,* January 1957.

33. FO 371/126467-AK1015/3, *Effect of Decree Suspending Constitutional Guarantees,* January 1957.

34. *Carta Semanal,* January 9, 1957.

35. Alcibíades Poveda Diaz, *Propaganda y revolución en Santiago de Cuba 1952–1958* (Santiago de Cuba: Oficina de la Historiador de la Cuidad, 2003), 220–24.

36. *Carta Semanal,* January 23, April 10, 1957.

37. *Carta Semanal,* January 16, 1957.

38. Lucrecia Ramos Estives, "Apoyo de la mujer santiaguera a la lucha contra la tiranía de Batista de 1952–1958," Research Paper, Universidad de Oriente, Santiago de Cuba, 1984, 22.

39. *New York Times,* August 1, 1957, 8; Ramos Estives, "Apoyo de la mujer santiaguera a la lucha contra la tiranía de Batista"; U.S. Embassy Havana, Dispatch 93, *Ambassador Smith Holds Press Conference,* July 31, 1957; U.S. Embassy Havana, Dispatch 107, *Ambassador Visits Oriente,* August 7, 1957.

40. *Carta Semanal,* April 10, October 23, November 6, 1957.

41. *Carta Semanal,* January 28, February 6, 1958.

42. Oscar Zanetti and Alejandro García, *Caminos para azúcar* (Havana: Editorial de Ciencias Sociales, 1987), 375–77.

43. *Bohemia,* March 3, 1957, 9.

44. *Carta Semanal,* January 28, 1958; María Modesta Coya, "El movimiento obrero en Santiago de Cuba 1952–1958, Universidad de Oriente," Research Paper, Santiago de Cuba, 1982, 76.

45. K. S. Karol, *Guerrillas in Power: The Course of the Cuban Revolution* (New York: Hill & Wang, 1970), 150; *Carta Semanal,* February 20, 1956.

46. Author's interview with María Antúnez, former PSP militant, Manzanillo, March 2009.

47. *Carta Semanal,* March 27, 1957.

48. Sección de historia del comité provincial del partido en Guantánamo, *Reseña histórica de Guantánamo* (Santiago de Cuba: Editorial Oriente, 1985), 131.

49. Ismael Alonzo Coma, "El Movimiento 26 de Julio en Guantánamo," Research Paper, University of Oriente, Santiago de Cuba, 1981, 46, 54.

50.  U.S. Embassy Havana, Dispatch 455, *Cuban Government Intervenes Communist Newspaper Hoy*, 1950.

51.  Javier Rodriguez, "José Antonio Echeverría y la Clase Obrera," *Bohemia*, March 10, 1967, 55; *Carta Semanal*, August 28, 1957.

52.  Reinaldo Suárez Suárez, of the Universidad de Oriente, generously gave me access to his personal collection of documents from the period, among which were a large number of leaflets published by the local branch of the PSP from the Havana suburb of Luyanó. (Henceforth, Suarez Collection.)

53.  *Bolos*, Suarez Collection, January 8, 13, 16, 18, 1958.

54.  "Compañeros," *Comité Revolucionario de Luyanó*, Suarez Collection, October 1957.

55.  "El Viernes 25," *Comité Revolucionario de Luyanó*, Suarez Collection, October 1957.

56.  *Carta Semanal*, October 23, November 6, 1957.

57.  "Compañeros," *Comité Revolucionario de Luyanó*, Suarez Collection, October 1957.

58.  IHC 1/8:13/26.1/1, Comité de Frente Unico de Trabajadores de la Rosalia, "¡Trabajadores!," 1958.

59.  IHC 1/8:13/27.1/1, Comité Obrero Revolucionario de San Miguel del Padrón, "¡Obreros Hermanos!," March 1958.

60.  Samuel Farber, *The Origins of the Cuban Revolution Reconsidered* (Chapel Hill: University of North Carolina Press, 2006), 156.

61.  Delio Orozco's interview with Ñico Torres-Head of the Frente Obrero Nacional, April 29, 1990.

62.  IHC 1/17/3/21/7-14, *Vanguardia Obrera* "Obrero ¡Hacia el FON!," December 5, 1957.

63.  Oscar Zanetti and Alejandro García, *Sugar and Railroads: A Cuban History 1837-1959* (Chapel Hill: University of North Carolina Press, 1998), 394.

64.  Yolanda Portuondo Lopez, *José Tey Saint-Blanchard, su última cita de honor* (Santiago: Editorial Oriente, 2006), 193–94.

65.  The University of Oriente organized a series of projects in the 1970s and 1980s requiring final-year history students to base their papers on interviews with surviving rebel activists. The records of the original interviews are lost, but the manuscripts are still available and have proved to be an extremely valuable source of information.

66.  Gabriela Mendoza Bú, "El movimiento 26 de julio en el sector ferroviario en Santiago de Cuba," Research Paper, Universidad de Oriente, Santiago de Cuba, 1988, 32–36.

67.  Facundo Alexis Rodrígiez López and Diosdado Martínez Rodríguez, "La huelga de 9 de abril de 1958 en la cuidad de Camagüey," Universidad de Oriente, Santiago de Cuba, 1984.

68.  Miriam Reyes Pérez and Ramón Batista López, "El movimiento 26 de julio en los municipios de Tunas y Puerto Padre," Research Paper, Universidad de Oriente, Santiago de Cuba, 53.

69.  Coya, "El movimiento obrero en Santiago," 31–34.

70.   *Carta Semanal,* August 7, 1957.

## 6. Two Strikes

1.   Oscar Zanetti and Alejandro García, *Caminos para azúcar* (Havana: Editorial de Ciencias Sociales, 1987), 372.

2.   My interviews with Francisco Monserrat, Alfredo Menendez, Alcibíades Poveda Díaz, Vicente Pérez, Francis Velázquez, and María Antúnez. I also attended a meeting of veterans organized by the Biblioteca Elvia Carpe in Santiago de Cuba. I was also able to discuss interviews conducted by other scholars: Luis Figueras's and Delio Orozco's interviews with Ñico Torres; Jana Lipman's interview with the coordinator of the MR–26–7 group in the U.S. base at Guantánamo; and Gary Tennant's interview with Octavio Louit. I am very grateful for their generosity. I have used the published recollections of Miguel Yaro, Pedro Santalla, and Ramón Alvarez from *Bohemia,* August 12, 1977, and drawn upon the twenty interviews conducted by Ismael Coma for his 1981 research paper, "El Movimiento 26 de Julio en Guantánamo," University of Oriente, Santiago de Cuba, 1981. Full details can be found in the bibliography.

3.   Luis Rolando Cabrera, "Sagua la Grande escribió su nombre en la historia, el nueve de abril," *Bohemia,* April 5, 1959, 36–39, 122–23.

4.   Armando Hart, *Aldabonazo, en la clandestinidad revolucionaria cubana, 1952–58* (New York: Pathfinder, 2004), 163; Julia Sweig, *Inside the Cuban Revolution: Fidel Castro and the Urban Underground* (London: Harvard University Press, 2002), 12, 13.

5.   *Revolución,* February 1957, 1.

6.   Manuel Fernándex Carcassés and Israel Escalona Cháldez, *Frank en la memoria* (Havana: Editora Historia, 2012), 96.

7.   Hart, *Aldabonazo,* 91–126.

8.   Sweig, *Inside the Cuban Revolution,* 25–28.

9.   Jorge Alberto Serra, "El Movimiento de Resistencia Cívica en La Habana," in *Memorias de la Revolución,* ed. Enrique Olutski Ozacki; Héctor Rodríguez, Llompart, and Eduardo Torres Cueva (Havana: Imagen Contemporanea, 2007), 231.

10.  Hart, *Aldabonazo,* 91–126.

11.  Delio Orozco, nterview with Ñico Torres, head of the Frente Obrero Nacional, April 29, 1990; Delio Orozco, "Manzanillo en los 50, rebeldía y revolución" (unpublished manuscript), 63–68; Delio Orozco, "Manzanillo: El Movimiento Revolucionario 26 de Julio y el apoyo a la Sierra" (Manzanillo: n.p., 1989), 67–70.

12.  Gladys Marel García Pérez, *Insurrección y Revolución (1952–1959 )* (Havana: Ediciones Unión, 2006), 42–50.

13.  Pedro Machado, "El movimiento obrero henequenero después del golpe de estado del 10 de marzo: Etapa conspirativa de Julián Alemán," 2011 This is an unpublished study of the henequen industry in Matanzas Province combined with a biography of Julian Alemán. I am grateful to the author for giving me access to his work.

14. These events are generally paid scant attention in the literature, with even the well-researched Ramón Bonachea book according the matter only three lines before turning to a long discussion of the effect of Frank País's death on the internal politics of the MR-26-7; see Ramón Bonachea and Marta San Martín, *The Cuban Insurrection, 1952–1959* (New Brunswick, NJ: Transaction Books, 1974), 146. Only Julia Sweig deals with it in any detail, in her *Inside the Cuban Revolution*, 46–49. Sweig's book is an important contribution to the understanding of the underground organization of the MR-26-7, particularly as it is based upon access to the normally secret archives of the Cuban Council of State, to which she was given rare access. However, detailed as her account is, the fact that it is based on the private papers of the leadership of the MR-26-7 means that she is mainly concerned with the decisions and actions of that leadership and pays less attention to the organization necessary to carry out those decisions.

15. Daniel Guérin, *Rosa Luxemburg et la Spontanéité Révolutionnaire* (Paris: Flammarion, 1971), 13.

16. José Alvarez, *Principio y fin del mito fidelista* (Bloomington: Trafford, 2008), 236–41.

17. Author's interview with Francis Velázquez Fuentes, rebel army veteran, Santiago, 2010.

18. Lucrecia Ramos Estives, "Apoyo de la mujer santiaguera a la lucha contra la tiranía de Batista de 1952–1958," Research Paper, Universidad de Oriente, Santiago de Cuba, 1904, 25, Caridad Miranda, *Trazos para el perfil de un combatiente* (Santiago de Cuba: Editorial Oriente, 1983), 294. Caridad Miranda's book contains is a rare photo of the funeral that shows a large group of women leading the funeral procession. The more common photo of the funeral, as shown on p. 297 of Miranda's book and many other places, including the Museum of the Revolution, was taken a few minutes later when the women leading the procession had passed from view.

19. Lazaro Torres Hernández, "La Huelga de agosto," *Bohemia*, August 12, 1977, 5; author's interview with Francis Velázquez Fuentes.

20. *New York Times*, August, 1957.

21. *Carta Semanal*, August 14, 1957.

22. Aleida Rodriguez Ramirez and Liduvina Ramos Cabrales, "El Movimiento Revolucionario en manzanillo de 1950 a 1959," Research Paper, Instituto Superior Pedagogico, Manzanillo, 1988, 72–74; Francisco Monserrat Iser, "Luchas obreras en Manzanillo" (unpublished manuscript, 2009).

23. Sección de historia del comité provincial del PCC en Guantánamo, *Guantánamo, apuntes para una cronología histórica* (Santiago de Cuba: Editorial Oriente, 1985), 41; Comisión Nacional de Historia Departamento Obrero II Frente Oriental "Frank Pais," *Provincia Guantánamo* (unpublished manuscript, 1980), 8–9; Coma, "El Movimiento 26 de Julio en Guantánamo," 58–61; Martha Albys García Faure and Margarita Canseco Aparicio, *Algunas Manifestaciones Políticas en Guantánamo* (Guantánamo: El Mar y la Montana, 2009), 73–75.

24. Torres Hernández, "La Huelga de agosto," 6.

25. IHC 24/3.12/1:2.3/1–56, *Informes del Jefe del BRAC sobre actividades subversivas*, September 1–9, 1957.

26. Torres Hernández, "La Huelga de agosto," 5–7; *Carta Semanal*, August 14, 1957; U.S. Embassy Havana, Dispatch 107, *Revolutionary Opposition Attempts General Strike; Frank País*, August 7, 1957.

27. Torres Hernández, "La Huelga de agosto," 7.

28. IHC 1/8:13/A1/1.1/27 CNDDO, "*Carta Abierta*," October 12, 1956; *Carta Semanal*, January 18, 25, 1956, and special issue, February 1956.

29. Torres Hernández, "La Huelga de agosto," 5–6.

30. *Carta Semanal*, August 21, 1957.

31. *Carta Semanal*, August 28, 1957.

32. *Carta Semanal*, August 21, 1957.

33. Javier Rodriguez, "José Antonio Echeverría y la Clase Obrera," *Bohemia*, March 10, 1967, 55; *Carta Semanal*, August 28, 1957.

34. Jon Lee Anderson, *Che Guevara: A Revolutionary Life* (London: Bantam, 1997), 297.

35. Orozco, interview with Ñico Torres.

36. "Porque nuestro partido apoya a la Sierra Maestra," *Carta Semanal*, March 12, 1958.

37. *Carta Semanal*, January 22, 1958.

38. K. S. Karol, *Guerrillas in Power: The Course of the Cuban Revolution* (New York: Hill & Wang, 1970), 153.

39. Bonachea and San Martín, *The Cuban Insurrection*, 173.

40. "Estudiantes" *Bohemia*, March 16, 1958.

41. Faustino Pérez, "La sierra, el llano: eslabones de un mismo combate," *Pensamiento Crítico* 31 (1969): 73.

42. Faustino Pérez, *Letter to Fidel Castro*, April 2, 1958, Suaréz Collection; Biblioteca Nacional José Martí, Sección Obrera MR 26 de Julio, *A los responsables obreros provinciales del MR 26-7*, March 17, 1958.

43. Sweig, *Inside the Cuban Revolution*, 126–31; Pérez, "Letter to Fidel Castro"; "El 9 de Abril de 1958," *Bohemia*, April 19, 1959, 111–12.

44. Sweig, *Inside the Cuban Revolution*, 44–45.

45. "El 9 de Abril de 1958," *Bohemia*, April 19, 1959, 59.

46. Jorge Ricardo Masetti, *Los que luchan y los que lloran* (Buenos Aires: Editorial Jorge Alvarez, 1969), 169–72.

47. This estimation of David Salvador is based on a letter from Robert Alexander to Jay Lovestone dated January 19, 1959, cited in Robert Jackson Alexander, *A History of Organized Labor in Cuba* (Westport, CT: Praeger, 2002), 206–7, 213. Also based on opinion of the British embassy as stated in FO 371/139397-AK1012/1, *Leading Personalities in Cuba*, July 31, 1959.

48. IHC 1/8:13A1/7.1/1, CDDO de Marianao, "*Viva el 1º de Mayo*," April 1958.

49. *Carta Semanal*, March 26, 1958.

50. *Carta Semanal*, March 19, 1958; *CNDDO l FON*, March 13, 1958, Suárez Collection.

51. Sweig, *Inside the Cuban Revolution*, 130–134.

52. "El 9 de Abril de 1958," *Bohemia*, April 19, 1959, 58–61, 111–12.

53. ANC, 15-26-1178, Venegas Calabuch, *Carta Abierta: En memoria de un nueve de abril*, 1959.

54. ANC 6-180-2794, MR-26-7, *Instrucciones al pueblo para el día de la huelga*, April 1958.

55. "El 9 de Abril de 1958," *Bohemia*, April 19, 1959, 58–61, 111–12. There is, however, not the slightest evidence for Ramon Bonachea's unsubstantiated allegations that the PSP collaborated with the police on the day. See Bonachea and San Martín, *The Cuban Insurrection*, 221.

56. IHC 1/8:13A1/1.1/74, CNDDO "*¡Viva el Primero de Mayo!,*" 1958; *Carta Semanal*, April 23, 1958.

57. *Carta Semanal*, April 16, 1958.

58. Table 6.1 was compiled from the following sources: "El 9 de Abril de 1958," *Bohemia*, April 19, 1959, 112; Clara Emma Chávez Alvarez, *Matanzas de rojo y negro 1952-1958* (Matanzas: Ediciones Matanzas, 2007), 163–67; *Carta Semanal*, April 2. 9, 11, 12, 16, 23, 1958; Cabrera, *Sagua la Grande escribió su nombre en la historia* (1959), 36–38, 122–23; Monserrat Iser, *Luchas obreras en Manzanillo*; Orozco, *Manzanillo: El Movimiento Revolucionario 26 de Julio y el apoyo a la Sierra*, 77–78; Rodriguez Ramirez and Ramos Cabrales, "El Movimiento Revolucionario en Manzanillo de 1950 a 1959," 76–78; Gabriela Mendoza Bú, "El movimiento 26 de julio en el sector ferroviario en Santiago de Cuba," Research Paper, Universidad de Oriente, Santiago de Cuba, 1988, 57; Jorge Andrews Thomas, "La huelga de 9 de abril en Guantánamo," Research Paper, Universidad de Oriente, Santiago de Cuba, 1982, 15–34; Facundo Alexis Rodrígiez López and Diosdado Martínez Rodríguez, "La huelga de 9 de abril de 1958 en la cuidad de Camagüey," Research Paper, Universidad de Oriente, Santiago de Cuba, 1984; Coya, "El movimiento obrero en Santiago de Cuba," 103.

59. Ignarra et al. to Fidel Castro, April 19, 1958, Suaréz Collection.

60. Dirección provincial de Las Villas to Dirección Nacional, April 30, 1958, Suaréz Collection.

61. Orozco, interview with Ñico Torres.

62. IHC 1/8:14/1.1/6, FON, "*Manifesto del FON,*" 1958.

63. IHC 1/8:14/1.1/7, FON, "*A los compañeros ferroviarios*" (1958); IHC 1/8:14/2.1/1-2, FON, "*Huelga General Revolucionaria,*" 1958.

64. Hugh Thomas, *Cuba, or the Pursuit of Freedom* (New York: Da Capo Press, 1998), 1002-7; Ernesto Guevara, *Pasajes de la guerra revolucionaria* (Havana: Editora Política, 2001), 245.

65. "Sabotaje Comunista," *Bohemia*, November 27, 1955.

66. *Carta Semanal*, July 4, 1956.

67. *Carta Semanal*, October 30, 1956.

68. *Carta Semanal*, March 12, 1958.

69. Harold Sims, "Cuban Labor and the Communist Party: An Interpretation," *Cuban Studies* 15/1 (Winter 1985): 55; *Cuba Socialista*, January 1964, 22–23.

**7. Last Days of Batista**

1. *Bohemia*, April 19, 1959, 111-12.
2. FO371/132164-AK1015/20, April 2, 1958.
3. FO371/132164-AK1015/28, May 9, 1958.
4. FO371/132164-AK1015/44, September 29, 1958.
5. Ramón Bonachea and Marta San Martín, *The Cuban Insurrection, 1952-1959* (New Brunswick, NJ: Transaction Books, 1974), 263; interview with David Salvador, January 9, 1959, in Robert Jackson Alexander, *A History of Organized Labor in Cuba* (Westport, CT: Praeger, 2002), 159, 167.
6. Partido Comunista De Cuba (PCC) Instituto de Historia del Movimiento Comunista y de la Revolución Socialista de Cuba, *Historia del movimiento obrero cubano*, vol. 2 (Havana: Editora Política, 1985), 352-60.
7. Fidel Castro, *La victoria estratégica* (Havana: Consejo de Estado, 2010); Bonachea and San Martín, *The Cuban Insurrection*, 226-65.
8. MR 26 de Julio-Sector Ferroviario, *Liberación Ferroviario*, August 4, 1958.
9. Dirección Provincial de la Sección Obrera del M.26-7 de La Habana, *Campaña del Mes del Soldado Rebelde*, Circular #2.
10. Joaquín Toirac Adames, "El Movimiento Obrero en la Base Naval Norteamericana," *El Managui (Guantánamo)*, 1988, 3-8; Jana Lipman, interview with the co-ordinator of the MR-26-7 at the U.S. base at Guantánamo, 2004; Thelma Bornot, "Esa tarde me pusieron a la frontera," *Santiago* 18-19 (June and September 1975): 187.
11. FO 371/132164/5-AK1015/47 & AK1015/56, 1958.
12. IHC 1/8:14/4.1/1-10, FON, "*Radio FON*," 1958.
13. IHC 1/8:13/27.1/2, Comité Obrero Revolucionario de San Miguel del Padrón, "*¡No Hay Que Confundir!*," 1958.
14. Julia Sweig, *Inside the Cuban Revolution: Fidel Castro and the Urban Underground* (London: Harvard University Press, 2002), 172-74.
15. *Carta Semanal*, August 6, 13, 20, 1958.
16. *Carta Semanal*, July 30, 1958; *Vanguardia Obrera*, July 14, 1958.
17. *Carta Semanal*, August 27, 1958.
18. Movimiento Revolucionario 26 de Julio Sección Obrera Nacional, *¡Hacia las Fabricas!*, August 28, 1958.
19. Vicente Perez, retired PSP trade union organizer, in the course of the author's interview with him in 2008 allowed me to copy an undated typewritten statement by the late Jesús Soto titled *La consitución del FONU en la clandestinidad*.
20. Luis Figueras of the Casa de la Historia in Guantánamo gave the author a copy of his notes of an earlier, undated interview with Ñico Torres titled *Semblanza de Antonio Torres Chedebaux*.
21. IHC 1/8:13A1/1.1/85, CNDDO, "*Salvamos la vida de David Salvador*," October 28, 1958; Soto, *La Constitution del FONU en la Clandestinidad*.
22. Archivo Las Villas, Colección de documentos del Movimiento Revolucionario "26 de Julio," Expediente 15.
23. FONU, *A Todos los Trabajadores del Pais*, November 10, 1958; FONU, *A la Clase Trabajadora del Frente Obrero Nacional (Unido)*, November 10, 1958.

24.    Movimiento Revolucionario 26 de Julio, *Viva el Frente Obrero Nacional!*, November 10, 1957.

25.    Soto, *La Constitution del FONU en la Clandestinidad.*

26.    IHC 1/8:15/3.1/24A.1, FONU *"Denuncia el asasenato de Carlos Rodriguez,"* November 28, 1958.

27.    Gladys Marel García Pérez, *Insurrección y Revolución, 1952–1959* (Havana: Ediciones Unión, 2006), 185.

28.    Author's interview with Alcibíades Poveda Díaz, head of propaganda in Santiago de Cuba for the 26th July Movement, Santiago de Cuba, March 3, 2009.

29.    Soto, *La Constitution del FONU;* author's interview with Vicente Pérez, communist trade union organizer from Caibarién, June 21, 2008; Figueras, *Semblanza de Antonio Torres Chedebaux;* Hugh Thomas, *Cuba, or, the Pursuit of Freedom* (New York: Da Capo Press, 1998), 1007, 1010.

30.    *Bohemia,* January 11, 1959, 102.

31.    Antero Regalado, *Las luchas campesinas en Cuba* (Havana: Editora Política, 1979), 162–65.

32.    Comisión Nacional de Historia Departamento Obrero II Frente Oriental "Frank Pais," *Provincia Guantánamo* (unpublished manuscript, 1980), 10; Sección de historia del comité provincial del partido en Guantánamo, *Reseña histórica de Guantánamo* (Santiago de Cuba: Editorial Oriente, 1985), 156.

33.    Pedro Cardona Bory, *Memorias del Congreso Obrero en Armas, Segundo Frente "Frank País"* (Cuba: Pilar Casada Gonzalez, ca. 1995).

34.    Sección de Historia, *Reseña histórica de Guantánamo,* 156; Comisión Nacional de Historia, *Provincia Guantánamo,* 10.

35.    Soto, *La Constitution del FONU en la Clandestinidad.*

36.    Pilar Quesada González, "El congreso obrero en armas," in *II Taller Científico Internacional, Movimiento Obrero y 1ero de Mayo: Memoria,* ed. Marcelo González Bustos, José Alfredo Castellanos Suárez, Luis Hipólito Serrano Pérez, Marco Antonio Anaya Pérez, and Alvaro González Pérez (Texcoco, México: Editorial Futura, 1999), 86.

37.    Sección de Historia, *Reseña histórica de Guantánamo,* 159; Cardona Bory, *Memorias del Congreso Obrero en Armas.*

38.    Lipman, interview with coordinator of the MR-26-7 group, U.S. base at Guantánamo.

39.    Figueras, *Semblanza de Antonio Torres Chedebaux.*

40.    Cardona Bory, *Memorias del Congreso Obrero en Armas;* Quesada González, "El congreso obrero en armas," 85–88.

41.    Testimonies of Arnaldo Milián and Alberto Torres in William Gávlez, *Camilo, Señor de la vanguardia* (Havana: Cincias Sociales, 1979), 340–43, 374–76.

42.    Ramón Simonea, *Testimonio de un viejo luchador,* 1982, Archivo Histórico Provincial de Sancti Spiritus, Fondo 70, Expediente 140, Legajo 3. This is a signed testimonial statement from Ramón Simonea, which may be found in the Sancti Spiritus archive. The author has a copy in his possession.

43.    José Bell Lara, Delia Luisa López García, and Tania Caram León, *Documentos de la Revolución cubana, 1959* (Havana: Editorial de Ciencias Sociales, 2006),

258–59; Horacio Díaz Pendás, *Textos sobre Historia de Cuba* (Havana: Editorial Pueblo y Educación, 2009), 263–63.

44. Testimony of Alberto Torres in Gávelz, *Camilo*, 379.

45. Letter from Camilo Cienfuegos. "*A los trabajadors de la ruta 35 y 48*," November 14, 1958, cited in "¡Vamos bien!" *Suplemento de Granma*, December, 31 1974, 46; Camilo Cienfuegos to Alfredo Milián, November 14, 1958, William Gálvez's personal collection.

46. Testimony of Alberto Torres in Gávelz, *Camilo*, 378; Simonea, *Testimonio de un viejo luchador*.

47. IHC 1/8:15/2.1/2-22, FONU, "*Informe de la conferencia azucarera*," December 1958.

48. Testimony of Arnaldo Milián in Gávelz, *Camilo*, 340–43.

49. Gávelz, *Camilo*, 284–86.

50. This was composed of Jesús Soto, Ursinio Rojas, José Maria de la Aguilera, and Lila Léon, a Havana office worker and member of the MR-26-7. IHC 1/8:15./2.1/1, FONU "*Conferencia de azucareros*," November 1958; Soto, *La Constitution del FONU en la Clandestinidad;* Cushion, interview with Vicente Pérez.

51. Soto, *La Constitution del FONU en la Clandestinidad.*

52. Testimony of Ursinio Rojas in Jaime Sarusky, "Camilo, el politico," *Bohemia*, October 27, 1972, 59–65; testimony of Ursinio Rojas in Gálvez, *Camilo*, 391–93.

53. Testimony of Mongo Simonea in Sarusky, *Camilo*, 59–65.

54. Testimony of Felipe Torres and Alfredo Milán in Gálvez, *Camilo*, 338–41.

55. Testimony of Tito Igualada in Sarusky, *Camilo*, 59–65.

56. Testimony of Gerado Nogueras and Tito Igualada in Sarusky, *Camilo*, 59–65.

57. Testimony of Ursinio Rojas in Sarusky, *Camilo*, 59–65.

58. IHC 1/8:15/4.1/1-2, FONU, "*Resolución de la plenaria azucarera del Norte de Las Villas*," November 30, 1958.

59. Efrén Córdova, *Clase Trabajadora y Movimiento Sindical en Cuba (1959-1996)*, vol. 2 (Miami: Ediciones Universal, 1996), 112.

60. IHC 1/8:15/3.1/1, FONU, "*Manifesto*," November 30, 1958.

61. IHC 1/8:15/4.1/3-4, FONU, "*Manifesto a las trabajadores de Las Villas*," November 30, 1958.

62. Testimony of Gerado Nogueras in Sarusky, *Camilo*, 63.

63. Testimony of Ramón Simonea in Gálvez, *Camilo*, 387–90.

64. Testimony of Gerado Nogueras in Sarusky, *Camilo*, 63.

65. IHC 1/8:15/2.1/30-32, Sindicato del central Natividad "*Mociones*," December 21, 1958.

66. Sarusky, in *Camilo*; Simonea, *Testimonio de un viejo luchador*.

67. Soto, *La Constitution del FONU en la Clandestinidad.*

68. IHC 1/8:15/2.1/2-22, FONU, "*Informe de la conferencia azucarera*," December 1958.

69. My translation.

70. Steve Cushion, interview with Alfredo Menéndez, Havana, March 2009.

71. Soto, *La Constitution del FONU en la Clandestinidad.*

72. IHC 1/8:13/36.1/3, Comité de Unidad Obrera de Las Villas, "*A Los*

*Trabajadores,"* January 6, 1959.

73. IHC 1/8:13A1/1.1/85, CNDDO, *"Salvamos la vida de David Salvador,"* October 28, 1958; IHC 1/8:13A1/1.1/102, CNDDO, *"A todos los trabajadores del país,"* November 27, 1958; IHC 1/8:15/1.1/1, FONU, *"A todos los trabajadores del país,"* 1958.

74. *Vanguardia Obrera* (Santiago edition), December 29, 1958.

75. IHC 1/8:15/1.1/1, FONU, *"A todos los trabajadores del país,"* 1958; IHC 1/8:15/3.1/1, FONU, *"Manifesto,"* November 10, 1958.

76. Sweig, *Inside the Cuban Revolution,* 159.

77. IHC 1/8:14/1.1/7, FON Las Villas, *"A los Compañeros Ferroviarios,"* 1958; IHC 1/8:15/6.1/1, FONU Ferroviario, *"A los Trabajadores Ferroviarios,"* 1958.

78. *Carta Semanal,* December 3, 1958; *Vanguardia Obrera* (Santiago), December 29, 1958.

79. Sweig, *Inside the Cuban Revolution,* 157.

80. *Carta Semanal,* December 10, 1958.

81. The MR-26-7 stated in 1957 that the term "imperialism" was "inappropriate to the American continent." See *Nuestra razón: manifiesto-programa del movimiento 26 de julio,* repr. in Enrique Gonzalez Pedrero, *La Revolución cubana* (Mexico City: Escuela Nacional de Ciencias Politicas y Sociales, 1959), 124.

82. IHC 1/8:13/40.1/1-2, Comité Municipal de Unidad Obrero de Santiago, *"Contra los Desplazamientos,"* October 1958; IHC 1/8:13/40.1/3-4-Comité Municipal de Unidad Obrero de Santiago, *"Contra los Bombardeos,"* December 1, 1958.

83. *Vanguardia Obrera,* various regional editions for Oriente Province from March to December 1958, most undated. Alcibíades Poveda Díaz, who in the 1950s was head of propaganda for the MR-26-7 in Santiago de Cuba, generously provided access to his personal collection of propaganda material (henceforth Poveda Collection), which gave a view of the implementation of the MR-26-7's politics in one of their strongholds and also contained a number of copies of *Vanguardia Obrera,* the MR-26-7's clandestine newspaper for workers, very few copies of which have survived elsewhere.

84. Alcibíades Poveda Diaz, *Propaganda y revolución en Santiago de Cuba 1952-1958* (Santiago de Cuba: Oficina de la Historiador de la Cuidad, 2003), 369–74.

85. Poveda Collection.

86. FO 371/132164-AK1015/69, *Report from Cable and Wireless manager in Santiago,* November 25, 1958.

87. FO371/132191-AK2181/3, *Trade Unions and Labor Situation in Cuba,* August 21, 1958; Economist Intelligence Unit (EIU), "Cuba, Dominican Republic and Puerto Rico," *Quarterly Economic Review,* 1958.

88. José Luis Padrón and Luis Adrián Betancourt, *Batista: últimas días en el poder* (Havana: Ediciones Unión, 2008), 234–36.

89. Ramón Barquín López, *Las luchas guerrilleras en Cuba: De la colonia a la Sierra Maestra* (España: Editorial Playor, 1975), 61; Padrón and Betancourt, *Batista: Últimas días en el poder,* 128, 134; Ernesto Guevara, *Pasajes de la guerra revolucionaria* (Havana: Editora Política, 2001), 263. Guevara gives the

date of the derailment as December 30, although other writers speak of the 28th.

90.  IHC 1/8:13/36.1/1-2, Comité de Unidad Obrera de Las Villas, *"ACTA,"* 1958; IHC 1/8:13/36.1/3-Comité de Unidad Obrera de Las Villas, *"A Los Trabajadores,"* 1958.

91.  K. S. Karol, *Guerrillas in Power: The Course of the Cuban Revolution* (New York: Hill & Wang, 1970), 167–68.

92.  Lazaro Peña, "Cuban Workers and People Resist Batista's Brutal Dictatorship," *World Trade Union Movement,* December, 1958, 18.

93.  "Alocución del Comandante en Jefe Fidel Castro, por Radio Rebelde, el 1ro. de enero de 1959," cited in José Bell Lara, Delia Luisa López García, and Tania Caram León, *Documentos de la Revolución cubana, 1959* (Havana: Editorial de Ciencias Sociales, 2006), 11–14.

94.  Burt Glinn, *Havana: The Revolutionary Moment* (Stockport, UK: Dewi Lewis Publishing, 2001).

95.  Fidel Castro, *Discursos de comandante Fidel Castro en el X Congreso Nacional Obrero* (Havana: COD de publicidad de la CTC, 1959), 8.

96.  Ruby Hart Phillips, *Cuba: Island of Paradoxes* (New York: McDowell, 1959), 38–43.

97.  This position is perhaps best articulated in Harold Sims, "Cuban Labor and the Communist Party, an Interpretation," *Cuban Studies* 15/1 (Winter 1985). For a more balanced view, see Samuel Farber, "The Cuban Communists in the Early Stages of the Cuban Revolution: Revolutionaries or Reformists?," *Latin American Research Review* 18/1 (1983): 59–83; or Caridad Massón Sena, "Proyectos y accionar del Partido Socialista Popular entre 1952 y 1958," in *1959: Una rebellón contra las oligarquías y los dogmas revolucionarios,* ed. Jorge Ibarra Guitart (Panamá: Ruth, 2009).

## 8. The First Year of the New Cuba

1.  IHC 1/8:15/1.2/1-2, FONU, "Llamamento del FONU," January 1959; IHC 1/8:15/1.2/1-2, FONU, "Manifesto a la Clase Obrera," January 1959; *Revolución,* January 17, 1959.

2.  *Bohemia,* January 11, 1959, 102; Mario del Cueto, "El 26 de julio en la dirección sindical," *Bohemia,* January 11, 1959, 50–55.

3.  IHC 1/8:13A1/1.1/104-6, CNDDO, "Carta a David Salvador," January 13, 1959.

4.  IHC 1/8:13A1/1.1/107, CNDDO, "Llamamiento a Concurrir," January 18, 1959; *Revolución,* January 21, 1959; *Gaceta Oficial de la República de Cuba,* no. 8, January 23, 1959.

5.  Francisco Pares "Estrateja Comunista en la Revolución Cubana," *Bohemia,* February 1959; "Fuera del FONU los comunistas" *Revolución,* January 26, 1959.

6.  "Entrevista," *Bohemia,* February 15, 1959.

7.  "Victoria Democrática en el Campo Obrero," *Bohemia,* September 27, 1959, 67.

8.  *Hoy,* January 31, 1959.

9.  IHC 10-126/2/62-92, PSP, "La Revolución cubana, su carácter, sus fuerzas y sus enemigos," May 1959, cited in Angelina Rojas Blaquier, *El Primer Partido*

*Comunista de Cuba 1952-1961*, vol. 3 (Santiago de Cuba: Editorial Oriente, 2011), 265.

10. "Charla del Comandante Ernesto Che Guevara," cited in José Bell Lara, Delia Luisa López García, and Tania Caram León, *Documentos de la Revolución cubana, 1959* (Havana: Editorial de Ciencias Sociales, 2006), 34.

11. *Revolución*, February 14, 1959.

12. *Revolución*, February 7, 1959.

13. *Revolución*, October 23, 1959.

14. "El X Congreso Obrero," *Bohemia*, November 29, 1959, 59-62, 78-79; *Revolución*, November 23, 1959.

15. James O'Connor, *The Origins of Socialism in Cuba* (Ithaca, NY: Cornell University Press, 1970), 193.

16. See, for example, Bell Lara et al., *Documentos de la Revolución cubana, 1959*, 23-24, 324.

17. Robert Jackson Alexander, *A History of Organized Labor in Cuba* (Westport, CT: Praeger, 2002), 198-203; Efrén Córdova, *Clase Trabajadora y Movimiento Sindical en Cuba 1959-1996* (Miami: Ediciones Universal, vol. 2, 1996), 67-78.

18. Samuel Farber, "The Cuban Communists in the Early Stages of the Cuban Revolution: Revolutionaries or Reformists?," *Latin American Research Review* 18/1 (1983): 65-67; Rojas, *El Primer Partido Comunista de Cuba*, 282-88; Antoni Kapcia, *Leadership in the Cuban Revolution: The Unseen Story* (London: Zed Books, 2014), 99.

19. "¿Qué opina usted del primer año de la revolución?," *Bohemia*, January 3, 1960.

20. See, for example, "Sin resolver," *Revolución*, February 5, 1959.

21. "Huelgas ¿Contra quíen? ¿Para qué?," *Revolución*, August 5, 1959.

22. *Hoy*, July 9, 1959; *Revolución*, July 9, 1959.

23. Efrén Córdova, *Castro and the Cuban Labor Movement: Statecraft and Society in a Revolutionary Period (1959-1961)* (Lanham, MD: University Press of America, 1987), 234-35; *Diario de la Marina*, June 10 and 11, 1960.

24. Conrado Bécquer, *El porqué de la congelación de los salarios, la productividad y los sindicatos en el proceso revolucionario* (Havana: CMQ, 1960).

25. Luis Figueras of the Casa de la Historia in Guantánamo gave the author a copy of his notes of an earlier, undated interview with Ñico Torres titled "Semblanza de Antonio Torres Chedebaux."

26. "Desfile," *Bohemia*, May 10, 1959, 102.

27. FO 371/148178-AK1011/1, *Annual Report for 1959*, January 1960.

28. FO 371/148342-AK2181/1, *Labor—Trade Unions*, December 1959.

29. U.S. Embassy Havana, Dispatch 1290, *Cuban Labor Leader Suggests Nationalization of American-Owned Electric and Telephone Companies*, December 18, 1950; U.S. Embassy Havana, Dispatch 1384, *Progress Reported in Nationalization of Autobuses Modernos S.A.*, January 3, 1951; U.S. Embassy Havana, Dispatch 1178, Weeka No. 3; *Railway Union Threatens General Strike If Government Does Not Nationalize United Railway*, January 18, 1952; FO 371/139488, *Expropriation of British Property in Cuba, 1959*; "Sucedio el 7 de agosto de 1960," *Bohemia*, August 14, 1960.

# INDEX